Ringing the Changes

Books by

Mazo de la Roche

THE BUILDING OF JALNA
MARY WAKEFIELD
YOUNG RENNY
WHITEOAK HERITAGE
THE WHITEOAK BROTHERS: JALNA—1923
JALNA
WHITEOAKS OF JALNA
FINCH'S FORTUNE
THE MASTER OF JALNA
WHITEOAK HARVEST
WAKEFIELD'S COURSE
RETURN TO JALNA
RENNY'S DAUGHTER
VARIABLE WINDS AT JALNA
✷✷
EXPLORERS OF THE DAWN
POSSESSION
DELIGHT
LOW LIFE AND OTHER PLAYS
PORTRAIT OF A DOG
LARK ASCENDING
BESIDE A NORMAN TOWER
THE VERY HOUSE
GROWTH OF A MAN
THE SACRED BULLOCK AND OTHER STORIES
A BOY IN THE HOUSE AND OTHER STORIES
THE SONG OF LAMBERT
RINGING THE CHANGES

Myself — London, 1936

Ringing the Changes

An Autobiography

by Mazo de la Roche

WITH PHOTOGRAPHS

An Atlantic Monthly Press Book
Little, Brown and Company
Boston · Toronto

ATLANTIC–LITTLE, BROWN BOOKS
ARE PUBLISHED BY
LITTLE, BROWN AND COMPANY
IN ASSOCIATION WITH
THE ATLANTIC MONTHLY PRESS

For Caroline
from first to last

Contents

Contents

Illustrations appear between pages 120–121.

Ringing the Changes

Prologue

ALTHOUGH I did not realize it at the time, or for many years afterward, that January day in my maternal grandfather's house was the most important day of my life. I can remember the dining-room, with its high ceiling, pale walls, and large window that overlooked the terraces, deep in snow. I can remember the feeling of excitement all about me. The family were awaiting the arrival of somebody — I was not certain who, though I did know it was a relative. It seemed that everyone who came to the house was some sort of relative. I was always the smallest, the only child, in a moving mass of grownups. Sometimes I was looking upward, trying to understand what they were saying; more often I was absorbed in my own affairs.

Now there were, besides myself, five people in the room. These were my mother, her parents, her sister Eva, and her young brother — always called Waugh. He had thick curling hair, so golden as to have almost a greenish cast, and rather greenish eyes. He had been a beautiful boy, but, when playing football, he had got his nose broken. In those days surgeons were not so clever at setting noses and the shape of his was left far from perfect.

We all were listening for the sound of sleigh bells.

3

Ringing the Changes

Now the silvery jingle of it came, sharp and clear on the frosty air. My uncle was the first to hear it. "There they are," he cried, and darted along the hall and out of the front door.

The others followed. I came last. The January cold rushed into the hall. The front lawn stood high above the road and was protected by a white picket fence. I could see on the road below the sleek bay mare and the bright red sleigh, with its bearskin rugs, one to cover the knees, the other to hang over the back of the sleigh. The mare was restive, tossing her head and pawing the snow. At each vigorous movement the bells, with which her harness was strung, quivered and sent out their gay chime. The largest of these hung above her shoulders. It was silver and had a special tone of its own — to me at once captivating and troubling.

I saw the massive figure of my father alight and go to the mare's head. He was followed by my Uncle George, who was carrying a large bundle. Those were all. Uncle George was young, small and slight. The bundle could not have been very heavy, for he strode quickly through the gate, along the snowy path, flanked on either side by high drifts, and into the midst of the waiting group in the hall. My father did not come in but again took his seat in the sleigh. The bells rang out joyously. He was taking his mare to the stable.

When I saw there was a child in the bundle I drew away. In fact, no one noticed me. All were intent on the bundle, from the top of which now hung, like limp petals of a flower, strands of silvery fair hair. Uncle George sat down in my grandfather's armchair and began to take layer after layer of shawls from the bundle. He did it with a proud, possessive air, as though he were doing a conjuring trick. Everybody stood about, waiting for the climax.

The climax was a small girl, sitting demurely on his knee, her thin little hands folded on her lap, while she stared about her, dazed by the sudden changes of scene which lately had befallen her. Her hair hung about her shoulders but was cut squarely into a straight thick fringe above her blue eyes. She had high cheek-bones, which then were considered rather a disfigurement, a square little chin and full curling lips. She looked as though she would never smile.

My mother and Aunt Eva were asking questions of her which she answered in a small voice. She just glanced at me. Then, suddenly bold, I came from my corner and stood facing her. I was just tall enough to rest my elbows on the dining-room table behind me. I was seven years old.

"This is Caroline," my grandmother said to me. "You two little girls must be friends. I think you'd better go off and get acquainted. Tea will soon be ready. Caroline must be starving."

Uncle George set Caroline on her feet. She came and put her hand into mine.

I held her hand closely and led her into the hall. The door of the sitting-room stood open on our left and that of the parlour on our right. Caroline stared about her, but her thin little fingers held tightly to mine.

"I don't live here," I said. "I live in Toronto."

"Oh," she said, as though not impressed.

"We just come to Grandpa's for Christmas," I went on, "and we've not gone home yet."

"That's a pretty dress," she said, touching the red and fawn of my dress that had a skirt and a little vest with stripes running round and a red bolero. I remember this dress because I so quickly outgrew it and it became Caroline's. I think I was rather a generous child, but I did not want to part with that dress.

"My Uncle Danford brought it to me from England," I boasted.

5

"He goes every year and always brings me a present. Have you been to England?"

"No," she said, "but I've been to the States — to the prairies."

That meant nothing to me. I pushed wide the door of the sitting-room, white walled, red carpeted and curtained.

"This is where we had our Christmas tree," I said. "It touched the ceiling and it was decorated."

"Oh," she said again, "and what room is that?" She peered into the parlour.

The fox terrier, Chub, circled about us as we climbed the stair with its white-spindled bannisters. Now he would dart ahead of us and rush back to meet us. Then he would hurl himself behind and nip our heels.

Half-way up the stairs I stopped in front of the niche where the great white owl sat. Here was something to admire — yet to be afraid of. Going up to bed all by myself, it was terrifying to pass him. Might he not at any moment swoop from his perch and alight on one's head? Covering my head with my hands, I would fly up the stairs, my heart pounding against my ribs.

But, with Caroline beside me, I found a new courage.

"He's pretty," she breathed, and stood on tiptoe to put her hands beneath his wings.

"He's a stuffed owl," I boasted, and I too put my hands beneath his wings. His beautiful amber glass eyes stared straight ahead of him. Oh, the delicious downy softness of the space beneath his wings — the intimate communion with him!

"He's pretty," breathed Caroline again. "Was he alive once?"

"Yes," I said, my imagination flying away with me, "he flew about in the woods and he killed things. He was a wicked owl. But then one of my uncles shot him and he was stuffed and put

6

on this perch, but at night he comes down and flies all over the house and hoots and cries. I've heard him."

I had expected Caroline to be frightened by this, but instead she gave a delighted squeal of laughter and scampered up the stairs, I after her, the fox terrier barking.

Upstairs I showed her my Christmas presents: the doll with bisque face, arms and feet and white kid body, the toys, the books. She held the doll in her arms for an ecstatic moment, then — "Can you sew?" she asked.

I had to acknowledge that I could not.

"I can sew," she said, "and I can recite 'The Jackdaw of Rheims,' all the way through. Should you like to hear me?"

She began at once:

> The jackdaw sat in the Cardinal's chair,
> Bishop and friar and monk were there —

And on to the end in her small clear voice.

A delicious intimacy was there between us, in that chill upstairs, with the grownups far below and the January sunset reddening the walls. Never before had I had a child in the house with me, a child who would go to bed when I went, have in common with me the activities of childhood. I was used to being made much of, the only grandchild on either side of the family, but I longed for a companion of my own age. Here was the perfect one.

I brought out my Christmas books, the favourite *Through the Looking-Glass*. We sat together at a table close to the window to catch the last of the daylight and read aloud, page about. I remember how carefully we sounded the *g* in gnat, our heads — hers fair, mine curly and brown — touching, our legs, in their long black cashmere stockings, dangling.

7

We heard steps on the stair. The fox terrier jumped off the bed. In a moment Aunt Eva looked in at us, her pretty face inquisitive.

"What are you little girls saying to each other?" she asked. "What are you talking about?"

At once she made us feel we had been caught in doing something naughty.

"Nothing," we answered.

"Nothing," she said. "Well, that's funny. Haven't you anything to tell, Caroline, about all the places you've seen?"

"No, ma'am," answered Caroline.

"No, ma'am," repeated Aunt Eva. "That's a funny way of talking. Where did you pick that up?"

"In the States," answered Caroline.

"May we have a lamp?" I asked. "It's getting dark for reading. I'd like a lamp."

"You may not. Do you think we want the house set on fire? No, indeed. Anyhow, it will soon be teatime."

She went, a firm, trim figure, always tidy, in spite of her fuzzy, bronze-coloured hair.

What we found funny in all this I cannot remember, but when we were left alone, we went into fits of laughter. We laid our heads on the table and it shook in our senseless mirth.

When we again looked at each other, it was through tears. We had laughed till we cried. A wild happiness possessed me. Yet night was falling, made even darker by the thick flurry of snow that swept against the window. The panes were covered by white furry frost. I scratched a clean space on this with my nail and peered out.

Down below the steep terrace, deep in snow, I could just make out the shape of the stable. A light showed in its window. The world was a whirling mass of snowflakes. The wind had been given a voice and with it blew screaming round the house, enclosing us in our own fastness.

I turned and could just make out the white disc of Caroline's face in the dusk. Should I tell her my secret? There was an expectant tilt to her pale head. Her thin hands were clasped as though in beseeching.

I drew a sigh. "I have a secret," I said.

"A secret," she breathed. "Oh, I love secrets."

"I'll tell you," I said, not able to stop myself, "if you'll promise never never to tell anyone else."

"I promise." And it seemed and was true that she'd die first. "I will never tell."

"It was a dream," I said. "First it was a dream — then I played it — all by myself. I play it every day. But now you are here, I'll tell you and we'll play it together."

"What do you call it?" she whispered, as though under the weight of a mystery.

"My play I call it. But now it must be *our* play. We'll play it together — if you think you can."

"I can play anything — if it's pretend," she said decidedly. "I've never tried it, but I know I can."

So then I told her.

Chapter 1

Maternal Forbears

I SOMETIMES have wondered why people write their autobiographies. It is possibly all very well for generals and statesmen who have their actions to explain, their failures to defend, but those whose work lies in the field of the imagination have no need to explain either their actions or failures — except to themselves.

In truth I feel that I scarcely know how to write an autobiography. The first person singular has always been repellent to me. The autobiographies of other writers have not often interested me. Of the few which I have read, some appear as little more than a chronicle of the important people the author has known; some appear to dwell, in pallid relish, on poverty or misunderstanding or anguish of spirit endured. They overflow with self-pity. Others have recorded only the sunny periods of their lives, and these are the pleasantest to read.

How easy to explain himself for the author who can point to distinguished forbears, statesmen, poets, painters. But, if he writes without this bolstering — if he writes to tell his own story, in his own way, knowing that the more he is written about by other people the less he will be understood — it is not easy. It seems to

10

me that even two biographers can make an enigma — a mystery — of any man, no matter how open his life.

When I look back on my great-grandparents, great-aunts, great-uncles, grandparents, aunts, uncles and parents, and consider their handsome looks, proud bearing and self-willed natures, I marvel that none of them ever did anything notable. They were, one might say, distinguished-looking nobodies.

First I shall tell of my maternal forbears, because my mother's family was much closer to me than my father's. I knew them much more intimately. They seemed closer to me, even though physically and temperamentally I resemble my father's family. My father's father I never saw. Whereas my mother's father, "Grandpa Lundy," was very near and dear to me.

He was the descendant of one Sylvester Lundy who had emigrated to New England from Devon in the seventeenth century. In the New World he and his family prospered, but when the American Revolution came, they were staunch Loyalists and were forced to leave property behind and make the long journey to Nova Scotia. There they settled and my great-grandfather married Margaret Bostwick, of another Loyalist family. These two moved westward to Ontario, but not again did they achieve affluence. They had a moderately large family, for those days, of whom my grandfather was the eldest son.

How well I remember him — his gaiety, his alertness, his icy tempers when he was angered! I loved him dearly; there was a strong bond between us. I regarded his tempers with curiosity, rather than fear. They never were directed at me. They were usually brought on by a visit to the house by someone to whom he had taken an unaccountable dislike. Frequently these dislikes were for an admirer invited to the house by Aunt Eva, his favourite daughter. Grandfather could sit through an entire meal in stony silence, while the family vainly tried to make conversation and the guest tried not to look embarrassed. Grandfather's chiselled aquiline features, his thick silvery hair, his ice-blue eyes lent themselves well to this frozen disapproval. But when he and Grandmother retired to their bedroom, then his anger was unloosed and Caroline and I, in bed in the adjoining room, would hear his voice endlessly reiterating the causes of his dudgeon. For he must have reiterated. No one could possibly have found something new to say for so long a while. Caroline and I never knew. I think we were not curious. He was always gentle and sweet to us.

To his sons he was a kind and indulgent father, but my mother, his eldest child, seemed to bring out the worst in him. She was highly excitable, highly emotional, and her childhood was a time of painful scenes between them. After what he considered a misdeed, he would place her on a sofa beside him and lecture her for an hour. During all this while she would fairly tear herself to pieces with sobbing. Her face would be disfigured by the salt flow of tears. After this the physical chastisement took place. Yet he was still a young man.

There were times when his love for my mother was roused and took an almost extravagant turn. I remember how once after she had had a long illness, he was convinced that the scent of pine, balsam and spruce would cure her "nervous breakdown," as it was called. He drove to the woods and returned with a mass of greenery, with which he decorated her room. Every space where one of the scented boughs could be hung, the very bed on which she lay, was given their weight. I remember peeping in at her, looking small and rather overpowered by all this — but grateful too for his solicitude.

One of her doctors was an object of his aversion. This doctor was a Scot, with a high-pitched disagreeable voice and rather an aggressive manner. Whether he and Grandpa had some unfortunate encounter, I do not know. More probably Grandpa simply disliked him on sight. In either case a visit from Dr. McKenzie was enough to send Grandpa into a state of frozen disapproval for two days. Once my grandmother was taken suddenly ill and the doctor, making one of his regular calls, went in to see her. While he was there, Grandpa returned, and the sight of the detested doctor, sitting by his wife's bedside, brought on one of Grandpa's worst tempers. He wheeled and left the room, but we children heard his wrathful voice late that night. Yet Grandma never complained!

Most hospitable and generous of men, friends and relatives might visit as often and stay for as long as they chose in his house. They were almost always Grandmother's relatives. He had several brothers, but of them none so dear as Dr. John Lundy of Preston. When he came, the two would embrace, then, clasping each other close, they would dance about the room, Dr. Lundy short, stocky, my grandfather tall and wiry, but both with the same fine aquiline features and thick silvery hair. Somewhere in their ancestry they had discovered a Quaker and they delighted to multiply him in the calling of each other "thee" and "thou." Somehow it seemed to make the bond between them even more palpably affectionate.

When my grandfather died, somehow in the confusion and shock no word was sent to Dr. Lundy till he had already seen the notice in the newspaper. Years later I came upon a tragic letter from the old doctor to my father. In it this sentence remains with me — "Daniel is dead, and oh, the callousness of the living!" The words still have the power to cause me pain, though at the time they were written I was little more than a child.

I have spoken of my grandfather as wiry. Indeed he had great vitality and a keen enjoyment of life. When he was seventy, the

13

year before his death, he walked thirty miles in one day. At that time Caroline played the banjo and I the guitar. I remember one winter's evening when he came in from a walk while we were playing a dance tune. He was wearing his topcoat, which had a black Persian lamb collar, and a wedge-shaped cap of the same fur, set at a jaunty angle on his silvery head.

For one instant he listened to the music, then, putting one hand on his hip, with the other removing his cap, he executed a lively dance. Faster and faster we young girls played — faster and faster he danced, till for laughing we could play no more.

That is one picture of him I like to remember. Another is of him sitting nursing his short, strong-smelling pipe while he brooded on his inventions. Several of these he had patented, but they never made any money for him.

When Grandpa sat buried in thought, I would steal up behind him, stroke his fine hair or perhaps suddenly tickle him. At this last he would start up with a shout. Never was anyone so ticklish. But he took whatever I did in good part. It was only my mother who angered him — my mother and Aunt Eva's admirers. One of these, and she liked him very much, was a young man named Carruthers. He was what was then called rather wild. He and Aunt Eva used to go riding together. One day her horse, a quiet beast from the riding stable, suddenly shied. Aunt Eva was thrown and the tendons of her hand were strained. I think my grandfather blamed this accident entirely on young Carruthers.

But finally, when Aunt Eva was past thirty, one acceptable suitor appeared. Goodness was written large on his white brow, beamed from his clear grey eyes. No one could possibly object to James. Even my grandfather liked him; but unfortunately he was tubercular. He lived only fifteen years after the marriage. There were no children.

14

A peculiarity of my grandfather's was that he could not correctly pronounce the name of anyone he disliked. Try as he would (and his efforts were so earnest they were almost painful) he could not give anything but rather a ridiculous rendering of the syllables. Of one name in particular — the bearers of which he despised — he had such a variety of pronunciations that I used to introduce their name into the conversation just for the pleasure of hearing him mangle it. Then he would give me a roguish look and produce still another horrid variation.

Except the newspapers (the *Globe* and *Saturday Night*) the only reading I remember seeing my grandfather indulge in was the novels of Dickens. He read them over and over. In politics he and his family were as strongly Liberal as my father and his family were Conservative.

What a contrast was my grandmother to him! While both were fair-skinned and blue-eyed, he was tall and thin, she short and plump. Where he was temperamental, she was usually tranquil. Throughout her long and troubled life she presented a courageous and uncomplaining front. One thing they had in common — their sense of fun. Both loved a joke.

Another thing they shared was the agony of grief over the death of their eldest son. Once a year my grandfather visited his grave and brought back a white rose. This he would put into her hand, without a word. The name of the dead son was never spoken in the family. To me, a child, it seemed something sacred and terrible. If by chance it was uttered, a shock struck all. Then a silence followed before talk could be resumed. We children learned to share this shock. None of the loved departed must be mentioned.

It was a black day in springtime when the dead son's clothes were hung out in the breeze to air. I can picture them now

— the suits, the velvet smoking jacket — still rounded by the imprint of his body — or was it the breeze that filled them out? As well as the smoking jacket there was a black velvet smoking cap with a gold tassel which once I secretly tried on, secretly peered at my reflection in the barrel of rain water and saw the glimmer of the pale face, the dark shine of the eyes, beneath the cap, and shivered at the nearness of death to me who was so small and so alive.

My grandmother's father, of English parentage, had been born in Kingston. He was for a time in the military force and his epaulettes, his sword were cherished by her family, as was the story of his skating down the frozen St. Lawrence bearing secret dispatches. As a child, I pictured him, skating at full speed, with Indians on our shore ready to scalp him and, on the other, Americans ready to shoot.

However, he early forsook the military and turned to farming. He married Caroline Macleod, the daughter of a United Empire Loyalist family who had come from Philadelphia. They had brought with them on their arduous journey into this northern land the deeds of the property they had left behind — sacrificed to their loyalty — but I do not think they were of any value.

This little great-grandfather, the mildest of all my forbears, seemed determined to be picturesque. When he bought the farm near the village of Sharon, he found that there was no Church of England, of which he and his wife were members, within reach, but there was within reach the Temple of Sharon, a place of worship soon to be erected. It was built under the direction of David Willson, the founder of a new religious sect, the Children of Peace. He was a man of strong frame and domineering mind. He was steeped in the writings of the Old Testament. He felt himself born to be a patriarch and a leader and was convinced that the field for his work lay in this sequestered, richly wooded part of the country. He had come from the United States, not poor, but possessed of oxen and money, rumbling over the corduroy roads till he found the very place he sought and believed he was led there by divine guidance.

David Willson gathered the pioneers about him and preached to them under the open sky. The autumn weather was benign, the crops had been bountiful. He stood there, dominant and strong, pouring out the noble words of the Old Testament, words of promise, of might, of peace.

My great-grandfather stood by his side, and after the exhortation he sang the Twenty-third Psalm in a tenor voice of a quality more beautiful than any these pioneers had heard. The two combined could not be withstood. The lonely, isolated pioneers surged forward to place themselves under David Willson's banner.

Peace with each other, peace with the world; a life of purity, of liberty, of spiritual beauty; not austere, for there were to be feasts and processions. There was nothing of the Puritan about David Willson. When their work was over, they would sing, and rejoice in the love that would bind them together.

All were of one mind in their desire to have a place of worship, a centre for their spiritual world. Without delay the foundations of a Temple were laid. The forest trees were felled. The Temple rose in three cubes, one standing above the other, and on the topmost cube a golden ball was to be raised and sheltered beneath a cupola. The Temple was to be painted white for purity. It was to have light from windows on every side, typifying Reason and Truth. Inside there were twelve pillars bearing the names of the Twelve Apostles. In the very centre, beneath the golden sphere, was a Holy of Holies, containing a model of the Ark which was only brought out on feast days.

What a day of rejoicing was the opening of the Temple! From all the farms and near-by hamlets the Children of Peace came at dawn of a summer day, the women and maidens carrying garlands, the men dressed in snow-white linen suits, the children with wreaths of flowers in their hair. The Temple stood shining in its purity against the dark trees. Before the door David Willson waited to greet his flock. The summer air echoed his sonorous words, tears of joy filled his eyes as he declared that he and his followers were but a handful of pioneers of Peace, the great army of which would, in time to come, drive all war from the troubled world.

At the end of his address my great-grandfather, clad in pure white, his golden hair and whiskers shining in the sunrise, was raised to the very top of the Temple. He unveiled the great golden ball and, poised beside it, sang, in a voice like an angel's, a hymn of dedication, of which he had composed both words and music. The words were still preserved in the family Bible.

HYMN FOR PEACE

I am a seeker after Thy peace, O Lord,
  With the rising sun in my face;
I stand holding my soul like a goblet
  To be filled with Thy grace.

I see spreading about me the fertile fields
  We have claimed from the wild woodland;
I see upturned faces of men who pray
  To be blessed by Thy hand.

Give us peace! Let strife be unknown to our babes!
  Let the hearts of our wives be calm!
Let death come to us, not in its terror,
  But in trust and in balm!

I came as a pilgrim from an old sad land —
I came as a hart from the chase —
I found refuge and joy in this Temple
And I found my Lord's grace!

The doors of the Temple were flung wide by two youths and the congregation marched in, singing the Doxology as they marched. The women laid their garlands at the base of the pillars. The rising sun filled the Temple with sacred fire. The men who had hoisted my great-grandfather to the top of the building remained behind to lower him again to the ground.

As the congregation were taking their seats these five young men, with the singer in their midst, came with free steps into the Temple and sat on the front bench beneath the dais where the leader and patriarch stood, his hands upraised. Dressed in white as they were, their cheeks flushed by exertion, their hair waving bright over their proud heads, they did indeed look like the sons of God.

My great-grandfather's eldest daughter, Louise, was my grandmother. His eldest son was the grandfather of H. R. Macmillan, of forest and fisheries fame, in Vancouver. His second daughter, Martha, married at seventeen the most affluent young man of the neighbourhood. He was the eldest son of Lewis Clement, one of a United Empire Loyalist family which settled in the Niagara peninsula and intermarried with the Chryslers. Lewis Clement married Abigail Emmet, a daughter of a Virginian family.

Squire Clement, as he was always called, did very well by his eldest son, but the son, James, was unable to settle down with his young bride. He was full of ideas which invariably cost money, ideas which carried him and his wife far afield before fruition evaporated. Once it was an orange grove in the distant Southern United States. Once it was a scheme for irrigating the Ameri-

19

can prairies. This involved the buying of heavy machinery which eventually sank into the prairie and he came away and left it there. Out on the prairie also he and his wife buried a little daughter, but the younger daughter, Caroline, a delicate infant when they left Canada, lived. She was born when her mother was almost fifty. She and I, though brought up as sisters, came of different generations. Her mother was my mother's aunt. There was a strong bond of affection between those two, as well as a considerable resemblance in appearance and nature. Both were almost wildly romantic, high-tempered and extravagant. I cherish a picture of them, taken when my mother was seventeen. She is seated at the knee of Caroline's mother, who at the time was thirty-six. It is a lovely picture, of dignity and gentleness, flowing skirts and folded hands. Both looked as though they were remote from the harshness of life, yet both, in a later period, knew much trouble. Both had clear soprano voices and loved singing, but my mother could never keep on the tune, while Caroline's mother was truly musical. I have been told how she and Uncle James sang charmingly together, without accompaniment — sitting side by side on a sofa, reading the score from the same book.

This recollection of her parents singing tunefully together was imprinted on the little Caroline's mind, her happiest memory of them.

My mother shall not be written of at length, here, for there will be much to say of her in the pages to follow. As a child, she was possessed by the wildest high spirits which got her into trouble at school and at home. Very young, she was sent to a small private day school, kept by a Miss Doucette. My mother has told me of being struck by a switch on her plump bare shoulders that were left uncovered by the low-cut neck of her dress, for Miss Doucette was a disciplinarian. The wild but sensitive child grew into a beautiful girl. She was just five feet three and charmingly formed, with beautiful shoulders, arms and hands. She had deep-set eyes of an intense violet. A few weeks before the writing of this, I had occasion to call Dr. R. J. MacMillan to come to my house. As he was leaving he turned to me and exclaimed — with no preface — "What a lovely woman your mother was!"

He had seen her only once and that on her deathbed!

I agreed and then he asked, "Have you a photograph of her?"

I said I had and he demanded, with his peculiar and pleasing mixture of authority and boyish eagerness, "Bring it to me. I'd like to see it."

I flew upstairs to bring the photograph. He looked at it long, repeating, "A lovely woman — one doesn't often see her like."

She was twice engaged before she married my father. I don't know what was my grandfather's attitude toward these suitors. I fancy that he was never given an opportunity to express an opinion. She was so impulsive, so eager for life that she fairly flew to meet it. The first of these suitors I met when I was seven. His name was Lount and I think I fell in love with him then, as had my mother, for the charm of his smile, the gaiety of his laugh. After the meeting he sent me a doll which I have to this day. She had a romantic aura, possessed by no other doll of mine.

Mr. Lount was followed by Mr. Van Norman, who won my mother's heart by writing romantic poetry to her. She cherished this, long after her affection for him had cooled. She kept it in a velvet-lined writing-case and once let me read it for a treat. I was greatly impressed, though I thought it rather high-flown and its extravagant adjectives embarrassed me. I was then in my teens.

However, these romantic attachments were as nothing when she met my father.

It was at a New Year's Eve dance, and throughout their married life this evening was set aside to be spent together to re-live that first meeting. They had had several dances — a schottische, a polka, and then a waltz. Never had she met any man who danced as he did, with such lightness and grace, though he was a big man, more than six feet tall. After the dance the two young people went and sat on the stairs together. They talked and talked. Afterward she could not remember what he said but only the deep, warm urgency of his voice and the brilliant depths of his brown eyes, raised to hers, for he sat below her on the steps. They went into supper together.

After supper they did not re-join the dancers but returned to the stairs.

As the ringing bells signalled the coming of the New Year, he asked her to marry him and she accepted him. The marriage took place not many months later. They were twenty-three and twenty-five years of age. I was their only child.

They had many things in common. Both loved country life, horses and dogs — she, in moderation — he, to excess. Both were extravagant in dress — for her, the most expensive shops — for him, the best tailor. Both — with the best intentions — ran up bills which afterward they found difficult to pay. Both were extravagantly generous to friends and family. Both demonstrative in affection. She quick in anger and retort. He slow to anger, forbearing, but when roused, violent in his rage. Both forgiving and ready to be won by kindness.

When young, she once gave a pedler at the door a new, expensive suit of my father's in exchange for a pair of blue Bohemian glass vases. And though he searched the streets for the pedler, my father never found him.

My parents, on occasion, would describe to me their impressions of each other at their first meeting — that meeting so fraught with destiny. My mother would listen to these praises of her beauty with pensive pleasure. But when it came to her describing him, she made him wince with the flowery adjectives she employed. His wavy dark hair; his luminous brown eyes, his teeth, his figure — till he would exclaim:

"What a sight I must have been! Stop — stop!"

He appeared unconscious of his extraordinary good looks. He talked well, was animated and witty. I have often thought that a fine actor was lost in him.

Chapter 2

Paternal Forbears

THESE were in every way a contrast to my mother's people. For while all her people were of Anglo-Saxon stock, my father's were Irish and French. His mother, born in Dublin, came to Canada with her parents when a child. They came in a sailing ship, taking six weeks to the passage. The young couple brought with them some quite good furniture, portraits of themselves in oils, and also a portrait of the husband's mother (my great-great-grandmother) with their eldest child, a little boy of three, standing by her knee. He had dark curls and wore a low-cut white dress and pale blue shoulder knots. I remember him on a special occasion of which I shall tell later, when he was an old man — my great-uncle. These forbears of mine were of the tall dark Spanish type of Irish and, though they came from Dublin and Cork, they were Protestants.

I do not know what became of two of these portraits, but the third, that of my great-grandmother, Fanny Danford, hangs in my dining-room to-day. She left it to her favourite daughter, whom she bore when she was past fifty years of age, and, at last, it came to me.

This Irish great-grandmother was a remarkable woman. By her charm, her fiery temper, her demonstrative affection, her dominating nature, she overbore her children and her children's children. While she lived she kept her stalwart sons about her, when they might have bettered themselves by going far afield. Her grandsons were guided by her rather than by their mothers. My father adored her. It was he who carried me, when I was three, to her on her deathbed. It is my first recollection of childhood. The tall house that seemed so dim and somehow forbidding, the long stairway thickly carpeted, the bedroom, with its four-poster bed, then — the sudden dip downward, as though my world had given way beneath me — the two long arms held eagerly upward to take me — the strong old voice, with nothing of death in it — "My little darling — my darling!" How fearful I was, in that dark embrace — I three years old, she ninety-four!

I was lifted up. I was rescued. I clasped my father's neck tightly as we descended the stair. I remember it clearly.

On her last birthday she had danced the mazurka with my father. It was he who, almost a year later, when she slipped and fell on the icy path in the garden, carried her into the house. She died not long after.

Of her sons I remember only one — the one whose portrait was painted as a tiny boy, with her mother-in-law. But her three daughters were well known to me. The eldest was my grandmother. The two others were Great-aunts Susannah and Fanny.

What a contrast to her mother was my grandmother! Placid, gentle, peace-loving. Yet she was capable of roundly asserting herself. I remember her coming into the billiard room in my Uncle Danford's house from her afternoon rest while my uncle and my father were engaged in a game of billiards. She towered in the doorway, massive in her long white nightdress. She had a particularly pleasant voice with a slight Dublin accent. Now she said, "I was woken by the sound of the billiard balls. I think you have forgotten

25

that it is Sunday afternoon. Please let us have no more of this."
She moved majestically away and the two sons, men in their fif-
ties, with shamefaced grins, hung up their billiard cues. But it
was seldom that she asserted herself.

It seems extraordinary to me that she and my grandfather de la
Roche should have married. From what I remember of her, from
what I have heard of him, I wonder what they had in
common; she, the single-hearted, inexperienced girl of twenty-
four; he, the-European, the scholar, the linguist — ten years
older. When she spoke of him to me, it was always with tempered
admiration of his great learning, as though it were a peculiarity
that had been with him from birth, that set him apart and yet was
not quite comfortable.

It seems extraordinary how these grandparents of mine — so
diverse — should have gathered together in this city of Toronto,
by way of Ireland, France, England, the movement of United
Empire Loyalists from America, and so produced my infant body.
How virile they were and yet how few descendants they had!
Their children, with eight marriages among them, produced only
two offspring — a quarter of a child to each marriage!

These two grandparents met in this way:

It was a mild spring morning and beginning to rain. My grandmother had just bought herself a new bonnet, trimmed with flowers and a satin bow. She and her little sister of eight, who was
carrying the bonnet box, came out of the milliner's and were con-
fronted by the shower. What were they to do? Return to the shop,
when their mother expected them home? Never — they must face
the rain.

Just then a young man in his thirties appeared before them —
not only appeared but offered them the shelter of his umbrella!
The bow with which he offered it, his unusual enunciation, with

the hint of foreign accent, his looks (my grandmother long afterward told me) fairly took her breath away. Like herself, he was
six feet tall but, while she was slender, he was stalwartly built. He
had auburn hair worn rather long, and grey eyes. He was smooth
shaven, an unusual thing in those days. As for his clothes — never
had she seen such elegance. His tall hat was worn at just the
right angle. His coat, of a dark blue, had silver buttons; his cravat
— oh, my grandmother had no words elegant enough to describe
his cravat!

His umbrella sheltered the sisters from the shower. The two
grownups walked in step, while little Fanny skipped alongside. He
escorted them to their door, talking the while with animation. He
showed great interest in the new bonnet and wondered whether
he would ever have the pleasure of seeing her wear it. She confided to him that she expected to wear it on Sunday. She sang in
the church choir. Would he perhaps be going to church? He hesitated, then said that he hoped to see her after the service. He did
not tell her that he was a Catholic.

At the door of the house, another bow, a murmured au revoir
and he was gone.

Indoors the two sisters dragged Susannah, the middle sister,
to the window, that she might glimpse him before he disappeared.

But they had not seen the last of him. When they came out of
church, the Irish family clustered about the widowed mother,
there he was, strolling along the opposite side of the street. Years
later my grandmother told me of her excitement at seeing him
there. He was, she declared, a being from another world.

Yet he appeared very willing to enter their world. He was lonely.
Obviously he admired the eldest daughter of the family. He looked
prosperous. He had family connections in Ireland, which made
him seem less foreign. Young de la Roche was invited to the

house in John Street. He became a frequent visitor. Before long, my grandmother, in spite of opposition from her mother and brothers, declared that in this man she had found the one love of her life. She was gentle but she was stubborn. She who had romped with her brothers, been a devoted and obedient daughter, now became a different sort of young woman — one who had ideas different from theirs on almost every subject. Her brothers were high-spirited, cocky. They rarely opened a book. The man she loved was indolent. He was a student — immersed in classic literature. He was a Catholic — not a very devout Catholic, perhaps, but still a Catholic.

Any liking the family had had for the man the favourite daughter now married soon evaporated. In truth it was succeeded by active dislike and that in time developed into hate. Everything he did was wrong. Even when he anglicized his name — even though he allowed his children to be christened in the Protestant church — even though he was kind (if a little aloof) toward my grandmother — they distrusted him. He had pretended (they said) to be well-off, yet the house into which the young people moved was small and sparsely furnished. For all his highfaluting ways, his disdainful air, he seemed to have little idea of how to support a family. Why didn't his aristocratic relations do something for him? Why had not the revolutionists killed off all of that name? This Irish family would have been in entire agreement.

Yet he had a great admiration for his mother-in-law. I was once shown a letter, written by him to my father, in which he most generously expressed both admiration and affection. "Her advice to us was always good," he wrote. "I wish we had more often taken it. Her wit, her fine spirit always have delighted me."

He was not what was called "a good provider." He spent extravagant sums for rare books. These came from booksellers in

London and Paris. He surrounded himself with books in French, Latin and Greek. The prices he paid for these made cruel inroads on their slender means, yet my grandmother did not complain. When she saw him poring over calf-bound, richly hand-tooled volumes in Greek and Latin, while others lay heaped on the floor beside him, she felt a gentle pride in being the wife of such a man. The common affairs of life, she felt, must not touch him. She protected him — waited on him.

He was able to get together a group of young men whom he tutored in the classics. That did not bring in much money, but still she adored him in her own quiet way. One day (and she herself related this to me) a needy stranger was somehow admitted to his study, where he sat by the open fire, wrapped in a Scotch plaid, reading. Only half listening to the man's tale of need, my grandfather absently felt in his pocket, pulled out a ten-dollar bill and gave it to the man. My grandmother seemed to feel more pride in him for this careless giving than anger.

Once the chimney took fire. He ran to the foot of the stairs and shouted up to her:

"Sarah, come — for the love of God! The house is on fire!"

Down she flew in terror. Somehow the fire was extinguished. Then she went upstairs and had a miscarriage. This she told me also without resentment. What he did was to her as a force of nature, his acts were as an act of God, and always she ended by exclaiming, "Whatever happened, his manners were perfect."

In their early life together she had two sons by him. I have a lovely photograph of her, her lace-mittened hands holding them close, the elder four years old, the other, my father, a year and a half younger. These handsome, healthy little boys as they grew received scant notice from their father, excepting caustic criticisms of their manners. If either of them had been of studious bent, it might have been different, but they were wild, with animal spirits, and had no interest in the dead languages. Their mother, their grandmother, their lively Irish uncles were enough for them. To them their father became an aloof, yet repressive, figure.

In the meantime, Susannah, the sister next my grandmother, had married and, in a material way, had married very well, for her husband was, in those days, counted a rich man. He was plain to look at, quiet, unaccomplished, rather dull. My grandmother pitied her sister, when she considered the contrast between their two husbands. But Susannah had handsome looks and high spirits, enough and to spare. She had inherited her mother's elegant carriage, her flashing dark eyes, her mordant wit. I have a photograph of her in which she looks more like an empress than an ordinary woman has any right to do. I have heard my grandmother say, "I am always twice glad of Susannah's visits — glad to see her — gladder still when she goes."

Well do I remember this great-aunt in my childhood. Her angular and colourless husband, departing this life, had left her with a large house in the country, a substantial income, also three tall daughters who took after their father, and a son with a splendid baritone voice. This son, Willy, was filled with the desire to study abroad. There were ample means, but his mother, because of the temptations of the Old World, refused to allow it. She kept her darling at home, where he grew up indolent — undistinguished — all his ambition gone.

Aunt Susannah would descend on us, always without warning, accompanied by her three daughters — four massive women, in the most expensive, overpowering mourning I ever have seen. It was remarkable, even for those days of deep mourning. Their full black cashmere skirts, edged by wide bands of crêpe, swept the

streets, their heavy crêpe veils hung to their knees. Their hand-
bags, gloves and shoes were of the blackest black. Wherever they
went their entrance was in the nature of a ceremony. In those
days McConkey's was the best restaurant in Toronto and when
Aunt Susannah and her daughters came to town, they always
lunched or had tea there. The towering procession they made as
they progressed to their table was enough to create a pause of
wonder, almost of consternation, on the faces of those present.
There was a funereal majesty about that entrance which I can
scarcely exaggerate. Remember, these four were all more than six
feet tall and Great-aunt Susannah was strikingly handsome.
The waiters knew her and one would hasten forward to arrange
the table. My great-aunt would seat herself, throw back her veil
and cast an appraising glance at her audience — for she was a
born actress. When she lay on her deathbed, she forced those
who nursed her to laugh at her wit even while they grieved. My
grandmother accompanied her occasionally on these visits to Mc
Conkey's and found them very embarrassing.

Though Great-aunt Susannah would not allow her talented son
to go to Paris to study music, she sent her rather colourless daughters abroad, under proper supervision. My father has told me how,
on their return, he who so greatly would have appreciated their
opportunities asked the eldest, "Well, cousin, what did you think
of Paris?"

All she could find to say was, "Well, they have very good clean-
ers and pressers there."

"My God," exclaimed my father afterward, "she wouldn't know
the difference between the Arc de Triomphe and the Toronto
Union Station!"

When my Great-aunt Susannah died, her daughters continued
to live in their large, rather ugly house, filled with heavy Victorian

31

furniture. They preserved their mother's room intact. Nothing was allowed to go into disrepair. Her very garments were kept in order and when her handsome sealskin sacque (as they then called seal coats) became unfashionable, they sent it to Dineen's and had it remodelled to the latest style. It was then returned to the clothes cupboard, where it hung for goodness knows how many years. I suppose that the thought of giving the coat to my grandmother did not occur to them, but how greatly would she have appreciated it!

To return to my grandmother and her two little boys — Danford, the elder, red-haired, pink-cheeked, devoted to his mother; Richmond, with his curling brown hair and large dark eyes, adventurous, not easy to control but clever and responsive to affection. They were a handful, these small boys, and before long the young mother was left to bring them up without a father's authority.

There was no outlet in this city for his talents, my grandfather decided, no appreciation of his powers. When he had arrived, he had brought with him letters of introduction, but he soon had quarrelled with the several important gentlemen to whom he was introduced, not hesitating to make light of the conventions they venerated and at the same time to show them how little he thought of their scholarship or theology. In truth, he could not get on with anyone, except my grandmother, and she was so gentle and good-humoured that she would have been difficult to quarrel with. He decided to go to the United States, that land of opportunity and, at least partial, cultivation.

I think my grandmother would have accompanied him. I think she would have followed him to the ends of the earth, had not her mother intervened, used all her influence against it. Who knew what might happen to her and to her two darling little boys in that strange land, with no one but an erratic, capricious, arbitrary husband to protect her! No — let him go by himself — a foreigner, without means — and see how he gets on. If he succeeds, how easy to follow him! If he fails — oh, he'll come back to you, Sarah, my dear, he'll come back — if he fails!

So — Sarah got everything ready for the journey, pressed his coats and waistcoats, of which he took such care, mended his fine linen, packed his travelling bags, dropping a few tears on the carefully folded garments. He himself packed his books. He said an affectionate good-bye to his two little boys, urging them to be good and obedient and to take care of their *maman*, till they again joined him. What he said was usually completely over their heads, so that they seldom understood what he meant. He visited his mother-in-law, making himself agreeable, kissing her hand in farewell. Then he laid his square white hands on his wife's shoulders, drew her to him and, with tears in his grey eyes, kissed her on either cheek and on the lips.

He was gone.

He tried posts in several American universities, but he found it difficult to settle down. His nature seems to have been a curious mixture of the capricious and the indolent. However, he did write regularly to my grandmother, giving her careful details of his life in America, and he did send her money. As his boys grew, he was anxious about their education. He could not understand why their tastes were so different from his. He planned courses of reading for them and urged my grandmother to see to it that their schoolmasters carried them out. At Christmas he sent presents of books in French, Latin and Greek. As the boys developed, he wrote impressive letters to them and when they replied, corrected their way of expressing themselves. He was eager to know which of the professions they wanted to enter and when he discovered that they had no bent for any of them, he was greatly disappointed. He was troubled by my father's spelling and when the boy was in his teens, sent him two ponderous calf-bound volumes of Johnson's dictionary, with quotations from Shakespeare and other great writers of the past to show the proper usage of each word.

I remember once seeing a bundle of my grandfather's letters to my father. They struck me then as extraordinarily cold letters from father to son, yet one paragraph stands out in my memory — as different. It read, "I am astonished to read in your last letter that you resent still a remark you say I made to you as a child. You write that I said you were no better than a dog about the house! I have no recollection of ever making a remark so unkind, but if I did I now sincerely apologize for it. My son — forgive me."

My father held the bundle of letters in his hand. We were in the process of making one of our frequent removals and he was sorting the things in his bureau drawers. He said, "I don't suppose you ever would want to read these letters?" Somehow feeling that he would like to make an end of them, I at once said no. "Then I'll not keep them any longer," he said, and one by one tore them across and tossed them into the wastepaper basket.

Suddenly I had a feeling of sadness at seeing them lying in fragments there. I picked up one and read in the fine foreign-looking writing the words "My son."

My grandmother appears to have been comfortably off. I expect that her mother helped her bear the expense of the house in John Street where they lived together after the departure of my grandfather. With them also was my grandmother's young sister, Fanny. They spoilt the two small boys, Danny and Richmond, to the satisfaction of all.

When these small boys were just entering their teens, my grandmother had a terrible shock. It came in the form of an anonymous letter from Baltimore, where my grandfather was now living. The writer of this letter declared that he was carrying on a love affair with a lady of high social position in Baltimore and advised my grandmother to lose no time in discovering the scandalous truth for herself.

I never have been told whether my great-grandmother was aware of her eldest daughter's reason for her impetuous journey to Baltimore. Though my grandmother was usually of a gentle, yielding nature, she could, when roused, be adamant in purpose. She lost no time in making her preparations. She packed her portmanteau, donned her best bonnet and fur-trimmed cloak and, leaving the household in the care of her staunch Yorkshire maid, Louisa, who was with her for thirty years, she set out on the long journey.

No word of her coming was sent to the suspected husband. She descended on him, like a massive avenging angel, with no flash of lightning or clap of thunder to signal her arrival.

She hired a cab and drove straight to his lodgings.

What did she find?

She found him in a book-lined room, books mounded on the floor beside him, while a volume of Greek drama lay open in front of him. Astounded by the sight of her, he leaped to his feet. Then he exclaimed, "My dear Sarah, how delighted I am to see you!" He embraced her and, with tears streaming down her cheeks, she untied the strings of her bonnet and threw it on the bed. She told of the reason of her coming.

Whatever was said in that interview the result was a complete reconciliation. She tidied the book-strewn room, mended his clothes, and at night climbed into the high bed with him where there was scarcely room for two large people. She stayed for a week in Baltimore. He took her about and showed her the sights. When she returned home, she was pregnant. She never saw him again.

35

A third son was born to my grandmother, a solemn little fellow, with a round dark head, narrow eyes and hands like his father's. His father named him François, which later became Francis. However, in these pages he shall be called by his proper name of François. He had the quality of studiousness his brothers lacked. He applied himself to his books with zest. He was well-behaved and obedient. While his brothers gave their demonstrative love to their grandmother, it was to his mother he clung. To his distant father he gave a wistful admiration.

My grandmother's elder sons were grown-up and married when word came of my grandfather's sudden death. He had gone to New Orleans to visit the descendant of a French family there. The heat had been great and he had died, in a park, of sunstroke. I am his only living descendant.

When the news of his death came to the family, my Great-aunt Fanny was visiting in the house. Great-aunt Fanny was for a moment shaken by the news; then she rushed to the sitting-room to tell her mother. Aunt Fanny was married to a doctor. One would think that she would have hesitated to burst in on an old lady of ninety, bringing such news without preparing her for it. But no — they were in complete accord in their feelings about my grandfather.

Aunt Fanny rushed in exclaiming, "De la Roche is dead! De la Roche is dead!" She threw her arms about her mother and the two embraced, repeating the words "He is dead!"

And what of my grandmother? My mother has told me how she went to her, found her in an abandon of grief, lying across the four-poster bed. She took my mother's hand and after a little was able to talk calmly of the dead man. To my mother he was a romantic figure and when she spoke of him to me, it was as of a man who should be forgiven much. From this bereavement my grandmother emerged a widow, clad in black, the woman I remember.

Even as a small child I was impressed by the serene dignity of her appearance. Never did she look in the least dishevelled or worried — her elegant figure, her long waist in a black bodice with white ruching at neck and wrists, and round her neck a long gold chain. She was proud of this chain, for it had been given her by her mother as a reward for nursing her through an illness. Fifteen guineas had been paid for it. When she was past eighty my grandmother gave it to me. She wore a cameo brooch and, on her silvery hair, a lace cap with little ribbon rosettes. She made these caps herself and she had at least a dozen of them, in bandboxes in her enormous wardrobe. Once, as a treat, she showed me the prettiest of all — the one she was to wear when laid in her coffin.

Always can I remember her hands, long, white and extraordinarily supple. They were inherited by my father, the one characteristic he had from her. I do not think these hands of Grandmama's had ever been used for anything more strenuous than needlework. They lay, long and white, on the arms of her chair. Sometimes she would raise them from the wrist and gently let them fall again, while she uttered a resigned "Heigh-ho."

When the word came of my grandfather's death, his eldest son took train at once to arrange for the bringing back to Canada of his father's body. He had opposition in this from some members of the family. "Bury him where he died," they said, but his son would not have it so. In the oppressive heat the young man packed twenty-eight cases of books, then, with his father's body, made the journey. So much did he go through on that journey that when it was over he had a serious illness. This young man had a fiery red beard and a temper to match it. He stored the books in the empty room above the stable behind his house, for there was no place for

37

them indoors. Certainly neither he nor his wife would have attempted to read them.

They were to be given to the youngest son, François, when he had somewhere to accommodate them and was old enough to appreciate them.

But the little boy of thirteen already appreciated them! He was allowed to spend all the time he wished among the books. Armed with hammer and chisel, he opened box after box and, with the books mounded about him, he read and read. A black-haired little boy, with high cheekbones and sombre eyes, he was never loved by his grandmother and aunts and uncles, as were his high-spirited brothers. A quiet little boy who liked Latin and Greek was not lovable.

He never tired of the stable and the books, no matter how cold it was. He tried to imagine what it would have been like to know his father, to have lived in the same house with him. On one occasion, when his reticence was unleashed, he told me of those long hours. Beneath his cold exterior he was highly emotional. I cannot remember what the occasion was or what led up to this burst of confidence. Never again did he refer to it.

What he told me was this: one dark afternoon in November — he had lately passed his fourteenth birthday — he opened, for the first time, one of the smallest of the cases. He always had a feeling of excitement when the lid of a fresh box was lifted and, beneath layers of newspapers, new treasures were discovered. Was ever a bookloving boy more favoured, he wondered.

But in this smaller box he discovered something different — bundles of letters! He had the right to read them, he thought, because everything in these boxes was his. Almost tremblingly he untied the first bundle. Perhaps he would in these letters find out more about the father of whom he knew so little.

My uncle's deep-set dark eyes looked sombrely into mine. "What I found," he said, "were love letters."

"Yes," he went on, "they were letters from certain ladies of Baltimore. It was not as though they were from only one woman. There were several and they all seemed very much in love with him. Of course, I had heard that he was a fascinating man."

I was young. I was embarrassed by these confidences from someone always so reticent — the uncle I knew least of all. I asked, almost in a whisper, "Did you read them, every one?"

"Yes," he said emphatically, "every blessed one of them. I didn't understand them, but I read on and on till it was almost dark. I was frightened. I don't quite know why. I made up my mind that nobody should ever read those letters. . . . There was a small rusty stove that had not been used for years, in the carriage house. I collected all the letters and thrust them into the stove, then I ran to the kitchen and got matches. In a few minutes there was nothing left of the letters but some scraps of charred paper."

Uncle François never again mentioned this to me, but to-day I picture the small boy, just entering adolescence — his confused imaginings — his frightened burning of the letters — the sudden impulse of the man to confide in me.

With a reticence equal to his I never told either of my parents of this incident. My mother would have been too interested. My father would have dismissed the affair with an amused and tolerant smile. No — I kept it to myself. I half forgot it. It is only now that it comes to mind.

And now I wonder what traits this grandfather bequeathed to his descendants — three sons and one grandchild. To my father, the middle son, nothing that I can discover. But eldest and youngest, it seems to me, inherited a leaning toward Catholicism. Surely it must have been in their blood. The eldest son, married to a

39

staunch Presbyterian, went to church with her, but his closest friends were priests. One of these, Father McMahon, I think his name was, died in my uncle's arms. The youngest son, François, made no outward sign of his Catholic leanings but astonished me by telling me, late in his life, that he went every day to St. Michael's Cathedral to reflect and pray. As for me, I had my period of that longing — but it is past.

In my impressionable schooldays the shadow of this grandfather lay across me. The best example I can give of this is that once, when I had come out at the head of my form in French, the teacher of French asked me if I got help at home. As a matter of truth I was given no help at home, but at the sudden question the shadow of my grandfather fell across me. I was sure he had helped me and I answered yes. For days, for weeks afterward I was troubled by this lie. I felt that I should go to the teacher and explain. But how to explain! I could not bring myself to do it — to try to make her understand that a dead man had helped me with my lessons. I felt there would be something shameful in that.

Chapter 3

Very Young Days

I WAS not born where I should have been, in my father's house, but
in my grandfather's. My mother was visiting there and made a call
at the rectory, where a member of the family was down with scarlet
fever. She contracted the disease. She was terribly ill and so not
able to go home to have her child. The labour of childbirth, during
the ravages of fever, undermined her health, which before this
had been superb. Never again had she such resistance.

Here I shall say something of the doctor who brought my miserable little body into the world, a fledgling of three and a half
pounds but — immune to scarlet fever.

This Dr. Bradford Patterson was such an individualist, so different from anyone I know today, that I should like to describe
him. As a very young man he had served as a surgeon in the
American Civil War. This experience, combined with keen intelligence, an iron nerve and no shrinking from the infliction of pain,
made him a very good surgeon indeed. He married three times and
it was his favourite boast that he was the only man living who had
sat down to Christmas dinner with his wife and his three mothers-
in-law, on the best of terms with all four. There was a tough, hard

geniality about him which possibly intimidated women, while the amorous glance of his light blue eyes flattered them.

I remember him well — his upright figure, his white hair and small beard beneath his lower lip — an "imperial" it was called — and his muscular, dominating upper lip. He adored women and when Caroline and I were almost full-grown, he would set us one on either knee and fairly beam with pleasure — if such a cold, egotistical countenance could be said to beam.

In winter he wore a topcoat of real sealskin with cap to match and carried a gold-headed cane. He was a great hunter. Each fall saw him off to the woods. Till he was past eighty he brought back his quarry and I tremble to think of the quail, partridge, pheasants, deer and moose which fell before him. The stuffed heads of wild animals hung above every doorway in his house and surgery. Tea in that house always meant to me scones and honey, preceded by paper-thin slices of dried venison.

The doctor's third wife was my Great-aunt Fanny. No child of hers lived, but my mother once told me how one night, in the middle of a supper party, Great-aunt Fanny went upstairs to her bedroom and there gave birth to a tiny body, perfect in every way but only a few inches long. Aunt Fanny herself had related this to my mother. For a long while the thought of this birth filled me with awe. I pictured the solitary woman, in the upstairs room, the laughing company below, the tiny baby — about three inches long — pretty as a little doll. I think that from my mother I inherited the power — or the weakness — of credulity, of wonder. Nothing has been too fantastic for me to believe. Yet, the simplest everyday things will fill me with wonder.

Great-aunt Fanny had been a handsome girl, tall and slim, with brown eyes and hair. Some years after her marriage an ulcerated tooth had infected her jawbone to such a degree that it was feared she might lose her life. A consultation was held, but no surgeon would venture to perform the operation. So Dr. Patterson himself performed it. It was successful, but from that time Great-aunt Fanny wore a narrow black velvet band round her head and beneath her chin which, because of the missing piece of bone, went off a little to one side. She was a fine pianist and the picture I have of her in my memory is of her seated at the piano, her hands flying over the keys, as though something wild and untamed by her life with that man were then let loose. Meanwhile he would sit listening with a pride that seemed to say he had invented both her and the piano.

This doctor and my Uncle François had the liveliest detestation for each other. The doctor hated my father's brothers, but for him he had real affection. Indeed, to know my father was to love him. Among the epithets hurled at each other by the doctor and Uncle François these two were relished by the family: the doctor called Uncle François "an educated ass," and Uncle François called the doctor "a brutally ignorant old quack."

Well, the doctor came to the house where my young mother was lying ill. The disease had not yet been diagnosed. He took off his sealskin cap, raised his head and sniffed the air. "I smell scarlet fever," he said. . . . A few hours later I was born, while outside a blizzard raged and the temperature fell to twenty degrees below zero. When my father saw me, he said to my mother, "Let me name this one and you may name all the others." And so he named me and there never were any others. Mazo had been the name of a girl to whom he once had been attached.

A little later he said to Mother, "I'll do almost anything for you, but never ask me to push the pram. I refuse to do that."

From being a delicate infant I grew into a healthy little girl, much humoured, yet affectionate and biddable. My memory goes

43

back to my very early days. It is an unusual memory that has brought me both pleasure and torment. Seldom have I been able to forget anything. A scene of pain or cruelty which I may have witnessed as a child returns to me to-day with terrific vividness. The first such happening I remember was the sight of a dog, running in terror through the street, with a tin can tied to its tail. There were boys in the street who doubled up in laughter and shouted at him. My astonishment that such a thing could be, my helplessness to prevent it, made an impression that years could not dim. It was some time later than this and we were living in a tall house in what was then called St. James's Square, overlooking the gardens of the normal school, when the first and only violent happening I ever saw in the street took place. It was early evening and almost my bedtime. The front door stood ajar and I stepped outside feeling adventurous, for I never was allowed outside alone at that hour. Suddenly I heard footsteps running. I saw two men, one young, the other old, running along the road. They were rough-looking men of the sort I had seldom seen. The younger obviously was chasing the elder. He bent, picked up a stone and hurled it after the old man. It struck him on his bald head and dark blood poured from the wound. They ran on and on, out of my sight, unseen by anyone but me.

I ran indoors, scarcely able to speak for excitement, but when I was able to tell what I had seen, no one believed me! I simply had imagined it. Such a thing would not happen in our quiet street. My father went to the door and looked out. No street could have been quieter, more respectable. He came back and set me on his shoulder. "It never really happened," he said. But I knew.

Childish fears, unreasoning terrors, I had like other children. Perhaps, being an only child, an imaginative child, they had a stronger hold on me. My first fear of all (I could not have been more than eighteen months old) was for a feather, a bit of fluff or down, blowing across the floor. Even now I can recall the trembling terror of watching its pale progress. There was no use in telling me that such a tiny thing could not harm me. I did not fear the largest dog. But of this airy, blowing thing I was deadly afraid.

This particular fear must have been the forerunner of a certain nightmare I had as a child when ill. In my dream I saw a dim tunnel and, rolling smoothly through it, an enormous ball that almost filled the tunnel. I stood in its way. Nothing could save me. At the same time I heard a distant roaring sound. A strange smell, the very essence of evil, stole through the tunnel. I woke crying and wet with sweat.

Once when visiting at Grandpa's I had tea with an older child. I was about six, she twelve, and she told me a story. It was about a woman who had a golden arm. She died and her husband greedily removed the arm and sold it for the value of the gold. When that very night he went to bed, he heard his dead wife trailing up the stairs in her graveclothes, moaning at each step, "Bring me back my golden arm! Bring me back my golden arm!"

After I was tucked up in my cot the horror of this tale possessed me. I lay covered in bedclothes, hands over my ears, yet nothing could shut out that terrible voice calling for the golden arm. Closer and closer came the ghost, past the stuffed owl in his niche to my very door. I felt that I should die of fright. Then came silence. The exquisite relief of silence. I breathed again. But the respite was only for a moment. . . . There she was with her terrible cry!

Over and over I endured the repetition of this misery — the trailing graveclothes, the approach, the wailing, the very rattle of

45

my bedroom door latch — the silence — the return. At last, in desperation, I climbed out of my cot and, as though pursued by all the devils of hell, fled down the stairs to the sitting-room, where the family sat in the cheerful lamplight at a game of cards. It was some time before I could make clear the cause of my terror. Then I was safe in my father's protective arms. But what a fine rage Grandpa was in! He had to be forcibly restrained by wife and daughters from marching straight to the home of the twelve-year-old and telling her parents what a wicked girl she was.

Remembering the quiet country roads of my youth, the exhilarating sights in the city, I feel pity for the child of to-day with nothing to see but the hideous mechanized traffic, making its stinking way, bumper to bumper, through the gloomy streets, nothing better to do than to learn at sight the makes of different motor cars. How different were the streets in those days! A dray would pass, drawn by a team of powerful draft horses — a butcher's cart, the butcher wearing his light blue apron — a splendid equipage, with coachman in fur cape — horses, horses, everywhere! Women, holding up their long flounced skirts — men who looked like gentlemen. In summer, fruit vendors, with their cry of "Strawberry, strawberry ripe! Two boxes for a quarter!" And they were quart boxes, not the miserable little pint boxes we buy to-day. There was an Italian boy I well remember who pushed his barrow of bananas twice a week to our door, with his musical call of "Ban-nana ripe, fifteen cents a dozen!" I even remember his name, Salvator Polito, and the big red bananas.

In those days everyone who had the use of his legs went for walks. To-day nobody walks for pleasure. You may walk for miles and meet nobody but yourself. In morning and afternoon people walked. In the evening they sat on their verandahs behind the shelter of syringas in flower, the white skirts of the girls billowing

over the steps. From indoors might come the sound of a piano.
Now and again one heard the clip-clop of horses' hoofs. Children
went to bed tired out by their play. Whenever they were free to
play they were absorbed in their games. What has happened to the
play spirit in the child of the present?

Not long ago I had lunch at the skating club and, looking down
on the ice, saw a dozen earnest children practising figure skating.
Over and over the little perfectionists, in their faultless skating
gear, repeated the monotonous figures. Nobody was forcing them,
nobody was urging them. They wanted to do just what they were
doing, each doubtless picturing himself as a champion of organized
sport.

I thought of our childhood's helter-skelter skating — hand
in mittened hand doing a crack the whip across the rink — skates
never quite fitting — skirts, flannel petticoats getting in our way.
I thought of the admiring group which would gather to see my
father execute the grapevine or the figure eight — he loftily ignoring them — pretending it was easy!

And the games of summer on the green, green grass!

London Bridge is falling down — Here we come gathering nuts
in May — The farmer views his lands — hide and seek — old
witch — this last throwing one into a madness of chase and pretended fear. Afterward the casting of oneself exhausted on the
grass, staring up at the blue sky or investigating the doings in a
tiny ant-hill . . . the winds in which one ran, all by oneself,
swifter, it seemed, than the wind, wilder than the tempest.

When I visited at Grandpa's I could see, far below the terrace,
beyond the stableyard, a railway line, over which several times a
day a train tootled. These trains were familiar friends to me, because, from the time I was five, my mother would put me on the
train in Toronto, in the conductor's charge, to go on a visit to

47

Grandpa's. I was a composed traveller, not in the least nervous, ready to enter into conversation with other passengers.

Quite early in the morning a certain freight train would pass and this train had the distinction of being a weather forecaster, because on the boxcar just behind the locomotive a painted moon showed the country folk what to expect in the way of weather. A full moon promised a fine day. A half-moon, I think, rain, and a crescent moon, storms. I lay in wait for this train and when I heard its whistle, gathered myself together for the race. I was fair to the train. Not till the locomotive was even with me did I begin to run. Always at this moment, but whether in fear of me or rage I did not know or care, the locomotive uttered an ear-splitting shriek. Matching it with a shriek of my own, I set out with flying legs and hair to outdo it. From end to end of the lawn we ran the race, the train and I, and always I believed I had won. Then with thudding heart I flew to the house to announce to Grandma what the weather would be.

But before long there came into my life someone who could run faster than I — one who could run on and on till he dropped panting to the grass, then, after a moment's rest, be up and at it again! This was a small boy named Leigh McCarthy. He was visiting in the house of his uncle, Judge Morgan, a neighbour of my grandfather, and I was visiting my grandparents. After all the years I remember well Leigh's looks. He was tall for his age and slim. I had to look up to him. He had a crown of curling fair hair and every day when he came to play he was dressed in white flannel shorts and jacket, and a little white shirt with a narrow lace collar. Round and round my grandfather's white house Leigh would run with me panting after him. His wild energy exhausted me, but still I panted slavishly after him.

One day we ventured into the street and had not gone far when a group of rough-looking boys surrounded us. I think one of them pulled my hair. In the frightening moments that followed, I forgot what started the fight, but there Leigh was, in their midst, fighting like a small fury, while I stood by trembling. It was soon over. The urchins vanished. Leigh and I ran back to safety, he exhilarated by the fight, though there were bloody nail marks on his flower-petal cheek, I strangely wishing he would go home. But no — he laughed in his joy — he caught my hand — we ran and ran!

One day a photographer came and took us to where there was a stream. He carried me across steppingstones, Leigh skipping be-hind, and sat me on a broad flat stone, with a fancy basket on my lap. Presumably this was to hold the fish that Leigh was to catch, for he was posed behind me with a fishing rod in his hands. Next the photographer found a place for himself and his camera. Wonder of wonders, he intended making a stereoscopic picture of us which one viewed through a contrivance held to the eyes. I still have one of these photographs.

At last the day came when Leigh was to leave. Quite early in the morning he came to say good-bye, not dressed as usual in white flannels but in a sober navy blue suit, with a little linen collar in place of the lace frill.

"Good-bye," he said soberly. "I'm going."

"Oh," I said.

"We can't say good-bye properly here." He looked up at the windows of the house. "We'll go behind those bushes."

I was accustomed to do as he said. We went behind the flowering currant bushes.

"Now," he said, "we must kiss good-bye."

Our faces shyly bumped together.

Then he was gone. I stood on the lowest bar of the gate, watching him run along the street and into his uncle's house. I walked slowly

49

back to where the high terraces sloped down to the railway. I felt oddly sad yet gave a little skip of relief. No longer should I be forced to run and run. I could be as lazy as I chose. I lay down on the grass, luxuriating in indolence, in freedom. I was my own again. . . .

Suddenly I heard the screech of a locomotive. The early train was coming! I sprang up — ready for the race!

Screaming together, the train and I raced in the morning wind. On the first freight car there was a crescent moon. I tore back to the house, into the room where Grandma was sewing. "Bad weather, Grandma," I called out. "Thunderstorms!"

Chapter 4

Secret Play
and Separation

I'LL TELL you my secret," I had said to Caroline that January evening when we had sat together reading *Through the Looking
Glass.* "I call it my play, but now you are here, we shall play
it together — if you think you can."

"I can play anything — if it's pretend," she had said "I've
never tried it, but I know I can."

So then I had told her.

First it had been a dream, an extraordinarily vivid dream, out
of which I had woken with the feeling that I had left something of
myself submerged in the dream, and also that I had brought
something out of it which would somehow make me different. I
cannot now remember what happened in the dream, but I well remember the characters who took part in it and have no reason to
forget them, for I have known them ever since. The odd thing was
that all these characters were males and that only two of them were
children, boys of about my own age. Yet, after all, that was
scarcely remarkable, because at this time I was revelling in volumes
of *The Boys' Own* and *Chum,* which had belonged to an uncle and

51

which I discovered in the attic. Talbot Baines Reed was my favourite author.

Caroline seemed not in the least surprised when I told her of these characters. She sat there in the wintry twilight, tiny, fragile, receptive as a crystal goblet held beneath a tap. When I told her the names of the six characters, she said, "Yes, yes, I'll remember." Never did she forget, either those or their personal appearances, which I minutely described.

The room grew darker. Through the clear space I had scratched on the frosty pane, I could see the new moon riding in the white surf of clouds. All is clearly etched in my memory.

We were called to tea and sat side by side. The grownups were pleased to see how well the two small girls got on together. Little did they guess the happy turmoil of the small girls' minds, their eagerness to be alone again that they might further explore the acting of the dream — the turning of themselves into *my* people, who were so soon to become *our* people!

I believe it is not unusual for children to invent playmates, sometimes grotesque, with which they amuse themselves in lonely hours. The Brontës had an imaginary kingdom. But I would find it hard to believe that characters invented by two children ever survived for so many years. As we grew to know them better, we ceased to *act* them. We *were* them. When surrounded by other people, we strained toward the moment when we could be alone together. Then, at once, magic enveloped us. The outside world became unreal. The vivid reality was our play.

At first we interchanged the characters. Sometimes I would be one, sometimes another. In this way, however, their different traits did not develop and before long we divided the six characters, taking three apiece. In time I discovered the need of a female character and invented a small girl, a sister to some of the existing "cast."

She was such a success that I added a woman — and another and another! There followed, after a few years, an orgy of new characters. Whenever interest slackened, up, out of my fertile brain, popped another member for the tribe. And such was the unfailing thrill of this, that we almost feverishly avoided the outside world. It was not always easy. I remember once, when we had hidden ourselves in the parlour and sat, in the darkness, entranced by our play, that suddenly I became aware of the presence of Aunt Eva behind the heavy curtain in the doorway. She was pulling my father by the hand and my acute ears heard her say, "Come on — let's find out what they're up to."

I sprang to my feet, as frightened as though I had been caught in something wicked — fearful that our play might be stopped. I had, the instant before, been a strong man, gripping the arms of my chair, in a moment of formidable decision. At the movement of the curtain, the sound of Aunt Eva's voice, I became, in a flash, a frightened child. . . . Then I heard my father say crossly, "No, I won't spy on them." And Aunt Eva followed him away, . . . I tried to recall what words I had been saying which might have been in that moment overheard. Yes — they were these: "Blount should grip the arms of his chair so hard that his knuckles turn white." And, in manly resolution, I had, with my small hands, been gripping the arms of my chair. The sweat of humiliation started on my forehead. But Caroline, once the danger was past, showed no perturbation. "Come on," she said, "be Blount again." And, in the darkness, we turned once more to the rapture of our play.

As I have said, more and more characters were introduced, as the years went on, into that unwieldy cast, yet unwieldy it never became to us — old people, middle aged people, babies, people of all classes, priests, schoolboys, engineers, maids of all work, actresses, horses and dogs. . . . I could at this moment, with little effort, name, give the ages and personal appearance of more than a hundred characters. None of these characters bears any resemblance that I can discover to any of the characters of the Whiteoak chronicles.

But though my imagination was early busy with these inventions, I also was trying to write. Caroline and I, with great effort, produced several issues of a newssheet. It was laboriously printed by hand and sold to the family for two cents a copy. Besides news it contained stories, verses and riddles. But, like many another literary journal, it failed through lack of public appreciation.

When I was nine someone gave me copies of a young people's paper. It was, I think, the *Youth's Companion*. In it was announced a short-story competition for children of sixteen and under.

Unconcerned by my youngness, I set out at once to enter the competition. Optimistic, though easily downcast, I saw no reason why I should not be the winner. With foolscap paper, pen and ink I began to write, and so on and on till eight pages were filled. The story was about a lost child named Nancy. Terrible times she went through but at last was restored to her mother's arms — my own heart ready to burst with emotion as I finished the story with a text from the Prodigal Son.

"But darling," said my mother, "do you think a child would ever be so hungry she would eat potato parings?"

"Nancy was," I said firmly.

"And do you think her mother would quote a text the moment her child was given back to her? It sounds so pompous."

This was my first experience of criticism, and how it hurt!

My father, standing by, exclaimed, "I'm dead sure I'd eat potato peelings if I were hungry enough and as for the text — it was the proper thing for the mother to quote. Don't change a word of it. It will probably get the prize."

Off he went to the letter box to post the manuscript.

No stamps for its return were enclosed, but a few weeks later, when I had ceased to think of it, a long envelope was put into my hand. Tremblingly I opened it and there was my manuscript returned! With it was enclosed a letter from the editor saying, "You are very young to have entered the competition but, if the promise shown by this story is fulfilled, you will make a good writer yet."

"Isn't that splendid!" exclaimed my mother, her pitying eyes on me.

I sat down on a low stool in a corner and covered my face with my hands. Sobs shook me.

Nobody came near me. The family stood about me, realizing that for the moment it was best to leave me to my grief. It was ridiculous, of course, but how well I remember it.

At last my father came to me. He led me to a table and placed two chairs by it. "Now," he said, "I'm going to teach you to play cribbage. It's a good game and you have no idea how comforting a game of cards can be." He took the pack from the cribbage box and set about dealing it.

Many years afterward I found, among my mother's things, the manuscript of "Nancy" and the letter from the editor — "You are very young to have entered the competition but, if the promise shown by this story is fulfilled, you will make a good writer yet." Dear, oh dear!

Caroline and I were sent to a small private day school kept by a gentle and charming Irish woman. I do not think I learned very much, but I spent happy hours there. Already I could read and this had opened up a new world, the world of books. I owned a great pile of books for children — *Alice in Wonderland* and *Through the Looking-Glass, The Water Babies, The Little Duke,* the Kate Greenaway books; these were my favourites. In those days the child had not the excitement of moving pictures and television. The young fancy was not spread out thin over many interests but concentrated on a few, and if he took to books, what a world of delight lay before him! At that time my Uncle Danford's business took him to London every year and each time he brought me a new book, a doll or a dress from a London shop.

By the time I was ten I read every book that came my way — *Oliver Twist* several times, *Old Curiosity Shop* once, for I hated Quilp and, even then, found the death of Little Nell too sentimental. But when our teacher read aloud *Misunderstood,* I was so overwhelmed that the reading had to be stopped. One of my uncles was given a book called, I think, *The Adventures of Hadji Baba.* He was no reader, but, on my next visit to Grandpa's, I found it, and "devour" is the only word which expresses my absorption in the adventures. I have no recollection of the story, but I remember Grandpa's discovery of the book, his brief scanning of it, his striding to the kitchen and before the frightened eyes of the maid, Victoria, taking off a stove lid and thrusting the book onto the coals. In fascination I had followed him. "But, please, sir," quavered Victoria, "why did you burn that nice book?"

"It was not a nice book, Victoria," answered Grandpa. "It was a very nasty book and I will not have my son tempted to read it."

Little did he dream that the small granddaughter, standing innocently by, was thanking her stars that she had finished the book before its destruction. I believed Grandpa when he said the book was wicked, but I could not believe that it had hurt me to read it. I concluded that what might be harmful to a young man could not hurt a small girl.

56

Other books of those days come crowding into my mind: *Carrots — Just a Little Boy, Spoilt Guy, Little Women* — though I liked *Little Men* still better — *The Bastables* by E. Nesbet. And the theatre! I could not have been more than six years old when I began to be a regular theatregoer. My mother and I went to matinees, I feeling very grown-up, and I saw some of the great actors in plays I could not understand and that sometimes frightened me a little but also gave me a strange pleasure. The tuning up of the orchestra, the ornate curtain poised to rise on that wonderful world filled me with a tremulous anticipation. Sometimes a friend of my mother's joined us and brought her little boy, Bertie, and we then went back to the friend's house for tea. I remember that Bertie had been given two birthday presents for which I greatly envied him. His father had given him a rowing machine to make him strong and his mother had given him a Bible to make him good. The rowing machine was in Bertie's own room and he (a pale, delicate child) got into it and showed me how it worked. He also let me hold the Bible in my hands, but only for a moment.

On the way home I enquired, "Mama, do you think I might have a rowing machine and a Bible?"

"Neither of them," she answered decisively, "is suitable for a child!"

I pondered this, not being quite convinced, but I was not a child who begged for things. I did not refer to the matter again, but many a time I pictured myself skimming along in the rowing machine, Bible in hand.

My mother and this friend of hers used to buy their clothes at W. A. Murray's and Stitt's. I can well remember the elegance of these two shops and how I noticed quite suddenly, one day when with them as they shopped, that they were beautiful women. I heard the silken rustle of their skirts, noticed their tiny waists,

their long gloves and how gracefully they held their lovely para-
sols. Yet I never longed for the day when I should be grown-up and
wear such things. I wanted to remain a child secure in the shelter
of my home.

What a contrast I was to Caroline, who so early learned to appreciate the pleasure of possessing pretty clothes; to whom it came
so naturally to learn to sew, to shop, to plan a modest wardrobe, to
keep her belongings in perfect order! We were so different, yet,
from that winter's day when she came into my life, such congenial
companions — never so happy as when together — ever indulging
our fancy in the vagaries of our play.

In those days we used frequently to spend our summers by Lake
Simcoe. Its shores were then unspoilt by motor traffic, its waters
untroubled by speedboats, and its few summer cottages surrounded by farm lands. We drove our pony along the dusty white
roads, blazing with heat, the pony so spoilt that when he saw an
orchard ripe with fruit, he would wilfully leave the road, cross the
ditch and stretch his neck to twitch an apple from the bough.

One day when we were bathing in the lake — my mother,
Caroline and I — my mother lost her wedding-ring. Vividly I recall the scene. It was our last bathe of the summer. All about the
greenish-blue lake, trees were blazing with red and gold, except for
the dark cedars. There had been frost. The air was cool but the
water was warm. All three of us wore blue flannel bathing dresses
trimmed with white braid. My mother was in the gayest spirits.
A child by either hand, she led us farther and farther out, over the
sand as fine as pepper, till the water reached our armpits. We
shouted and sang, tugging at her hands, begging to go still farther.

When we came dripping out of the lake, she looked down at her
hands. "My ring!" she cried out. "I've lost my wedding-ring!"
Her consternation, the anguish in her voice startled us.

"We'll find it for you," we cried. "Don't worry — we'll find it."

We three ran back into the lake. We peered. We held our noses and put our heads under water, the better to see. We snatched at bits of shell, at bright pebbles, but the inscrutable sand had swallowed the ring.

When we had given up hope, we returned shivering to the shore. My mother sank to a boulder and again looked with unbelieving eyes at her bereft hand, her fair hair hanging wet on her shoulders.

"Won't Papa buy you another?" I asked.

"Of course. But it won't be the same. It's a misfortune to lose one's wedding-ring. Things will never be quite the same for me again."

And the sad part was that this was true.

Shortly afterward Caroline and I were separated for nearly two years. My parents and I removed to the town of Galt, though just why this was I did not know. As children accept the changes in their lives, I accepted this without question. However, I have a feeling that the move was made for the sake of my mother's health. She had suffered for some time from bronchitis, and our relative, Dr. Lundy, declared that the low situation of Toronto was to blame and that the dry air of Galt, set in the hills, would cure her. He lived in the near-by village of Preston and it was he who first established the value of its mineral springs.

My mother was used to moving about. She often remarked that, during her married life, she moved seventeen times. Caroline and I have held to this tradition, never remaining more than a few years in one place. My volatile father so often had some new enterprise to tempt my mother and she, eager and enthusiastic, was never unwilling. At that time he had an agency for the importation of French wines into Canada. He went frequently to

59

Montreal. He was very much at home among French people. I have heard him say, "When I am with the French, I am French. When I am with the English, I am British."

This removal was looked forward to with a great deal of pleasure. Pleasurable anticipation was a strong quality of both my parents. Festivals of all sorts, birthdays were eagerly prepared for. There were presents on every occasion. On your birthday — so great was your importance — you were confident that the family could never have survived without you. I shared these buoyant emotions but had also a dark strain of melancholy. From the heights to the depths has been my Celtic inheritance.

I do not even remember Caroline's and my parting. We accepted the fact that I was to go to Galt and she was to remain with other relations without question. My mind was filled with the excitement of the change. During all the while I lived in Galt I remember writing to her only once. Then I wrote to her as one of the characters in our play. He was a young man named Bernard. In this letter I told her of my fine score at cricket and enclosed a picture of myself in cricketing costume, cut from the *Illustrated London News* — a fine, upstanding young man. I was eleven!

We did not take a house in Galt but had two bedrooms and a sitting-room in the Queen's Hotel. Before going there to live, my mother and I had paid a visit to the town, in the house of her cousin, a daughter of Dr. Lundy, just to make sure that my mother would find it congenial. This brief visit is memorable to me because it was then that I discovered the wonder and beauty of the world, as something separate from myself. Before that morning, when something in me awoke, never again to be unconscious, I had felt no more appreciation of my surroundings than a young animal. I was cold — I was hot — this flower smelled sweet — this russet apple tasted good! I was very conscious of the separate scents of my parents — the smell of my father's shaving lotion, his cigar, his tweeds, and a perfume he used on occasion, called Jockey Club. I was conscious of the sweet smell of my mother's flesh and of her favourite perfume — New Mown Hay. But, until that early morning in Galt, all my emotions were instinctive. Cherry trees in bloom, the song of robins, the wild whistle of the locomotive, the distant roll of thunder, all were a part of the voluptuous procession of my days. I did not consciously stand in wonder. Not till that spring morning in Galt.

I had been put to sleep on a couch in a small library next to the bedroom where my mother slept. I was restless because of my strange surroundings and woke early. For a moment I could not discover where I was, then I felt the thrill of being in the midst of unknown rooms, with little-known relatives sleeping in them — but I felt safe, because there, in the next room, was my mother.

The window stood open. The sun, like a great red flower, had just risen, throwing its petals of fire across the world. I sprang out of bed and ran to the window, the air, ineffably sweet, stirring my nightdress, my hair. . . . Across the road from this house, there was a small field or pasture and in it, reflecting the sun, a pool. I stood entranced by the miracle of colour — the blue of the sky, the vigorous green of the grass, the carmine of the pool so conquered me that it seemed they had been invented for me and me alone, in that moment of sunrise. . . . And, as though this were not enough, three snow-white ducks appeared, like actors in a play, crossed the pasture and entered the pool. As carefree as angels they floated, dived, breasted the carmine waters or gently drew together as though in love.

I gazed and gazed. I felt that never again should I be the same. Yet when I joined the other children at play, they saw nothing different in me. I told no one of this experience but cherished the memory of it for secret musing.

When my mother saw the rooms engaged by my father at the hotel, she said that she could not possibly live with such furniture, so we took train for Toronto and from Murray's and Kay's (stores which no longer exist) they bought carpets, curtains and furniture. We stayed at the Queen's Hotel, which no longer exists, and when we rose from the table, I shook hands with the waiter and thanked him for the nice dinner, as I had been taught to do after a party.

"We don't usually," said my mother, "shake hands with the waiter."

To draw attention from my lapse I remarked, "Papa is forgetting some of his money."

"That," said my father, "is for the waiter."

"It's better," I remarked, "to shake hands with him."

The new furnishings transformed our apartment in the hotel. Handsome carpets took the place of dun-coloured ones, long reseda-green curtains hung at each one of the deep windows, with their built-in seats for which Kay's had made fitted cushions. These stand out in my memory because of the hours I spent curled up in them, the curtains drawn between me and the outer world, reading, reading, reading.

And there was plenty to read. We had brought a few books with us — the volumes of Shakespeare which my father's father had sent him on his twentieth birthday — the heavy calf-bound volumes of Johnson's dictionary which had been sent him when he was seventeen. I am ashamed to say that I once sold the Shakespeare, illustrated by steel engravings and with favourite passages marked by my grandfather. It was one of those impulsive things I have so often done and often regretted.

My father had bought a bookcase and handsome sets of Dickens and Scott. Even while I admired the new furniture I could not keep my eyes from the books. How happy we were going to be in Galt! My parents were gay, animated. They went from room to room, from window to window, admiring. "From this window you can see a church!" "From this window you can see another church!" "And there is a glimpse of the river." "And in front there is a little park with a cannon in it." All three of us thought we had discovered a wonderful town.

My mother's cousins came and admired. Dr. Lundy came and prophesied that my mother's cough would soon be cured. We settled in and began to make many friends. But there was one great lack in my father's life. He had sold his horse and trap. He had sold his Gordon setters. The fox terrier, Chub, which he had given me on my second birthday remained with my grandparents. A hotel was no place for a dog, my mother said. She could do very well without a dog. Actually, she said, her married life had been over-run by dogs.

In spite of this my father appeared one day with a pug puppy in his arms. He set it down on the carpet.

"Whose puppy is that?" demanded my mother.

My father gave an ingratiating smile. "Yours," he said.

The pug was a present for her and what could she do but be pleased? Yet it was I who fed the pug, took him for walks, and later worried over him.

I found it thrilling to live in a hotel, with the constant coming and going, the dining-room with its rows of white tables at which sat strangers. Yet this was a residential hotel and we soon made friends with other guests. The floor above us was almost entirely occupied by an English army captain, his wife and six children. Captain Dickson was retired and what pleased me about him was that he had a twin brother exactly like him. I had thought that only children were twins. This handsome, lively family, living beneath the same roof with us, soon became close friends, but my closest and dearest friend was Mina Sylvester, who lived directly across from the hotel in a house surrounded by a low brick wall. Every morning I could see her father, Dr. Sylvester, come out of his surgery, drawing on a pair of yellow kid gloves, while a groom stood holding his horse. The doctor would then mount to the driver's seat of the trap, the groom spring up behind, and with a flourish of the whip, the horse would be off and the round of calls begun.

Mina was more like Caroline than any other child I had known — the responsive companion, ready to fall in with all my inventions, my imaginings. One of my inventions at this time was an aerial system of communication between the doctor's house and the hotel. From a tailor we bought very large spools, from the hardware store a ball of twine. One spool was attached by a nail to a window sill of our sitting-room, the other to a window in the Sylvesters' house. These revolving spools were the support of the cable of twine and from the twine there depended a tiny basket. It took us all of one June day to get this invention into working order, with innumerable trips across the road and through the little park. By evening it was perfected and, tired out, gloriously tired out, we went to bed.

Next morning we were up at six. It was a sunny morning and there by the window sill the little trolley waited. I was beside myself with impatience when I saw the spool turning, saw the twine moving on the spool, beheld the little carrier making its way, high above the road, across the square. Safely it reached the window sill and there in the basket was a note from Mina! It read:

"Hello — you silly old goose."

And beneath was the drawing of a goose.

I did think the event merited something more romantic, but that was Mina's jocular way. She would have nothing to do with sentiment. Therefore I wrote my reply in a similar spirit. It was:

"Send me six cherries, you lunatic, or it will be the worse for you."

Back through the sunny air the tiny carrier toddled. Back it came to me bearing six cherries from the Sylvesters' tree.

It was a Saturday morning. There was no school. Nothing to interfere with our delight in this marvel. When, from my window, I saw farmers coming to market with their produce draw in their teams to gaze in wonder at the little carrier moving above, I felt such pride as Marconi or Alexander Bell must have felt in their achievements.

For one glorious day there was no flaw in our pleasure. We never tired of sending messages. Even the grownups were impressed. . . . Then — just at sundown — the twine broke — the basket fell. No longer an aerial messenger travelled from the hotel to the doctor's house, only two lengths of string dangled uselessly from two spools. "Perhaps it is just as well," said Dr. Sylvester, "for people going to church might not care to see that contraption in action."

Mina and I went to the same private school. It was kept by a Miss Blain, in her family's residence. I remember it as a large, rather gloomy house, surrounded by evergreen trees. I do not think I learned much, but it was a pleasant little school.

I do not remember ever doing any homework. My mother was ambitious for me, but never did she supervise my study or my practice of the two instruments on one or other of which she hoped I should excel. These were the piano and the violin. A handsome upright piano had been bought in Toronto and installed in our living-room. There also had been bought (for me, I realized with apprehension) a violin. My mother pictured my fingers rippling over the keys of the piano. She pictured me standing, tall and graceful, the violin tucked beneath my chin, while, with the airy bow, I drew sweet music from the instrument. I do not think she considered what grinding work must go into the production of these pleasant sounds and never could she have brought herself to force me to practise. Her cousin advised her to engage Professor Baker to teach me.

How well I remember Professor Baker — his slender figure, his upright carriage, his clear blue eyes and grey moustache! He was an Englishman and, like his father, a professional musician since childhood. His father, he told me, would as soon knock him down as look at him.

I learned to look forward to Professor Baker's visits with dread. Four times a week he came to teach me and no sooner was the strain of one lesson over than I began to dread the next. All his other pupils were grown-up. He had no way with children. His method was to give me pieces far too difficult for me, a few bars at a time, and for days I would reiterate those deadly bars, with dogged hopelessness. Years passed before I recovered my liking for music.

I can picture him now, with a look of cold fury on his face, as I stumbled miserably through my exercise. He would leap from his chair, snatch it up as though about to hurl it to the floor, then, controlling himself, mop his forehead and sit down again. But of the two instruments the violin caused me the greater suffering. With my head wet with sweat, my lip trembling, I was put through the ordeal. Stoically I never complained, but one day the professor, in a voice of fury, ordered me to go to my mother and tell her to cut my nails short. I went to her and held out my hand, not able to speak. She gave one look at my finger ends, almost bleeding from his pressing them on the strings, then she said, "Stay here, dear, for a moment."

I heard her voice, clear and decisive. "I will not have my child treated so harshly."

I heard him apologize. Never after that was he so rough with me, but still my music lessons were looked forward to in dread.

About this time I gave up childish reading. I spent my happiest hours in one of the deep window seats living with the novels of Dickens and Scott — *David Copperfield, A Tale of Two Cities, Rob Roy, Quentin Durward.* My mother cared little for Scott, but she delighted in Dickens, the Brontës, Jane Austen. Another favourite of hers was Rhoda Broughton, though what pleased me most in her books was their lovely titles — *Red as a Rose Is She* and *Cometh up as a Flower.*

All three of us read everything that came our way, with uncritical zest. Often my father and I read the same book at the same time, his six feet three extended in an easy chair, my growing length draped against his chest. So I remember reading *The White Company, Harry Lorrequer, Allan Quatermain* by Rider Haggard. In this last book there was a young warrior named, I think, Umslopogaas, whom we very much admired. From this time, for many years, my father called me by this name. In fact, he had a variety of names for me, beginning from the time the news of my conception was first broken to him. The three of us, and, later, Caroline, had secret names for each other that the outside world never knew.

I think it was in these days, when first we began to read together, that the bond between my father and me strengthened into a deep understanding and we became the most loved of friends. As he waited for my slower grasp of the page to catch up to his, as his large shapely hand was raised to turn the page, a palpable emotion stirred within us. My love for my mother was instinctive. I took her devotion for granted. But he was my hero, my protector, my gay companion. . . . As I grew older and young men appeared on the scene, I invariably compared them to him, to their disadvantage — till the day when one arrived who could better bear comparison with him.

Evenings in front of the fire in our living-room we in turn entertained each other. My mother would recite a poem by Tennyson, her violet eyes dimmed by emotion as she enunciated:

> Break, break, break,
> On thy cold gray stones, O Sea!
> And I would that my tongue could utter
> The thoughts that arise in me.

The trouble was that she would recite the verses in the wrong order.

"That's not right, Bertie," my father would interrupt. "You have them in the wrong order."

"Who is reciting this poem?" she would cry.

"You are," he would growl, "but you've got it wrong."

"I can prove I'm right."

Simultaneously they would pounce on the volume of Tennyson.

Then he would recite "The Wreck of the *Julie Plante*" and my mother and I would listen entranced, picturing the sinking of the little vessel "wan arpent from de shore." Meanwhile the pug sat on his knee, its prominent eyes fixed mournfully on his face.

I could scarcely bear to wait for my turn. I stood up taut, declaiming:

> 'Twas brillig, and the slithy toves
> Did gyre and gimble in the wabe . . .

It was not enough for me to recite the "Jabberwocky." I must act it. Once I snatched up an ivory paper knife and, as I cried:

> One, two! One, two! And through and through
> The vorpal blade went snicker-snack!

I flourished the knife and somehow — I never knew how it happened — the blade struck the back of my mother's hand and great red drops of blood came spurting out. In consternation, in shock, I threw down the paper knife and bent over her hand. With eyes full of concern for my pain, she cried:

"It's nothing — it didn't hurt at all!"

One evening my mother said to my father, "We should do some serious reading. It will be good for us and good for Mazo to hear. There are those volumes of Shakespeare your father gave you. Let's read one of the plays aloud."

"We've seen Irving and Ellen Terry in them," he said. "And Robert Mantell. That ought to be enough."

"That will not help our child. It will be splendid for her to hear us read them. Let's begin with *Othello*. I'd love to do Desdemona. You can be the Moor. We'll divide up the other characters."

He became as enthusiastic as she. They drew chairs to the table and laid the volume before them. The pug and I were audience.

At first the reading went well. Then my father read words that made my mother recoil. She cried, "Oh, you shouldn't read that — not in front of *her!*" and she cast a solicitous look at me.

"How was I to know what was coming?" he demanded.

"Anyone could see what was coming!"

"Why didn't you stop me, then — before I said it?"

"I tried to stop you but I couldn't."

"Anyhow," said my father tranquilly, "she wouldn't understand — not any more than that pug."

69

My mother cast doubtful looks on both me and the pug, and we, feeling embarrassed, slunk into the next room.

My mother was always trying to protect my innocence, while my father seemed to think it was its own protection. His favourite author was Balzac and he encouraged me to read him. Together we discussed *Père Goriot*. Tears were in my father's eyes. He was easily moved to laughter, but tears were not embarrassing to him. I remember, when we went to see Martin Harvey in *The Only Way*, how we cried together at Sidney Carton's last words — "It is a far, far better thing that I do than I have ever done. It is a far, far better rest that I go to, than I have ever known." To see a play with my father, to be moved to emotion, either happy or sad, in his company, was to me a pleasure not to be outdone by any in the company of my contemporaries. He and I read books together, drove together, walked together. I contrasted him with the fathers of my friends, who were often stern or fault-finding or repressive. The thought of sternness or punishment in connection with him was unthinkable. As for my mother, she always wanted me to do what I wanted to do! Yet both were high-tempered people.

As for me — their offspring — I am weak as water, always only too ready to be guided by those I love, my only defence the ability, like water, of sometimes slipping from under.

During the year that followed our arrival in Galt my mother's health did not improve as Dr. Lundy had expected it would. That same troublesome bronchial cough afflicted her, especially at night. Her lips were so very red and her eyes so bright; she seemed to be in a constantly feverish condition. The strange thing was that her cousin, Derita, a daughter of Dr. Lundy, and herself married to a Dr. Wardlaw, was at this time on her way to her death from tuberculosis. Dr. Wardlaw attended them both and I remember seeing them together, talking and laughing, and how I wondered at the strange resemblance in their sparkling looks.

Dr. Wardlaw provided my mother with what was called an "inhalor," a sort of muzzle, with a medicated sponge in it. This she wore by the hour and it did give her some relief. But the constant dosing with cough mixture to which she was subjected took away her appetite and almost ruined her digestion. More often than not she could not bring herself to go down to meals in the dining-room but had a tray brought up to her.

To make matters worse my father's business took him to Winnipeg and Vancouver. He would be away for six weeks. When I saw the effect on my mother of this long absence, I too felt a great foreboding. It was as though doom hung over us. Even he looked sober when he said good-bye. And when he had gone, one thing after another transpired to make me apprehend the strangeness of life and the possibility of death.

One morning I was woken by a roaring sound. It came from the direction of the river, which had lain frozen beneath the grey stone bridge. But now the ice had broken and the river, in tumult, was carrying great blocks of it through the town. I ran to the window and could glimpse the broken ice, rocking, whirling, almost ready to tear down the bridge. I could scarcely wait to eat my breakfast, so eager I was to stand on the bridge, to look down on that wildness.

Mina could not go with me, for she had somehow contracted measles. I ran alone, past the church, through the throbbing air, to the bridge. Down below I could see the river, churned up, dark and threatening, as it struggled with the ice. And there was something else! Among the uprooted trees, the débris of the flood, I saw a poultry house, with the poor hens inside, staring wildly through the broken roof. Then came a slab of ice and on it the body of a

71

sheep, with a little lamb beside it. I stood fascinated, asking myself how such things could be. And as I stared, the body of a cow passed beneath, and after that a black and white cow, still living, with precarious hold on the ice.

It was a long time before I could tear myself away from the strange scene below. When at last I did, I ran back to the hotel to tell my mother of all I had seen. "Mama — Mama," I began, but she cut me short. "I can't bear to hear of it!" she cried. Then I saw that she had drawn the curtains across the windows which overlooked the river.

My mother's health did not improve with the coming of spring. The troublesome cough continued and more especially at night. The pug slept in a little box room across the passage from our bedrooms, and whether the coughing disturbed him I do not know, but every night he would begin to whimper and at last to fill the air with his mourning. I could have slept through all this undisturbed, not so my mother. Her voice would penetrate my dreams, calling my name. Half-dazed, I would go into her room. "You must stop that puppy's crying," she would say. "He will disturb the other guests. Take your slipper and give him a good slippering." Then she would turn her face to the pillow to smother her cough.

Slipper in hand I would cross the dim gaslit passage and open the door into the darkness of the box room.

At my coming, the pug would rear himself in joy and lick my hands as I felt for his soft velvet body. Then I would whack him with the slipper. I cannot remember, in all my life long, doing anything so painful to me.

He would be quiet then and I would go back to my room, tumble into bed and in a few minutes be fast asleep — but not for long. My mother's voice would wake me, calling to me to go and quieten the pug. It was the same story over and over. Whatever my distress

I did not dream of disobedience. What I wanted was to take the puppy back to bed with me, but I was an obedient child. I even reached the point where I felt a kind of anger at him for being the cause of so much misery. Why should he have licked my hands in love when I was going to beat him! One night I saw tiny sparks fly from his coat as I applied the slipper. Aghast, I threw it to the floor and sat down beside him. At once he was comforted, but I covered my face with my hands. For the first time in my life, I felt alone — alone. A great sadness engulfed me. In this building, full of people, I was alone. . . .

The door was ajar and by the shaft of gaslight I saw, when at last I rose to go, a small wooden box containing some odds and ends of no value. The litter of this small room was familiar to me, but I had not before seen this box. Among the things in it was a small book in a red leather cover. It looked old and shabby. I picked it up and read the title:

CHAMBERS'S
Historical Questions
With Answers
Embracing Ancient and Modern History

I turned over the opening pages. There were about a dozen questions on each page. They were in italics, the answers in plain print. I know, because the book is in front of me at this moment. It is the only thing that I have ever stolen.

The questions were such as:

What is a Demagogue?
What is Anarchy?
What was the condition of Egypt under the Ptolemies?
What is meant by Cosmogony?

These were dry indeed; but wait! On the next page was the heading: ANCIENT HISTORY — GREECE, ITS LEGENDS AND MYTHOLOGY.

The following pages were a never to be forgotten experience. I doubt if questions and answers so deliberately unpicturesque ever gave so great delight to a reader. On and on I read, while the pug snuffled peacefully. I was not in Galt. I was in Greece. . . . I was with Proteus, the keeper of the sea-calves of Neptune. I was with Psyche. I was with Narcissus — with Hero and Leander!

I do not know how long I read, but at last I stole back to bed and hid the book beneath my pillow. My mother had stopped coughing.

In the days that followed, I often looked at the many handsome books which had been given to me, but thought none so precious as Chambers's book of questions and answers. Every night I went into the box room and sat with the pug, reading, reading. I felt the rapture of the convert. But it was not to Christianity I was converted. I had become a pagan, worshipping at the shrines of the bad old gods.

I was growing fast. My mother was five feet three and I was almost as tall. I had lost my colour and looked all legs and eyes and hair. One morning she said, "Let's hire a boat and go on the river this afternoon. It will do us both good."

Those were days of simple pleasures. The thought of us two on the river filled me with happy anticipation.

The river no longer seemed a dark menace, flowing through the town, but a beckoning promise of delight. My mother no longer seemed shut away from me by illness but again had become a lovely companion.

We hired a small boat. I proudly took the oars, while she established herself in the stern with the rudder. How gay we were and how brightly flowing the river! They say that its shores are greatly changed since those days, but then they were pretty, though rather rugged. Everything interested us — the reflections in the dark water — the clouds mirrored more shapely than in the heavens. My mother held a parasol over her shoulder and trickled her white hand in the water.

"This will do your cough good," I said.

"Oh, yes," she agreed, "I feel better already."

After a time we drew into the shore and pulled the boat to a safe place. She was a little tired and sat down on a boulder to rest, while I wandered along the shore.

When I found myself alone, the strange emotions to which I had been subject of late took possession of me. To be alone — alone! Yet loneliness was what I most feared. On and on I wandered, sometimes picking up a stone to feel its strange smoothness against my cheek. I forgot my mother. I forget everything but my obsession with the river and its shore. . . . At last I came to a dark little cave and in it I hid myself.

I did not hear my mother's voice calling. I was only conscious of her coming when she appeared in the opening of the cave, looking distraught and calling my name, in both relief and anger. She had been so frightened. How could I treat her so? She had imagined all sorts of dreadful things. It was growing dark. It was beginning to rain. . . . It was indeed damp and there was the long rough way back to the boat. She began to cough.

Soon after this my father returned from his trip to the Pacific Coast. Every few days letters had come from him. They were eagerly awaited and read, but he had seemed very far away. When, through the window, we saw him alight from the hotel bus, then heard his step in the passage, actually saw him in the flesh, it was like rain after drought. We ran to him, clinging to either shoulder, while he looked down into first one loved face and then the other. If he thought my mother looked ill he did not tell her so, but he did marvel at the way I was growing. The pug snuffled and danced with joy about us.

"Oh, what we have gone through with that dog!" cried my mother. "Night after night he has kept everyone awake with crying — though lately he has been quieter."

My father bent to fondle the pug, which, because of its emotion, made a fresh puddle on the carpet.

Now the porter brought in my father's travelling bags. We gathered about the table to see our presents unpacked. The things he had brought! From the coast a Chinese porcelain figure — a table-cover embroidered in a rich design — beaded bags worked by Indians — and, as each article was displayed, he mimicked the strange foreign character from whom he had bought it.

We could picture them all. We laughed — almost we cried, in the joy, the relief, of having him with us again.

For himself he had an embroidered Indian hunting jacket of white buckskin, given him by a chief, and when he had donned it, my mother and I stood lost in admiration.

Before long he had found a home for the pug. I do not remember its going or where it went. My mother was thankful to be without a dog and my father seemed resigned. But it was not for long. He appeared one day leading a tall white French poodle. It was clipped in proper Continental style and wore an expression of cold superiority.

"Whose dog is that?" cried my mother.

"Yours," he returned, with an ingratiating smile. "The poodle, you must know, is the most intelligent of all dogs. He'll be a wonderful companion for you."

76

"I don't need a companion," she said. "How much did you pay for him?"

Up went my father's expressive eyebrows. "To tell the truth," he said, "I can't remember. There was such a lot of barking and talking and I was so taken up by studying his pedigree — he has a most distinguished pedigree — I'll show it to you now."

As they bent together over the pedigree, the poodle gave a disparaging look about the room, then climbed on the sofa and laid his head on the pillow.

But, for all his fine airs, the poodle did not last long. No one was free to minister to his wants. My father was often away. I was occupied by school and music lessons. My mother was more and more often confined to her room. As the pug had disappeared, so did the poodle.

My father was pensive for a few days, then he said to my mother, "Well, if I can't have a dog, do you think I might have a canary?"

He looked so innocent and yet she felt him to be so full of guile that she laughed.

"What are you laughing at?" he asked.

"You!"

"You don't want a canary, then?"

"I'd love a canary."

So the very next day he appeared, carrying a handsome cage and in it a handsome canary which happily sang and scattered seeds in all directions. But that evening my father said to me, "Bring me a sheet of paper and I will draw you the nicest dogs you ever have seen."

We sat down by the table together and he sketched Scotch collies, beagle hounds, fox terriers, spotted Dalmatians. He could draw any breed of dog but, for a human being, only one sort, a

77

wooden-looking creature which, if a woman, wore a bustle, and, if a man, a cut-away coat. As for cats, he would not waste his talent on them, he said.

The following winter my mother's health grew steadily worse. The "inhalor" did not help her cough, and the various mixtures she took for it were ruining her digestion. Suddenly, or so it seemed to me, it was decided that we should go to live with my mother's parents, who had lately moved into Toronto. There she would have proper care and quite soon be well again, my father said.

During that winter I had been subject to hours of strange melancholy. The sense of my own smallness and helplessness in the world oppressed me. The constant coming and going in the hotel made me more aware of my aloneness. I watched myself as an actor alone on a great stage. The spectacular and elemental Greek gods, on whom I brooded, were more congenial to me than my schoolfellows. I would stand long on the bridge watching the dark flow of the river below. There was no such flood as there had been last spring, but one day I witnessed a happening on the bridge which left an indelible impression of calamity on my mind.

Some farmhands were driving a small herd of cattle across the bridge to be slaughtered. One of them, an immense white beast, refused to cross. The others had been driven over, but no matter how he was beaten and prodded, he refused. Again and again they had him on the bridge, but each time he eluded them and plunged back, wild and exhausted, to the safety of the road. There was a nobility in him. He would accept his doom there, but he would not cross the bridge.

I watched horrified and at last saw him sink to his knees, a great white bulk, about to die.

When I returned later, he was gone, but there was a pool of blood at the edge of the bridge where he had been slaughtered.

78

At last the time came for us to leave.

My father was to remain behind to see to the packing of our belongings, the crating of the furniture. Dr. Patterson, who had attended my mother when I was born, now came to watch over her on the train journey.

In what was then called a "parlour car," he sat solid and self-important, his hand on my mother's wrist, as the train steamed out of the town.

Chapter 5

Adolescent
Pleasure and Pain

In my maternal grandfather's house at this time there were eight in the family — my grandparents, my parents, my aunt, my two uncles and myself. Caroline, who had been staying with other relatives, was coming to join us. I could scarcely contain myself for excitement. With a child's acceptance of change, I had not sorrowed over our separation. Now, with reunion at hand, I rejoiced that the separation was over. My father and I were on our way to meet her at the railway station. He held my hand as he still did when we walked together. But I danced rather than walked. My spirit flew ahead of me to meet Caroline. Would the train be late? Should we have long to wait?

The city seemed large to me, but compared with to-day how quiet, how peaceful, it must have been! My grandfather's house was in the west end, quite near the lake. Where there is now by the lake shore a railway line and apartment houses, there were fields of tall feathery grass and daisies which we children called marguerites. There were a few large houses with gardens by the lake. People of foreign birth were unknown there, with the exception of a Chinese

who kept a laundry and a long-bearded Jew with his cry of "Rags
— bones — bottles!" who drove a decrepit horse.

My grandfather's house was one of five that stood on a tree-
shaded street that ended in a kind of wooden terrace with seats,
overlooking the lake. It had a deep stone porch where there were
in this Maytime boxes filled with geraniums in bloom, lobelia and
pansies. There were hanging baskets with already luxuriant growth.
I was eager to show everything to Caroline.

When my father and I arrived at the station, the train had come
and gone, and there she was sitting waiting for us, looking somewhat forlorn and much smaller and paler than I had remembered.
My father at once took possession of her travelling bag and found a
carter to bring her trunk. She had been ill and she walked slowly
and quietly, but when we had reached home and she had been
greeted by the family, we ran upstairs to our bedroom and shut the
door. She took possession of the drawers that were to be hers and at
once began to lay her things neatly in there. My father had bought
a handsome new bedroom suite for us and I was proud to show it to
her.

Suddenly I asked, "Do you remember our play?"

"Of course I do," she answered. "I'd never forget."

"Do you think you could play it now?" I asked.

"Let's try," she said.

Our past was very short indeed, yet it seemed to us a long while
since the days when we had lost ourselves in living the characters
I had created. We could not yet return to the mysterious fascination of our play — not till I had shown Caroline every corner of
the house, had told her of the friends I had already and so easily
made, not till we had walked to the lake and she had gazed in
wonder at that great expanse of greenish blue which seemed to us
an ocean. We could see the white sails of a yacht and the streamer

of smoke from a schooner. How quiet it was! Quietly we savoured the joy of being together once more. We did not put our arms about each other's waists, as most girls would; we did not look into each other's eyes; but, gazing at the lake, we talked and talked, and at last, without effort, took up our parts in our play again. The characters were few, their doings were wildly imagined, but — oh, the fascination of it! The sun was lengthening the shadows of the freshly leaved trees before we turned homeward.

A new life began. Caroline was not considered strong enough for school but joined a few other girls in a private class. Also she had lessons on the banjo, rattling off marches and polkas, her thin fingers flying, her long fair hair falling about her face. In the midst of all those grownups we had our secret life. During the school week we were separated most of the day, she spending much time with my mother, whose health had not improved. The bond between them deepened in these days, so that they became the most congenial of companions. They had the same tastes. They craved beauty to surround them. They loved pretty clothes, elegance in furniture, pictures, ornaments. My mother would go to any length to acquire some object that took her fancy and when she possessed it, did not tire of it but cherished it always. Her family, especially her parents and sister, deplored this as extravagance and took no pains to hide their disapproval. But Caroline was always heart and soul on my mother's side.

It was marvellous to see how Caroline improved in health and looks. Even I, a child, was conscious of it. From being a sallow little girl, with high cheekbones, she became round-cheeked, red-lipped, full of a gentle vitality. Soon she had reached her full height of five feet, but I went on and on growing. My face became more pointed, my eyes more eagerly enquiring, my hair longer and thicker, my body longer and thinner. Caroline was serious. I was always ready to smile. She was shy. I was forward. Both were what to-day would rightly be called ridiculously sensitive. A rebuke from a grownup would dissolve us in tears. But there were few rebukes. We lived sheltered in the family, our pleasures were simple. A "treat" was enough to supply conversation for days. Strange it would seem to a "teen-ager" of to-day to see Caroline and me setting out for a picnic accompanied by my grandmother with as much pleasure as if in the company of those of our own age. When Great-aunt Susannah came to see us, trailing with her her three six-foot black-clad daughters, she would grin at me in delight and say to my mother, "Ah, your child is the image of my family and, mark you, she'll be just as tall." The three daughters would smile deprecatingly and my mother would cast on me a fearful and protective look and I would try to telescope myself down to her height of five feet three. It was not fashionable for a girl to be very tall, but my mother's anxiety was for nothing, as I grew to only a scant five feet eight.

One of our pleasures of those days was the weekly band concert in the grounds of the Home for Incurables. In those days a spade was called a spade. If a person were incurable, so he was called, and no fancy name was given to his place of residence. So also there was an Idiot Asylum and an Insane Asylum, and I cannot discover that the occupants were any more miserable because of this frankness. An undertaker had not yet become a mortician or his establishment a "Parlour" or a "Home."

On the night of the band concerts we children never gave a thought to the "Incurables." We saw the bandsmen pass carrying their instruments. Twilight was beginning to fall. We heard the first strains of music vibrating on the placid summer air. As we neared the gardens we saw the flare of the torches against the blackness of the trees, saw it caught on the brass of the horns. We

83

submerged ourselves in the sauntering crowd. The young ones sauntered with their elders or gathered in decorous little groups, but when the band broke into "Soldiers of the Queen" or Kipling's "Recessional," a confident patriotism moved our hearts.

At one of these band concerts I was strolling among the formal flower beds, filled with red geraniums and asters, with the son of one of our neighbours. His name was Gordon and he was my first tentative "boy friend." Another boy, whom I had met just once before, joined us. He talked to me, volubly yet with odd stammerings, ignoring Gordon, who, all in white, walked sulkily on my other side. After a little the intruder left us and Gordon broke out, with a violence which astonished me, "What a fool that fellow is! Upon my word I've never seen such a fool!"

The next day the odd boy came to our door. He did not ask for me but handed the maid a handsome tennis racquet and asked her to tell me he had brought it for me.

I was pleased to have the racquet, because I had just begun to play tennis with Gordon. I never saw the boy again. Yet some instinct warned me not to tell Gordon where I had got the racquet. I think I shrank from hearing his disparagement of it and the other boy.

Gordon was the only friend of ours who possessed a tennis court. It was rather a lumpy grass court which would not be tolerated by the young experts of to-day, but we had a great deal of fun playing on it. Gordon's widowed mother would sit in the shade of the trees, with a friend or two, watching us.

She was a tall, handsome, fair woman with four tall, handsome sons who all were at home. Gordon, the youngest, was later to go to the Royal Military College at Kingston. But, though I saw Gordon almost every day and took his friendship for granted, it was his eldest brother I adored. Caroline adored him too, but there

84

was no jealousy between us. He was remote, as inaccessible as a Greek god, and looked remarkably like one. He had spent several years in a crack regiment in Ireland, till his polo-playing, his other expenses, became too great for his mother's patience and he was forced to sell out and return to Canada. The sight of his tall lithe form, clad in Irish tweeds, was enough to send us silly little creatures scurrying to the windows to rhapsodize over his passing. Once when we were spending an evening with 'Gordon, playing a game called Crokinole with him and his mother, she brought in the eldest son and presented us to him. He showed us his stop watch that he had used in the races in Ireland. He wore a wrist watch, considered in those days rather effeminate, but not effeminate on him, oh, no, not on him! Everything he did was perfection. Gordon also worshipped him and eventually he married a very rich wife, which was just what he needed.

Gordon had made a new friend, somewhat older than himself. His name was Willie and he was already shaping to his later role of a dashing young man about town. He dressed well and had a superior air. One evening Gordon invited us to his house to meet Willie. When we arrived, we found that Gordon's mother was away for the evening. We four young people were alone. We had a sudden feeling of untrammelled gaiety. Willie performed on the piano with spirit. He could sing the songs from the comic operas. He played dance music too and Gordon danced in turn with Caroline and me. Then I played a polka, a schottische, a waltz, and Caroline danced with Willie. We were noisy. Gordon and Willie laughed loudly. At home, because of Mother's illness, we had to be quiet. The piano was not to be heard at night.

After a while we began to indulge in ridiculous games. One of these, introduced by Willie, was called Zoo. I do not remember how it was played, but I do remember that the dining-room chairs

85

were piled in a corner of the room to form cages. What animals we were I cannot recall, but we were sitting on the floor in these cages when, without warning, Grandpa's tall, straight figure appeared in the dooray.

"Put on your jackets," he said to Caroline and me, ignoring the boys, "and come home."

His austere, pale face, his stern voice rendered the boys speechless. Caroline and I snatched up our jackets. She snatched mine, I hers, which was much too small for me, and we struggled into them as we hurried after Grandpa, who was already on his way to the street. He did not scold us as we skulked homeward by his side. His icy silence was enough to make us quail.

How different it would have been if my father had come for us! He would have danced with us, doubtless played the game with us. He had taken dancing lessons as a youth from Professor Davis at his Dancing Academy in Church Street — the same Professor Davis who now taught us. The old dancing master well remembered my father as a pupil, and my father looked back with pleasure on his dancing lessons. Although he was six feet three and weighed two hundred pounds, he was extraordinarily light on his feet. My mother's bedroom was large, and now that she was confined to her bed, it had become a gathering place for us. She would tell of dances they went to, when she was well and strong, and beg my father to show me the steps of dances which were popular then — the gavotte and another the name of which I have almost forgotten — some such name as Vesuviana. The pair of us would dance for her pleasure and she would sit up in bed, smiling and bright-eyed. She would seem her old self again.

At this time Caroline and I were what might be called religious — that is, in the outer forms of religion. We went devotedly to the services of our church. We had been confirmed. We looked on

Father Ingles, our High Church rector, with reverence, his word as infallible. Yet, I think, there was no real Christianity in us. We were intolerant of other creeds. We were fascinated rather than uplifted by the ritual of our church. The six o'clock communion service, after the walk through the Sabbath-quiet streets, the church with the sparse early-morning congregation, the twitter of birds outside the open windows, the sibilant murmur of the rector, as he gave us the bread and wine, drugged us as though with lotus. Frequently we went again to the eleven o'clock service, this time accompanied by my father, in regulation frock coat and top hat. He liked the service, the excellent singing of the choir, but the dreary sermons bored him and he had a way of surreptitiously looking at his watch that filled me with anxiety. The movement of his hand, the bend of his massive head, the secretive glance of his large dark eyes seemed to me so obvious that I feared Father Ingles from his pulpit would see him. And so one day he did and dreadfully paused in his discourse till my father blandly returned the watch to his pocket.

When we girls went alone to church, we were invariably escorted home by Caroline's first admirer. His name was Donald and he belonged to a family of attractive sisters. However, he himself was not attractive, being plain, stodgy and rather dull. His admiration for pretty Caroline was so patient, so humble, her lack of interest in him so chilling, that I, walking between them (for she never would have him next her), felt a kind of scornful pity for him. Our two families were not acquainted, but his mother, persuaded, I am sure, by her only son and he in the throes of calf-love, sent a formal invitation to Caroline and me to spend an evening with them. Donald's sisters also were on hand. Their house was much grander than ours, but Caroline was not impressed. Throughout the evening she was drawn into herself, shy and cold.

87

To make up for it I was my most expansive. It was easy to see that Donald's mother liked me much more than she liked Caroline. However that may be, this little affair was over. Donald grew up and became a successful barrister.

As I remember, we and our friends talked not at all of sex or marriage as a reality, though we were enthralled by it in romantic fiction and the theatre. The reason for this, I think, was that the times were hard. There was little money in the hands of young men. Their salaries were too small for the support of a family. They knew that when they married, they must provide a house and furniture. They would have felt eternally disgraced if they had crept into an apartment and their brides had taken a job, as so sensibly is done to-day. Not that girls of that time ever had jobs. The young men were thirty or more before they dared contemplate marriage. The thought of working in the holidays to make extra money did not, as I recall, enter their heads. All were completely dependent on their fathers. My young uncle spent his holidays in sailing and playing tennis and must petition his mother for spending money.

As for us growing girls, sex was scarcely a reality. Indeed we felt something ugly in the word. We were captivated by the romance in stories like *The Prisoner of Zenda* and Richard Harding Davis's *Princess Aline.* We cried our eyes out over Kipling's *The Light That Failed.* The theatre was our weekly treat. There was a stock company at the Princess Theatre and we could have seats at twenty-five cents each and saw a great variety of plays, from *The Private Secretary* to *Lady Windermere's Fan* and *Camille.*

Of all pleasures the theatre was the greatest and before long I began to write plays for Caroline and me to act. Quite satisfied we were, at first, with the family as audience, but later, with two friends, we gave a play for a group of grownups. This was to be performed at their house. These two sisters did a scene they had dramatized from one of Scott's novels. I wrote the play for Caroline and me. It was called *A Passage at Arms,* and a swashbuckling performance it was. My part was that of a dashing cavalier. Caroline was an innkeeper's daughter and wore a sprig-muslin dress with panniers.

The audience already gathered below, we four girls, in great excitement, put on our costumes. My long curling hair under a plumed hat looked very well. So did my velvet jacket, with wide lace collar and cuffs. It was my legs that caused the trouble. I wore a pair of red woollen underdrawers belonging to my grandfather. As my tunic was fairly long and my boots, with their buckram tops, reached to the knee, only my scarlet-clad thighs were visible. My family had seen me in the costume and found it highly effective. Not so my friends' mother, who was a prudish mid-Victorian, if ever there was one. One glimpse of my legs was enough. She forbade the production of the play. She was kind but she was firm, and her daughters and Caroline sorrowfully and silently accepted the ban. But silence was not one of my characteristics. I strode up and down the passage, weeping aloud. Sobs shook my tunic. My sword (lent to me by my father from his collection of weapons) clanked miserably at my side.

Then appeared Charles, the older brother of my friends. "Stop crying," he said to me. "I'll see what I can do with Mother." A little later he ran up the stairs with the joyful news that the ban had been lifted. On with the play! And what a success it was — none seeming to enjoy it more than our friends' mother.

From this time there grew one of the pleasantest friendships of my life. I think my friendship with Charles was almost platonic, though not entirely so, for sometimes I almost loved him and sometimes, I think, he almost loved me. Together we discussed books and through him I was led to read Henry James, Gissing and Arnold Bennett. He was elegant, in a quiet way, very proper — because of the vitiating propriety of his family life. He wrote beautiful letters in the most beautiful handwriting. He enjoyed a kind of delicate sparring with me. I think we tried very hard to converse like *The Dolly Dialogues*.

That one-act play of mine was the first of a number I wrote, always for a cast of two. Almost always Caroline was the heroine and I the hero. Always were the costumes picturesque. The most successful was one in which I was a gipsy fortune-teller. The scene was in Spain during the Napoleonic wars.

But Charles soon had a wonderful idea. It was for an evening of *tableaux vivants*. As he was of a scientific turn of mind, he would arrange the lighting. We two, his sisters and a half dozen boys were to be the subjects of the tableaux. For weeks we thought of little else. My grandparents' house was to be the scene of the party, as it had a large double drawing-room. The carpet was covered by grey linen, for dancing after the tableaux. My mother was to spend the night at a friend's, as her nerves could not endure the racket.

What a scene of gaiety it was! Charles saw to it that the lighting was effective. One of his sisters made a charming Madame Butterfly. I was cast as "A daughter of the Pharaohs." I was in my bedroom, making up for this tableau, when Charles tapped on the door. He had a question he must ask me. But when I opened a crack of the door, he discreetly stepped backward into the passage. Through the crack we held our whispered consultation. Our shyness was rather ridiculous but, I think, somehow touching. When the dancing began and I was doing a polka with Gordon, who was wearing his uniform of the Royal Military College, I should have liked to dance with Charles, but he had sought out my grandfather and with him was discussing something scientific.

Even my grandmother had a part in a tableau and very pretty she looked. I remember making up my father as a Roman soldier and exclaiming, "Look at yourself in the glass! Aren't you superb?"

In the tall pier glass he surveyed himself with some satisfaction and said, "How comfortable this rig is. Why can't men always dress this way?" Well may he have asked this, for, in hot weather, a half dozen starched collars would melt on his neck in one day. When I consider the complicated discomfort of the clothes we then wore, I feel pity for us and admiration for the way we coped with them. The people of to-day, bare-headed, lightly clothed, with the air playing on their sun-tanned skins, should be serenely happy and as good as gold.

The morning after the party, there were Caroline and I perched on the sofa beside my mother (for she had early returned from her friend's house) telling her of all that had happened. Oh, how she would have liked to see the tableaux — the dancing! But more and more often she remained in her bed. Her cough had left her but left her with digestion and nerves so impaired that she was no longer capable of enjoying a normal life. She began to be afraid of being alone. Dr. McKenzie seemed unable to do anything to help her.

My education was not being neglected. There was my practising of the piano. There was my homework, for I was attending a collegiate institute. No longer were my music lessons a misery to me. I now had lessons from a brilliant young pianist, Millicent Evison. From her I learned an appreciation of Chopin, though practise as I would I never could play with fluency. Really I had more to do than I had the strength for. Always the practising of the piano seemed the last straw.

Millie Evison was as fond of the theatre as was I, but she had

91

198756

a keener conscience. While I was always ready to waste the lesson time in talk of plays and actors, she would firmly draw me back. Later she gave up her career in music and went on to the New York stage. Only a year or two ago she wrote to me — a voice from the distant past. In the letter she recalled seeing a meeting between my father and me, when he had just returned after a journey. "I was moved," she wrote, "to see the joy you both felt in being together again. I have never forgotten it."

And how, during these adolescent years, fared our play — that great secret — that wonderful invention for the wasting of time, for the enthralling of the imagination? The answer is that it throve — it flourished only too strongly. Every hour that Caroline and I could snatch was spent in its delight.

As I say, every hour that could be snatched was spent in our play. Barely would I have settled down to my studies in the evening when the door of the little study would be gently opened and Caroline would slip into the room, invitation in her eyes. She would draw up a chair beside me. "Who shall we be?" She would ask. My mind would fly among those familiar characters, choosing which to begin with. These characters were not yet loved by us for their qualities. Often they were cruel. Their adventures were ill-considered. We were in no way bound by time but would pass over a year in no more than a minute. The various parts were interchangeable, so that a character would be bandied back and forth, acted differently, as Shylock by different actors is differently portrayed. Their fascination for us never for a moment flagged. If anyone came into the room, we would pretend that Caroline was hearing me recite what I had to memorize. But my homework would remain undone until the time when I should have been in bed. Then I would sit up late to finish it, already half asleep while I undressed.

When winter came, my mother's health grew steadily worse. Her suffering from nerves was excruciating. I have seen the cords at the back of her neck stand out like the taut strings of an instrument on which some wild tune is played, while her dark blue eyes would have a look of strange intensity. She was so ill that the atmosphere of her condition permeated the household. When I entered the house after school, it descended on me. Even in the classes I was conscious of its oppression, but I was not old enough to feel acute sympathy for her.

One difficulty of her illness was that she now must have the presence of a man always in the house. This masculine presence was, she thought, a protection to her. However, it was not easy to have a man always on hand. My father was frequently in Montreal or Quebec. My grandfather had to attend to his business. My younger uncle was attending the university and his older brother, who had returned home with a delicate wife and baby, was not often in the house during the day. He was in financial difficulties and was anxiously trying to better himself. My grandfather would come from his office whenever possible, to be within call, but it was not always possible.

Then my father had an idea. It was to bring an uncle of his, an elderly widower, to stay in the house. This Uncle Bryan was the tiny boy in the low-cut dress and blue shoulder-knots and silky black curls whose portrait, painted with his grandmother, had been one of those brought from Ireland by the family. Now, though he had spent the greater part of his life in Canada, he looked and spoke like an Irish gentleman of the old school. Let me describe him. He was well over six feet tall and only a little bent. His wardrobe must have been quite elegant when new but had obviously not been added to in many years. There was a greenish cast to his black broadcloth coat. His top hat was of an antiquated shape. He wore

93

large cravats and a seal ring and always carried a heavy walking-stick. His smooth-shaven lips wore an expression both urbane and devil-may-care. Curly brown hair grew in his ears. He had lived an adventurous life, it was said, but I have never known how it was employed. I was told, however, that, as a young man, his spirits were so high that he had been known to ride his horse through the countryside shouting at the top of his lungs for the sheer joy of living.

When Uncle Bryan arrived, he made a formal call on my mother in her bedroom, but from that time it was enough for her to know he was in the house, to hear the creak of his boots as he went up and down the stairs to the top-floor room he occupied.

He was an inveterate card player and must every evening have his game of euchre or cribbage. Grandpa did not play cards, but there would be Uncle Bryan, my father, one of my uncles and myself. Caroline would be sitting with my mother. I don't know how I managed to get on with my studies, yet, somehow I did. On Saturdays we would sit in the smoke-filled room (two pipes and a cigar all going), three men and a child playing cards, for the greater part of the day. On Sundays, after the morning service (Uncle Bryan was a devout member of the Church of England), again we played.

Grandfather and Great-uncle Bryan took to each other at once. They were a great contrast, yet each found in the other something to admire, and each in the other's company was livelier. When a circus came to the city, they decided to go to it together. Grandpa said to Grandma, "As you know, Louise, I have not been to a circus in many years and I care nothing for them, but the old gentleman is anxious to go and I don't see how I can get out of accompanying him." Grandma agreed that it would be only the polite thing to do. . . . Uncle Bryan said to my father, "I've given up circuses and all that sort of thing. I don't take any interest in 'em. But the old gentleman, your father-in-law, will be terribly disappointed if he doesn't see this circus and I've promised to go with him."

And so they went off happily together. . . .

Consternation seized Grandma, Caroline and me when shortly afterward Uncle Bryan was (so he said) obliged to leave us for a week on business. What business could he have that was half so important as this business of keeping my mother's nerves in a bearable state of being? My father was in New York. He had depended on his uncle to be always within call, and now he left us for a whole week.

Grandma and Caroline were not subject to extremes of emotion. What must be, must be. To me no possibility of panic or fright seemed too remote for belief. I pictured to myself what might happen when my mother discovered that Great-uncle Bryan was not in the house. It might mean the snapping of that slender cord that bound her to reason. It was the sound of his movements in the house that reassured her — his deep-toned voice, his resonant laugh, the creak of his boots as he went up and down the stairs.

Suddenly an inspiration came to me. I would be the instrument to save my mother from fear! She should not be without the sounds of that masculine presence. In Uncle Bryan's bedroom I found a pair of his boots. I put them on and creaked heavily down the stairs, along the passage, past my mother's door and down the other stairs to the hall below, where Grandma and Caroline breathlessly awaited me. I was trembling from nerves but laughing too. The deception worked. Thereafter, several times a day, I mounted and descended the stairs, wearing my great uncle's boots, even, in my girl's voice, forcing a deep "Ha!" from my throat as I creaked along the passage.

It was a triumph. It took a load off our minds. I even, after a fashion, reached a point where I enjoyed playing the part of the elderly man.

My mother suspected nothing. The dreaded week passed. Again the house seemed full of men. My father also having returned, I relaxed in the sun of his presence. Uncle Bryan was there, in person, and I no longer had to wear his boots.

Another memory comes to me. This one concerned not with boots but with skates. I had among my Christmas presents that year a fine new pair. Caroline and I were eager to go to the rink with Charles and his sisters. But, on that evening, my mother was having a bad time with her nerves. When I went to say good-bye, I could see that she was suffering. For a moment I wavered. I pictured the rink, heard the music of the band, the ring of skates on ice. I wanted to go, but I could not make up my mind to leave her. I hesitated. I could hear the voices of my friends in the hall below. I looked down at the face on the pillow.

"Would you like me to stay with you, Mama?" I asked.

"No, no, you must go with the others." But I could see the longing, the fear, in her eyes.

"I don't very much want to go," I said.

"You don't want to go? Not really?" Relief in a flush of colour flooded her face.

"No — I really don't want to go," I said. "I'd rather stay here with you and do my Latin."

I leaned over the bannister and called to those waiting below, "I'm not going. I've Latin to do."

They crowded at the bottom of the stairs.

"But surely you'll come. The band plays tonight."

"I must do my Latin." I turned back to the bedroom.

As I sat there, bent over my book, one hand shading my eyes, my mother said, "Your hand looks very thin, Mazo. Are you sure you eat enough?"

"Oh, yes, I eat plenty." My eyes turned from the Latin grammar. I stretched out my hand and examined it. "It is rather thin," I agreed, "but that's because I grow so fast."

"I suppose it is," she sighed, then, "Are you sure, my darling, that you didn't mind not going to the rink?"

"I didn't mind in the least." And by that time I did not mind. "I'd rather stay at home with you," I said.

And never did I again go to the rink or put on my skates.

These incidents are perhaps too trivial to record, yet such happenings sometimes influence character, even more than important ones. These two happenings stand out with great clarity to me, and may have helped, for all I know, to make me the woman I became.

My mother's physical and mental suffering so increased that winter that she at last agreed to consult another doctor. Dr. Algernon Temple was called in, and I remember my trepidation as his verdict was awaited. I do not know what I dreaded, but the fear was there.

Dr. Temple was in truth very grumpy about the treatment my mother had been given. She had been starved, he said, till she was too weak for the exercise she needed. Peptonized milk, toast, water, boiled rice never would cure her. She must have underdone beefsteak and she must have a trained nurse to see that his orders were carried out. A load of responsibility rolled from our shoulders when the capable nurse entered the house. She had not an endearing nature. We all disliked her and my mother grew to hate her hard, domineering presence. However, the treatment was efficacious. Week by week my mother's health improved. Once more she began to have a lively interest in life. When the nurse

97

had gone and the fresh foliage of the maple trees shaded the quiet street, my mother took little walks leaning on my father's arm. I remember that she wore a fawn-coloured cloak with a little cape trimmed with fur, even in the summer. I remember how she became once again interested in inviting people to the house.

Now a new family, and to us a remarkable one, came to live next door. They were a family of South Americans. A revolution or some political crisis had made it necessary for them to leave their country for a time. Now suddenly they appeared on our quiet street, exotic, mysterious, unlike everyone we knew. There were the parents, a number of children, a nurse for the youngest, and two black servants. The father spoke little English, but the mother and children spoke it with fluency. It would be difficult for young people of to-day to understand the fascination these foreigners had for us. Neither we nor our friends had travelled. The minds of these strangers appeared at the first as a closed book to us. But they were very friendly. The eldest daughter, somewhat older than we, became before long our inseparable companion. Her name was Inez and she was the first girl we had met who talked of her love affairs. It both embarrassed and amused us. These recitals always ended by the suitor's exclaiming, "I will marry your daughter, *señor*, in spite of anything you may do to prevent it!" We learned a little Spanish from Inez and thought it fun to show this off when we went into town on the street car.

Inez often spoke of her elder brother Roderigo, who later on was expected to join them. Then one day he appeared. He was good-looking and incredibly sophisticated. We introduced Gordon to the brother and sister and the five of us were much together. We cycled together. Together we went to McConkey's and ate *meringues glacées*, vanilla ice cream with little crescent-shaped cakes, iced and sprinkled with coconut. It was not long before we discovered that Inez had made a sofa cushion for Gordon's room and that Gordon had given her a silver chain bracelet. For the first and only time in my life I experienced jealousy. I did not want Gordon for myself. When I had been smoking a surreptitious cigarette with him, at night on the verandah, and he had put his arm about me, I had swiftly withdrawn. I was like a highly strung filly that will not endure a hand laid on her. As I say, I did not want Gordon for myself, but neither did I want Inez to have him. I became cold toward them, and so three of our quintette were no longer happy, for Gordon and Inez appeared no happier than I.

What of the other two?

I noticed nothing till the five of us were spending an evening together with the South Americans in their house. Then I had a glimpse of Roderigo and Caroline in a dim corner, where they were sitting because, he said, he had a headache. But he looked perfectly well and I saw that, with an impassioned expression on his dark face, he was holding Caroline's thin little hand in both of his and caressing it. The worst was that she seemed to like it — she who had always been so unkind to poor Donald.

I had a new feeling toward her — a feeling of hurt anger, as though she had broken some unspoken pact. But I said nothing. We pretended that nothing was different, yet I guessed that there occurred other meetings between her and Roderigo. Then I discovered, I do not know how, that Caroline had confided in my mother. I was left out. I was alone.

My mother was romantic. She would have done anything in her power to help the youthful lovers, but it was impossible. One great obstacle was religion. The South Americans were rigid Catholics. My grandfather was as strongly Protestant. He had disliked these foreigners from the start. Neither of the young people had means. Roderigo was dependent on his father. Caroline was far too young.

Everything was settled by the news that our neighbours were leaving almost at once to return to South America. A great upheaval took place next door. Children and servants were running in all directions. Roderigo and Inez were to be the first to leave. They and Caroline and I spent our last evening together. We were subdued. Though we swore friendship, I think we knew it was the end.

Next day Caroline and I went to the railway station with Inez and Roderigo. The waiting for the train seemed interminable. Already the brother and sister were in spirit far away. When they had left us, Caroline and I went to the old public library in Church Street. We were thinking of giving a three-act play and we wished to consult the catalogues. We stood side by side and I remember seeing how the tears fell from Caroline's eyes onto the ponderous volume in front of her. That night she wept after we had gone to bed, but I turned my back, understanding nothing of what she felt. A few days later she had an attack of palpitation of the heart and Dr. McKenzie was sent for. Then indeed I felt as though my little world were shaken. I did not know what to do.

One evening she was feeling better and we walked together in the twilight to the lake. We sat in the daisy field where daisies, buttercups and clover were past, and tall feathery grasses had taken their place. We watched the new moon shining above the quiet lake, and my child's heart was softened and I talked to Caroline of Roderigo, with some sort of understanding and sympathy. We felt older, seasoned in the strange ways of the world. . . .

But what could I do to make her smile again?

As an inspiration came the thought of our play. In the past summer it had been pushed aside, for new pleasures, though never forgotten. Now, I thought, I would bring it out, dress it in brighter yet more subtle colours — make it so interesting that, in the pleasure of it, we should forget all else.

How well I succeeded! New characters were introduced. All the characters, of both sexes and diverse stations and ages, were divided equally between us and remained so always.

They took on a new significance. Their relations with each other became more intense. The passing of time too became controlled. No longer would we hasten through a year in a few days or anchor a loved character to a desired age. Two of them had remained at fourteen and fifteen years, regardless of passing time. One thing I could not yet control was my desire to invent new characters. At every slightest flagging of interest a new character would be brought in to swell that cumbersome cast. Yet never did we forget any of them or leave them to languish in the wings. Quite suddenly a minor character would be given a star part and emerge with a lasting importance.

Now we learned something new. That was to feel affection for our characters. Certain ones we grew to love, as beings quite separate from ourselves, yet irrevocably bound to us, since no other actor would ever play that part. . . . During our play one of these characters met a violent end. We had not been prepared for the devastating effect this would have on us. All the night through we mourned and cried our eyes out. It was only at dawn that we fell into an uneasy sleep.

The next morning my mother remarked on my pallor. "And you have such blue rings about your eyes," she said. "Are you sure you are well?"

"I'm perfectly well," I answered, feeling strangely guilty.

Never again did we risk such a bereavement in our play, and what is more — this particular character was, after a time, raised from the dead, to live a happy, flourishing life as a farmer. As I say, never again would we risk such a bereavement — there was quite enough of suffering in our own lives.

Such was the fantastical double life lived by Caroline and me inside the close circle of the family. So enthralling did the play become, so diverse and fascinating the characters to us, that often when we glimpsed our friends coming to see us, we would escape through a side door and go to the lake, where we could uninterrupted pursue our game.

I had a feeling of antagonism toward Gordon, a feminine desire to punish him. One evening Caroline and I laid a trap for his vanity. We prepared it for the time of his daily call, which usually came at dusk. His white duck trousers and blue blazer could be glimpsed beneath the heavy boughs of the maples, in the light of the street lamps. He walked with leisurely unconcern.

I had a new sailor hat which Gordon had never seen. I put this on my head at a jaunty angle and with it a veil, something to which I had not before aspired. As we saw Gordon's stalwart figure approaching I seated myself in a dim corner of the porch where the flowers and vines from a window box overflowed and filled the air with their scent. I sat in what I thought to be the attitude of a much travelled woman of the world. Gordon drew near. Languidly I half rose as Caroline introduced us.

"Lillian," she said, in an affected voice, "I should like you to meet our friend Mr. McGrath. . . . Gordon — Miss Stacy."

I bowed distantly and gave Gordon a limp hand. He seated himself on the steps and we politely conversed, I in a refined American accent. Through my veil I could see him giving me admiring looks. Several times he had expressed a desire to meet Lillian Stacy, an American girl who had recently moved into our neighbourhood.

The quiet of the street, the scent of flowers, the moonlight glimmering through the leaves, all were romantic. The trouble was that Caroline and I dared not meet each other's eyes. We were shaken by inward laughter. After a decent interval I rose and said I must be going. Gordon at once offered to escort me home.

As we left I had a glimpse of Caroline supporting herself against a pillar of the porch.

When I had Gordon to myself, I said cooingly, "I've been wanting so much to meet you, Mr. McGrath."

"I feel just the same about you," he said.

"I don't know why it is," I said, "but ever since I first heard of you . . ."

"Ever since I first heard of you" — his voice was warm, almost tender — "I've been wanting . . ."

"I hope you're not disappointed in me," I said.

"Oh, no," he got out. "I think you're — you're wonderful."

Never before had Gordon said anything like this to me!

"You're so different from any of the men I meet abroad," I murmured. It was too easy. I was almost ashamed for him.

He bent to peer beneath the brim of my hat. He saw the malicious glitter in my eyes. I broke into derisive laughter.

He wheeled, striding homeward and leaving me to follow alone. The next day he left for the Royal Military College, without saying good-bye.

That summer my grandfather died. Great-uncle Bryan had departed. My mother no longer required a nurse. Each month saw an improvement in her.

Then one day my grandmother said to me, "I'm a little anxious about your grandpa. I notice that when he works in his flower border, he quickly tires. It's not like him."

Grandpa seemed just the same to me. I did not want to feel worried about him. I put the troubling thought out of my mind. Then suddenly he was very ill indeed. He would not have Dr. McKenzie called in, but I was sent hurrying for a doctor who lived in the next street. He came, and that evening Grandpa was suddenly much better. He appeared, wearing shirt and trousers, in the doorway of the sitting-room, where Caroline and I were sitting with Grandma. Caroline had her banjo on her knee and I my guitar, but we were not playing, because of Grandpa's illness.

Now how different everything became! He exclaimed, with his old gay smile, "Strike up the band! I'm well again."

We broke into a tune and, putting one hand on his hip, he executed some lively dance steps.

But the very next day his suffering was greater than ever. Another doctor was called in. Grandpa refused to go to the hospital, so an operation was performed at home. After that we could see that he was dying. Yet I could not let myself think about death. It was too strange. It was like the middle of the night and the wind howling outside.

In that year I always seemed to have a pencil in my hand, always making sketches. Once when I went to sit with Grandpa, I took my drawing block. He was asleep and his hands were loosely clasped on the counterpane. I thought how beautiful they looked and I made a drawing of them, as he slept.

After a while he woke and said, "Mazo, how can I ever repay you for your kindness to me?"

My mother came into the room. She was going to stay with a friend while Grandpa died. She bent over him and kissed him tenderly, but she could not speak.

Later on I felt great shame that I should have made a drawing of a dying man's hands, while he lay there helpless. It seemed somehow disloyal, but always there was in me that urge to create. I tore the drawing into small pieces.

After that I did not sit with him, but when I looked into the room, I would see my uncle, his youngest son, lying on the bed beside Grandpa, one arm about him, holding him close, as though he would protect him against what sought to destroy him. My uncle's golden head lay on the pillow close to Grandpa's.

One of Grandpa's brothers came to stay in the house. This was Great-uncle Sylvester, who was not tall like Grandpa but had the same fine aquiline features. The day after he arrived he came downstairs to Grandma and, standing in the doorway of the dining-room, he said quietly, "Daniel is gone."

Grandma had been drinking a cup of tea, for she had eaten nothing. She set down the cup and ran up the stairs. I hastened after her and saw her kneel beside that still figure on the bed.

All the blinds were drawn, making twilight in the house at noonday. A long streamer of crêpe hung on the front door. The luxuriant window boxes and hanging baskets of flowers that Grandpa had cared for bloomed on as though nothing had happened. Only a few months before, Grandpa had walked twenty-eight miles in one day without fatigue. Now he would never move again. He lay in his coffin in the dim "back-parlour," and I went there with my father to look at him.

There was nothing to fear. All signs of suffering were gone from his face. It was white as marble and he seemed about to smile. My father, so full of health and strength, stood looking down into the coffin. "Poor Grandpa," he said, and tears ran down his cheeks.

Grandma asked me to cut a lock of hair from Grandpa's head for her. That night I went alone into the parlour. I was not afraid. I would not cut the hair from the front, which looked so beautiful. I raised his head a little and was astonished to find how heavy it was. I cut off a silky silver lock and put it away in a little box to give to Grandma later, but I never could bring myself to do it, because I feared it would upset her, and at last somehow it was lost.

Every time I came upon Grandma, sitting calm in her rocking chair, I would perch on the arm of it and sit and stroke her forehead. Yet instead of comforting her, it always made her cry. I felt very strong and capable, as though I were no longer a very young girl, almost as though I had the helm of the family ship in my hands and could guide it.

I went up to the attic room where, in a box, was a quantity of heavy crêpe worn in a former bereavement. I cut a wide band from this and sewed it on the left sleeve of my little grey jacket. I thought it was the proper thing to do.

Chapter 6

The First Flight

AFTER the death of my grandfather we moved to Jarvis Street. My grandmother gave up housekeeping and she and my youngest uncle came to live with us.

We must have been a gloomy-looking family, clothed in black as we were, for even teen-age girls, such as Caroline and I, went into mourning in those days. But, though our outward appearance may have been mournful, we girls and my mother were full of pleasurable anticipation of life in that house. It stood in what was at that time one of the most spacious and fashionable streets in Toronto. I do not remember when it began to degenerate, but its downhill trend has been steady. In my youth it represented solid dignity and peaceful permanence. Judges and pillars of the Methodist church, such as the Masseys, lived there, also Sir William Mulock, chancellor of the university, and that fine historian, Professor George Wrong. The trees in summer formed an arch overhead. The pleasant clip-clop of horses' hoofs could be heard.

Our house had lofty rooms with a handsome white marble mantelpiece in almost every one. My mother took great pleasure in buying new things for this house. From that time the improvement in her health was remarkable, though there were certain things she still would not do. She would neither venture into crowds nor would she travel by train. But she now was able to give my father the companionship his genial nature craved. Through the long years of her illness no one ever heard him complain of this lack in his life. I can remember how, when coming into her room, flushed from tennis, I would find him sitting with her, reading aloud or, more often, just giving her the strength of his presence. How often his stalwart frame must have hungered for something beyond the sickroom!

Yet, in spite of his devotion to her, he was in certain ways a trial to her. The chief one of these was his habit of acquiring dogs. When we removed to the house in Jarvis Street, he already had two dogs — an irascible Maltese terrier named John and a beautiful Scotch collie, Queenie. We had not been long in the new house when Queenie produced a litter of four puppies. After that appeared Biddy, a highly pedigreed Irish terrier whose puppies (she was bred to an expensive sire) were to be sold at high prices. But her litter consisted of nine bitches and we discovered that she never had been known to have a male puppy. Somehow the care of the dogs devolved mostly on me. I loved them but found them a great responsibility, especially when neighbours complained of their barking.

Three of Queenie's puppies were sold — the fourth, Lorna, we kept. Queenie was expected, the following winter, to have another litter. She did not sleep in the kennels with the other dogs but had a little back bedroom of her own upstairs. As she grew heavier she seemed to find the climbing of the stairs too great an effort. She just sank down, a tawny heap, at the bottom and raised beseeching eyes to us. So Caroline and I carried her up the long flight to her room. As the time for her accouchement drew near we hastened eagerly each morning to see if anything had happened in the night. But no — Queenie lumbered down the stairs, eager for breakfast and the new day. We began to think we had miscalculated, for she grew heavier and heavier. Sometimes we scarcely could carry her up the stairs, for laughing. What was she going to produce? A baby elephant?

It turned out that she was simply hoaxing us, while she grew fatter and fatter from lack of exercise.

Before long another dog was acquired by my father, this time an English brindle bulldog. My father agreed he did not need another dog but convinced us that this dog, of champion stock, was a valuable possession. She was not a lovable dog and the feminine part of the household were unanimous in declaring her to be a nuisance. I called her Aggerwator after a character in Dickens, so named by her cockney husband because she so greatly aggravated him. But her proper name was Wanda.

She actually was a valuable dog and later on my father sold her for a high price. When the new owner called her by name, she just looked at him stupidly.

"I'm afraid she isn't intelligent," he said, and essayed again — "Wanda! Wanda!"

She ignored him.

"I wonder if she's deaf." Her new master plainly was worried.

"Try her with Aggerwator," said my father laconically.

The effect was immediate. When she heard the beloved name, she bounded with joy.

In those days we had great snowfalls and I remember taking the dogs for walks up Jarvis Street on winter evenings at sunset when the street was deserted. Biddy, the Irish terrier, was especially overjoyed by this. She would fairly fly across the snowy lawns in rhythmic leaps like a deer and I would feel as full of joy.

Sometimes Caroline and I would snowshoe over the bridge into

Rosedale and beyond to the countryside. We were good walkers and though we would have delighted in seaside and mountains we made the most of our visits to Lake Simcoe and the Ontario countryside. An observer might have called us little stay-at-homes who knew nothing of travel, but how wrong a conception of our life! For we travelled when we willed, in the freedom of our play. Well we knew the rugged shore of a certain island off the west coast of Scotland. We explored sandy beach and wooded hill of England. After reading Henry Harland's novels of Italy, that became our favourite country, for a time, and Roman Catholicism our favourite religion. Indeed, a large number of our characters became Catholics overnight. With no spiritual struggles we transferred them and enthusiastically they accepted the change. The other characters remained in our own Church of England and this gave variety and added interest. One family in particular, whose most important member was played by Caroline, obstinately clung to tradition, even though Caroline at the same time was portraying a Jesuit priest and doing very well in that role.

We two belonged to a small orchestra of boys and girls who played on the banjo, mandolin and guitar. We had a great deal of fun out of this little orchestra and even went to near-by towns to play at concerts, and, of course, there were incipient affairs of the heart, though the memory of Roderigo made Caroline supercilious toward these provincial youths, and I retained my dislike of being touched. An attempt at hand-holding, a hand stealing toward my waist were enough to make me fiercely withdraw. I loved to attract, but to hold bored me. Also there was something almost boyish in me. I looked on sex as rather silly. There was so much that was more interesting.

Caroline talked of becoming a teacher of the banjo and indeed she, at seventeen, had several pupils, but her greatest interest lay in the life of home. She sewed beautifully and made herself charming clothes, while I was comparatively helpless with a needle. Always we had pretty clothes, though there never seemed to be much money about. In our family there was a perennial scarcity of money, yet seldom were we denied what we wanted. The wants of Caroline and me were not extravagant and this was in contrast to my parents, who, as long as money was available, believed in spending it as quickly as possible. Possessions never greatly mattered to me. I can admire without desiring, and have a horror of debt.

I had been ailing and Dr. McKenzie, in his dictatorial way, declared that I must not enter the university. I had not the stamina, he said. I accepted this without great disappointment, for I did not yearn for hard study and examinations. I felt sure there were other things in life for me. . . . As I have said, I was eternally sketching. At school I had ornamented my textbooks with drawings. I decided that, above all things, I wanted to study at the Ontario School of Art, and later go to Paris. My parents were delighted. "I myself will take you to Paris," said my father. "We will go together and have a wonderful time." Always he and I were planning to travel together.

G. A. Reid was my teacher at the School of Art. He was a bearded, good-humoured man whose wife also was an artist. Her paintings of flowers had a gentle grace and beauty. My mother was charmed by the Reids and at once set about acquiring pictures by them, several of which I still possess.

I was rather good at pen and ink drawings and vaguely dreamed of a time when I should become an illustrator of books. But, in my teens, all my dreams were vague. Time seemed endless, the future mysterious but always propitious and without pain.

The large room at the School of Art where we worked was in

winter bitterly cold. I remember how snow, drifting through a crack in the skylight, would settle on the floor in a ridge and not melt. I used to carry a bottle of milk to drink with my lunch and often it would be frozen. Yet we always were jolly, ready for any distraction. There would be a cry of, "Come quickly and see Lady Melvin-Jones pass!" And we would fly from drawing-board and easel and crowd to the windows to admire the splendid equipage, the horses shining in silver-mounted harness, the coachman and footman in livery, and Lady Melvin-Jones and her handsome daughter looking regal indeed.

I could scarcely wait to show my drawings at home. Wherever I was I always strained toward the return home — to my father, the loved protector — to my mother, a part of myself — to Caroline, partner of my imaginative excursions.

Soon after the death of my grandfather, my Uncle Walter had succumbed to an attack of typhoid fever. Never shall I forget the tragic calm of my grandmother's face as she saw him carried to the ambulance. The drastic treatment he was given in the hospital quickly broke up the fever and he returned home, only to spend a year of indifferent health before he again went down with the fever.

This time the old stand-by, Dr. McKenzie, was called in. The fever, he declared, must run its course to the crisis at three weeks — then we should see what we should see! My mother undertook the nursing.

Looking back, it is strange to think how she who, for so many years, was the care, the focus of anxiety for all the family now became the untiring nurse of her brother. For the many long weeks of his illness, she was always there, changing his bed-linen, preparing his food, giving him his medicine, till he emerged from the ordeal, gaunt, large-eyed, and wearing a little sandy beard. From this time on she cast off the habits of invalidism and her naturally staunch and spirited nature asserted itself.

Something new was stirring in me. I discovered that I wanted to write a story — one that I might send to a magazine. It must be done in secret, so that if I were not successful, no one need know, and, if I were, it would be a lovely surprise for the family.

For some reason I chose to write about French-Canadians, in this, my first, venture. Why I did this I do not know. I was not a French-Canadian. My connection was with Old France — yet something in me drove me to place the scene of this story in Quebec. I shut myself in the dim end of the huge sparsely furnished drawing-room. I wrote the story in lead pencil (as I have written all since) and then copied it painstakingly in pen and ink. The thought that it should be typed never entered my head.

I have little patience with writers who declare that all their works are composed in agony of spirit. This agonized creation seems to me affected, for, in truth, imaginative writing is one of the most delightful of occupations. It is exacting, it often is exhausting. It demands everything the writer has it in him to give. He must believe in the characters if he is to persuade the public to believe in them. What the writer of fiction needs — first, last, and all the time — is a public. Its interest is the steady wind that fans the fire of his creative ability. All his "agonizing" will not create a public for him.

My first stories, however, were written in a kind of calculated agony. I had the idea that I must work myself up into a state of excitement before I could write of what was in my mind. I would lie on the sofa in the dim room, my body rigid, my mind hallucinated by the pictures that passed before it. Then I would rise, take up paper and pencil and write. Again I would stretch myself on the sofa. Again I would write. I remember my reflection in the old gilt-framed mirror that hung above the sofa, the glitter in my eyes, the flushed cheeks, as of one in a fever. And so in this way the story was completed.

Related long afterward, in cold blood, it sounds rather ridiculous. But I think it is rather touching too, because I was so very young, so ignorant. I am sure that most twelve-year-olds of to-day are more knowledgeable than I was at that time.

In secrecy, then, the story was finished. In secrecy it was posted to *Munsey's* magazine. I did not know that I should enclose return postage.

I waited.

At the hour for the postman's call I was on hand to be the first to get the mail. From an upstairs window I would see him coming. I would tear down the stairs, my heart hastening its beat. Weeks passed. Then came a small envelope from *Munsey's* — not the dreaded long envelope containing my manuscript — and in it a note from the editor saying that he had much pleasure in accepting my story. I flew to where my mother and Caroline were sewing.

"I've written a story," I said, "and it's accepted and I'm to be paid fifty dollars for it."

My mother began to cry. "How lovely," she said through her tears.

"So that's what you were up to," said Caroline. "We've been wondering."

They were very pleased but scarcely surprised. They said they knew I had it in me to write a good story.

I had had little money in my young life. To me it seemed something of which there was a perpetual shortage in our family. I made up my mind that the cheque for this story was to be spent on a present for my mother, something she could keep always.

Caroline and I went to Junor's store and there we discovered an ornate lamp, the base of wrought iron, the bowl of bronze, the shade of beautiful amber glass, like a full moon, and on the side of the shade a golden dragon. How much was it? Fifty dollars — the very price!

My mother was delighted. This lamp was just what she had longed for, she said. A few years later she broke the shade and one would have thought the end of the world had come, so devastated was she. But then, she was highly emotional. She took things very hard; yet in the great troubles of her life showed wonderful self-control.

When the magazine containing my story appeared, I was strolling along Yonge Street. In the window of a stationer's shop I saw the latest number. I went in and asked if I might look at the index page. I was allowed to see it, and there, in print, was my name!

I had no money with me and ran along Maitland Street home for the price of *Munsey's*.

At that time my paternal grandmother was visiting us, and my father was determined that his mother should appreciate what I had achieved. He was going to read aloud my story to her. Not that she had expressed a desire to have it read. The fact that it had been accepted was enough for her. I never knew her to read anything but the Psalms of David and of these she knew quite a number by heart. Her visits to us were something of a strain, as she had become, through the years, accustomed to the conventional atmosphere of the house of her eldest son, Uncle Danford, with whom she lived. I remember being dreadfully homesick there, even during a short visit. The house was too tidy — the meals too regular — the carpets too thick — Auntie Ida's dominance too evident. And when Grandmother came to visit us, I think she was in her turn depressed by the contrast to the precise order to which she was used. She had forgotten the high-spirited family of which she had once been a part.

Now, when I had my first story accepted, she was to hear it read aloud by my father. He had placed two chairs side by side in the dining-room. He took her hand and led her with ceremony to one of them.

"Do you think there will be time before lunch?" she asked, with a yearning look toward the table upon which the maid had already laid a white cloth.

"A full half-hour," beamed my father. "So sit down and prepare to enjoy yourself."

"Is this story true?" asked Grandmother.

"No, no, it is purely imaginative." Dramatically he began to read aloud, and she to endure.

Never could I forget the picture of them sitting there — he with a small dog on his knee, another between his feet; she a stately figure in her black silk dress, with ruchings of white at neck and wrists, and a long gold chain. Her cap, of white lace and ribbon rosettes, was on a foundation of wire. She herself made her caps and, during all the years I knew her, I never saw her do anything more arduous than this and the making of patchwork quilts. Those quilts were quite handsome, being of silk and satin with a wide border of black velvet. She scorned any material but what was absolutely new. One she made for each member of the family and when at work on the one destined for me, she met a young man who came to the house frequently as my friend. She was favourably impressed, especially by the young man's height, and at once set about making the quilt six inches longer.

Now, with a resigned "Heigh-ho" and a lifting and a dropping of her shapely white hands on the arms of her chair, she listened to the reading of the first published story of her loved granddaughter — the only grandchild of hers ever to be produced. And she listened with every evidence of boredom.

Yet she was not to escape. My father was determined that she was to hear that story.

After a few miserable moments I slunk from the room.

When I returned, the lunch was being brought to the table. My father, looking somewhat subdued, was heaving my grandmother to her feet and she gratefully was approaching the table. Her ordeal was over. The little Yorkshire terrier was dragging *Munsey's* magazine under the sofa.

It was during this same visit of my grandmother's that I persuaded her to dress up in a suit of my father's. Why or how I did this I cannot remember. Probably a perverse mischievous spirit in me wanted to see the undignified transformation and I always had a persuasive tongue.

However that may be, I got her secretly into a light grey suit, trousers, shirt, tie, waistcoat and jacket. It was the first time in my life when I had seen her divested of her noble armour of the day, though once on a memorable night when I was about twelve I slept with her in her four-poster because of the sudden visitation of Great-aunt Susannah and her three daughters.

My father's suit fitted her surprisingly well, for she was nearly as tall as he and well proportioned, but above it rose her head with its lace cap. Quickly I brought his grey Homburg and she allowed me to replace her cap with it. She rose to her full height and surveyed herself in the pier glass.

Oh, the transformation! With the change of clothes she had become a rather rakish-looking old gentleman-about-town, with a strong resemblance to her brother, Great-uncle Bryan.

I had never seen my grandmother smile in the way she now smiled at her reflection. She looked positively devil-may-care. With a jaunty walk she went toward the room where my mother was brushing her long golden-brown hair.

"Good-afternoon," said my grandmother.

The brush suspended in the air, my mother regarded the apparition in the doorway with first amazement, then unbelief.

"I don't make a bad figure of a man, do I?" said Grandmother.

My mother could not speak for laughing.

Then my father came in. He gave the seeming old gentleman a look of astonishment, then exclaimed, "Uncle Bryan!" and held out his hand.

"It is I," said my grandmother, in her pleasant Irish voice, and with a shout of laughter he clasped her to his breast.

Such a picture they made, the two of them, that my mother and I were helpless from laughter. Caroline came running. Grandmother herself laughed till she was crimson in the face and her hat tilted to a rakish angle. Surely she had never had such fun in Auntie Ida's primly ordered house.

In truth she laughed so hard that my mother became a little alarmed and brought smelling-salts and held them to Grandmother's nostrils.

My father sat down on the side of the bed and Biddy, the Irish terrier, seeing him there, felt emboldened to climb up and lay her head on the pillow.

Chapter 7

Clipped Wings

IT WAS not long before I wrote a second short story. This too was of French Canada and I wrote it with the same vehemence that I had put into the first. But this one was not written secretly. My mother and Caroline knew what I was about, and before I sent it to the editor I read it to them.

Like the first, it was accepted and a cheque for fifty dollars was sent me. Again I spent it in presents — twenty-five dollars for a stylish beige raincoat for my mother, ten dollars for a swarthy plaster head of Cleopatra, also for my mother, and the remainder for a long silver necklace for Caroline which she still treasures. For some reason my father and I got nothing out of these first earnings. They must be spent headlong, with a bang, on those two.

I felt strong and full of power. I was exhilarated by my success. I sold one story after another. I was still going to the School of Art. I was taking French lessons too from Monsieur Masson in St. Joseph Street, who went every morning to Mass in the church across the way from his house. But I had a feeling that my education was not what it should be and I arranged for certain lectures at the university. Looking back, I can see myself ploughing through deep snow in Queen's Park, my heavy serge skirt encrusted with snow to the knees, stopping every so often surreptitiously to straighten out my petticoat, which somehow managed to work itself into a hampering ball between my legs.

The short stories I wrote at that time were written not only in the first heat of inspiration but with considerable care for the right phrase and with anxious thought for the handwriting itself. If the look of the manuscript did not please me, I meticulously copied it again.

There was one story that I thought of as my best. Mother and Caroline agreed that it was my best and I posted it with a feeling of happiness. Yet weeks passed — more weeks than the usual time taken to acknowledge receipt of a manuscript — and still no word from the magazine. A strange unease took possession of me. There was a tremor in my inmost being. I could not understand it. I went to the post office where I had bought the stamps for the postage. The girl at the wicket remembered me. Yes, she remembered me well and the odd thing was that just after I had left someone had found a ten-cent stamp on the floor.

I turned away. Yes, that had been my stamp, I knew. My manuscript was lost. It had had no postage on it. . . . Strange how the pavement appeared to slant — as though falling away from me. I had a feeling of strange excitement, yet I felt weary as never before. When I returned home, I found that the floor sloped away from me as the pavement had done, as though into an abyss. I could think of nothing but the lost manuscript.

At one of the theatres the morality play *Everyman* was shown. Caroline was not interested in this, so I went to it alone. For years I shrank from hearing this play mentioned, so acute had been my suffering while watching it. I did not know what was wrong with me and why these new and frightening sensations.

I kept them to myself, but one day, it was early in Lent, I went

My mother's mother

My mother's father

My father's father

My father's mother

My mother at about thirty years

My father at about thirty years

Myself at two years

Myself and Leigh McCarthy

My mother at seventeen and
Caroline's mother at thirty-six

Myself at eleven years

Caroline — London, 1937

Myself with Bunty — 1923

Myself — a recent photograph

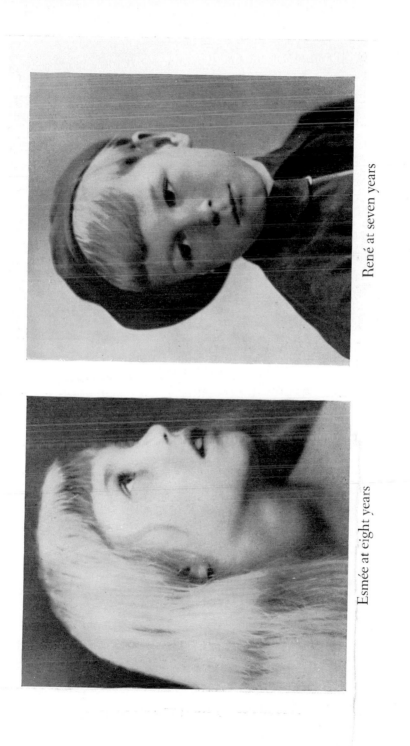

René at seven years

Esmée at eight years

Vale House — Windsor

A corner of my study — Vale House

to St. Michael's Cathedral and knelt at each of the stations of the Cross — perhaps hoping for a miracle. I do not know.

The walk home seemed long and I was tired. I went to the sitting room where my mother and grandmother were sewing. This was not the grandmother who was tall and stately but the short, maternal grandmother — the best loved, whom I called Grandma.

Standing in the doorway of the room, I looked in at them as though I were an alien. I told them where I had been and what I had done, but I did not tell them why. For I did not myself know. I told them with an air of defiance, as though to show that I no longer belonged to them.

Grandma, strongly Protestant, gave me a look of scornful displeasure and my mother exclaimed, "All day I have felt something hanging over me — a cloud — I did not know what it was." Grandma turned away from us both.

I went up the stairs. It was a handsome staircase, broad, with delicate white spindles beneath the mahogany handrail. I clung to this as I mounted the stairs, for I felt unutterably tired and I had no certainty of balance. I sat down on the side of my bed. The room looked unfamiliar. This thing that had descended on me had come with ruthless speed. I was trembling all over.

But the following day I felt better. I made up my mind that, with all my strength, I would struggle against this blight which sought to destroy me.

Sometimes I am inclined to make fun of modern psychologists, with their pat jargon, yet I suppose, if an understanding doctor had been brought in, he might have helped me.

But it was Dr. McKenzie who finally was sent for. He came and stood by the bed and looked down at me, with his jeering smile. "Well, you've got yourself into a pretty pickle," he said.

121

He left me a prescription and dropped in once or twice more to see me. I was to stay in bed, he said, till I had recovered. My father was in Quebec at the time and my mother wrote to tell him of my illness. One sentence of his reply remains with me — a cry from his heart — "But I don't want her to be ill! I want her to be strong and well and happy." He had suffered so much from my mother's long illness.

Of the weeks that followed I have never talked to anyone, and never thought to have written of them. They passed, in confused procession. I took what seemed gallons of Dr. McKenzie's prescription. My mother, who, so short a while ago, had nursed my uncle through a siege of typhoid fever, now nursed me — bathed me, brushed my long hair, carried endless trays to me — with never a hint of weariness, never a word of complaint.

My father returned and came and sat by me, with that rueful smile he had when things went wrong. Once I heard my mother say to him, "I've never felt so sorry for anyone in all my life, as I feel for Mazo."

I did not hear his reply, but for the first time, hearing my mother's words, I felt pity for myself and my shattered hopes. I buried my face in my pillow and wept.

It was my mother who nursed me through this long illness, but it was Caroline who slept with me, whose rest was broken by my tossing — my inability to sleep. It was she who held me close in her arms when despair threatened me. . . . One night my uncle, coming home late, heard us talking. He came into the room and stood, a dim figure, at the foot of the bed.

"How are you?" he asked, and I answered in a strangled voice:

"I'm done for — I shall never be well again." And, from my fevered brain, I brought out the fear that haunted me — "I'm going to die — like Grandpa died."

He gave a short, angry laugh. He laid his hands on the foot-board of the bed and leant over us. "You couldn't," he said. "You couldn't — not even if you *tried*."

His voice came out of the darkness. "There's plenty of time for you to develop. You're only beginning. What you need is a different doctor."

But we never considered consulting another doctor. Dr. Mc-Kenzie was our doctor and, though we had not seen him for more than a month, my mother still had a strange confidence in him, a confidence he had never done anything to merit.

Now my father went to see him and to ask if it would be all right to move me to the Reids' studio, which we had taken for the summer. It was in Indian Road, which at that time was almost in the country.

The doctor's jaw dropped. "Why," he said, "I thought she would have recovered by now. I'll come round and see her."

He came, and the tension his presence always evoked in me made me refuse to acknowledge that I was worse, rather than better. I just looked at him in hate.

By this time I was too weak to walk down the stairs to the carriage. My uncle carried me and I lay back among the cushions — a ghost of the girl I had been.

Shortly before this I had had a letter of acceptance from the editor of the magainze to which I had sent the story I feared was lost. But the letter, and the cheque that followed it, meant little to me. I was done for — I was finished — I would never write again!

The panelled walls, the beamed ceilings of the studio, the sweet air from the near-by fields were tonic. The field in front of the house, with its tall waving grasses where harebells grew, filled me with a new hope. Here I would recover. Far away seemed the room where I had suffered, though it was only a few miles.

Indian Road was at that time not paved, but was served by a sandy road. A little way up this road lived Wylie Grier, the artist. He used to come to use our telephone, always surrounded by his horde of handsome children.

Pine trees surrounded the studio and my bedroom window looked out on them. Its door opened on a gallery which overlooked the high panelled studio, but this bedroom was plastered. Its walls and ceiling were rough and it was my torment to discover on their grey surface horrible faces that mouthed and grimaced at me. Fear had become my companion, my imagination no longer my delightful servant but my cruel master. All that happened was exaggerated. When my pet canary was asphyxiated in his cage from the fumes of a gas heater, all that night I relived his suffering. . . . Yet I improved. I began to take short walks. I learned again to sleep — to be lively, as was my nature.

In the late summer Caroline went to visit friends in New York. What a preparation — as though she were off to the ends of the earth! What planning, what buying of material and making it into blouses and dresses, and how lovely she looked in them, with her fine fair hair and clear blue eyes!

When Caroline had gone, my mother and I passed long days together. She read aloud to me books from the Reids' shelves — *Villette, Wuthering Heights, Lorna Doone.* Yet we counted the days till Caroline's return. So close we lived inside the family that the smallest break in that circle was a cause of wonderment and concern. And when the absent one returned, what rejoicing. . . .

She looked so tiny and yet so strangely experienced. My mother and I sat on either side of her, as she drank coffee, absorbing all she had to tell. And, of course, she had presents for every-

body. Out of her slender purse she had bought presents for everybody.

When we were alone together, I asked, "Have you forgotten
our play?"

"Never." She gave her gay little laugh. "Never for a moment.
Let's do it now." And so we did.

Chapter 8

The Long Years

DURING that summer I became physically much stronger. I regained much of the strength I had lost, though never did I regain it all. I still could not concentrate on the reading of a book. One day I had occasion to write a postcard. I thought I would write it in pencil, as I had no pen with me. I sat down by a table and took the pencil in my hand. How strange, how beautiful it was to hold it! My pulse quickened. Just to write — even to write a postcard . . . to do that for which I was made.

But I could not write. My hand and arm were as though paralyzed — as though made of wood. A pain shot through my head. My forehead was wet with sweat. I was helpless to write. I could not force the pencil to move.

All that day, and the following day, I suffered the sensations with which my illness had begun. The floor would appear to sink away in front of me. I would seem about to fall, and a great weariness possessed me. I concealed this, for I could not bear to bring anxiety to those I loved.

So, now and again, I would make the effort to write and each time would fail. Nearly a year passed before I was able to write a letter. In truth I look back on the three succeeding years with a feeling of confusion. I can barely recall the times when I thought it might be possible for me to write —my attempts — my failures — my near despairs. . . .

The effect on me of this illness of the nerves was to make me more dependent on those about me. I had been rather an independent girl — somewhat sure of myself, I fear, though I don't think anyone would have called me conceited. But now, like a child, I wanted to be told what to do. This desire to have decisions made for me has clung to me the rest of my life. In fact, I am weakly amiable — too ready to agree.

The following year we again went to the Reids' studio. I was by this time able to write letters and had an interesting correspondent in a young Scotsman named Alastair. We had been introduced in letters by relations of his in Canada. The romantic interchange of letters with Alastair suited me very well. His beautiful handwriting, his sentimental descriptions of Scottish scenery, his boyish reflections on life were stimulating. Above all, he was far, far away — a great recommendation — for my physical strength was precarious.

In the late summer I was sent, on the advice of Dr. McKenzie, for a complete change of air and scene, to the Georgian Bay. I went by myself, to a hotel at Pointe au Baril kept by the Oldfields. This was an unusual family — born, reared, spending their lives by these wild waters. A primitive place the hotel then was, standing exposed on a rock at the opening into Lake Huron. Its patrons were mostly American fishermen and their wives.

I am wondering whether such individuality could now be found in a group of American holiday-makers. No pair of those Americans were like the others. They were not interested in each other, but I was interested in them and they in me, probably because I was the only Canadian — a young girl, alone and fragile. I must have looked fragile indeed, for once, when I had left the verandah and returned a few moments later, I was just in time to hear one of the women (she was a Jewess and very kind-hearted) say to another, "That young girl is not long for this world. She looks just like my sister, who died in my arms two years ago —" and she burst into tears.

There were, in the hotel, a New England professor and his wife, and her room was on the third floor next to mine. The partitions were thin and every night I could hear her (as she could hear me) striking the walls with a slipper to kill the big water spiders perching there. Every morning, sharp at eight, the professor would knock at his wife's door.

"Is that you, Professor Watmough?" she would call out, and he would answer:

"It is I, Mrs. Watmough. Good-morning."

"One moment, please," she would respond, and then the door would open and he would enter.

In discreet tones they would converse. I would wonder what about. There were another professor and his wife in the hotel. This pair were convinced that, having come to the Canadian wilds, they would revert, as far as possible, to the primitive life. But this was done in a decorous manner. They walked stealthily in Indian file, wearing moccasins, and her hair hung in two plaits to her waist. Both were giving their hair an oil treatment, so that it glittered oilily in the sun. Sometimes they invited me to go for a row with them, when suddenly — I never knew how the moment was chosen — he would lay down his oars and ejaculate the single word "Teeth!"

Instantly, from some recess, both would whip out toothbrushes, and, without embarrassment, they would set to work vigorously to clean their teeth in the Georgian Bay.

He was a small man, rather austere — though kindly — and to my mind he took a dim view of life. He would gaze across the dancing waves and say, "Do you realize, young lady, that we are born but to die? For a few years we have lovely flesh" — and he would look almost accusingly at me — "then how soon it fades! We are doomed from the day of our birth."

At the next moment he might give the order for tooth-cleaning and I would watch fascinated, as their tooth paste troubled the waters.

Very different were the New Yorker and his daughter. He was a widower, a wealthy man, and his daughter was accompanied by a French maid. Father and daughter were devoted to each other, but I was surprised to see how she would quite casually tell him to go to her room to fetch her handkerchief or jacket. The white-haired man would cheerfully mount the long flight of stairs — after a day's fishing — while the healthy young girl lounged below. Well, in my family, the women, unless they were ailing, waited on the men!

These New Yorkers were very nice to me, inviting me to join them for sailing in the boat they had engaged. I was pleased by this, for they ignored their own countrymen. The daughter was a girl of great charm. She had with her a scrapbook filled with newspaper cuttings concerning the society doings in which she had part. There were pictures of her riding in Central Park or going to the opera. She and I sat side by side in the hotel sitting-room, looking at this book. I longed to tell her that I wrote short stories, but a sudden shyness overcame me and I could not bring myself to speak of it. I thought I should like to put this attractive girl into a story. By this time hope of again being able to write had returned to me. The story even took form in my mind. Later on I did write it.

Ringing the Changes

One more guest at the hotel remains in my mind. This was Mr. Craig.

Christian names were not so lightly bandied about in those days and he remained Mister Craig, though he came each summer to the hotel. He was a reticent, even sombre man — a sufferer from insomnia. His best sleep of the year came to him in the Georgian Bay, he said.

Mr. Craig owned a handsome skiff and every evening he went rowing in it, to tire himself physically. Even after that I would hear him pacing up and down the pier, long past midnight. One evening he abruptly asked me if I would go out in the skiff with him. I accepted gladly, for I admired him as a strong and skilful oarsman and sometimes the evenings seemed long.

It was glorious to skim between the islands, with the sunset blazing red behind us and the pine trees, black as thunder, on either side. The channels between the islands were narrow, the air so clear that every fern frond, every mossy ledge of rock was reflected with exquisite accuracy in the water. So perfect were these reflections in detail and colour that there was nothing to choose between solid rock and liquid image. They were alike as the two sides of an Indian totem pole.

As the sunset radiance faded and the large northern stars were reflected in the dark water Mr. Craig steered the skiff into the open bay. His thin brown arms moved in rhythmic strength and a look of peace came into his face.

"Are you cold?" he asked.

I denied that I was cold, but he tossed his jacket to me. Then, with his rare smile, he said, "It helps me to have you with me." I did not tell him that I knew what it was to suffer from nerves, but I felt that somehow we comforted one another. It was late when we returned. The pier was deserted. I tiptoed up the stairs to my room, feeling that these hours had been the best of the twenty-four.

Every evening I went on the lake with Mr. Craig.

A small crowd would gather on the pier to watch us set out. Everyone admired his lovely skiff and his masterful handling of her. Even when the waves were tumbling beneath the northern stars I felt no fear. I had complete confidence in his boat and in his own powers.

One night the bay was so rough that the group on the pier gave an apprehensive look at me as Mr. Craig steadied the boat while I clambered in. One of the men remarked:

"Do you think it's safe to go on the water tonight? There's a gale rising."

"If I didn't think it was safe I'd not be going," Mr. Craig answered tersely.

"Well, you've a great responsibility there," said the man.

"I don't need to be told that."

It was amusing and rather exciting to me to see how little it took to make Mr. Craig's temper rise. And, as though the skiff responded, it fairly leaped upon the waves. Soon we were swallowed up in the singing darkness and the group on the pier dispersed. We remained out much later than usual and when we parted, Mr. Craig said, "No walking on the pier for me tonight. I shall sleep like a top."

But the following morning one of the women guests drew me aside and said, "Do you know that you are getting yourself talked about, my dear?"

"Talked about?" I repeated astonished.

"Yes — criticized for going out every night in Mr. Craig's boat. Do you think your mother would approve?"

I said I hadn't thought about it. Indeed, I knew that if it had been possible for both my grandmothers to be in the boat with Mr. Craig and me, they would have heard nothing to alarm them.

"I am sure your mother would not approve," insisted the lady, with a compelling look.

I considered these remarks during the day and when that evening Mr. Craig came to me where I sat, as though waiting, in my usual seat on the pier, and asked, "Are you ready?" I answered, "Thanks, but I think I'll not go this time."

His smile turned to a frown. "I know what has happened," he said bitterly. "Those busybodies have been gossiping. Surely you don't mind what they say."

"I think I do mind." I looked him straight in the eyes.

"Then I'm greatly disappointed in you," he exclaimed hotly. "I could not have believed it possible. I thought you were above such pettiness."

If he had remained to urge me I might have weakened — I do not know. But he turned abruptly away and went to his boat. I never exchanged another word with him. Two days later he returned to his home. When I saw his place at table vacant, I thought, "Well, I needn't bother about him any more. His insomnia may be better or worse — it doesn't matter to me."

I went to my room, found a sheet of paper and wrote the title and first paragraph of the story about the girl from New York. I reflected happily that those evenings on the Georgian Bay had been good for my nerves. Again I could write.

But it was slow going. A very little each day — and sometimes that little was too much, and I suffered for it.

The hotel was by this time almost empty, but I could not leave, because the money to pay my board had not arrived. I waited and waited. The third floor, where I had my room, was empty but for me and the spiders. The nights were cold, the stars bigger and brighter, the pine trees on the deserted island took kingly possession.

At last the money arrived and I arranged to leave. But a gale came down from the north and lashed the water to fury. My luggage and I stood waiting rather pathetically on the pier. The steamer, hours late, wallowed in, past the lighthouse, but when the hawser was thrown over a post, the heavy rope snapped like twine and the boat staggered on, unable to stop. I must wait three days for the next boat.

Up to the third story I was returned with my luggage. I began to wonder what winter would be like at Pointe au Baril.

It was very cold and I thought I would make myself a hot drink. I had with me a little travelling stove, fed by methylated spirits. I lit it, but the flame was feeble. It required more of the spirits. I must have been excited, for instead of putting out the flame before I added the spirits, I poured the liquid straight from the bottle onto the flame.

A blaze shot ceilingward. I screamed, but only the spiders heard me. Out in the night the gale howled. The great waves beat on the enduring rocks. When I had somehow quenched the flames, I peered into the looking-glass. My eyebrows and the fringe of hair on my forehead were gone! I crept into bed and pulled the bed-clothes over my head.

Four days later I arrived in Toronto, the manuscript of my story safely under my arm. It was Exhibition time. The windows of the greengrocers were blazing with ripe peaches — the streets seething with visitors from out of town. I telephoned the studio. Mrs. Reid's voice answered. She told me that at the end of August my family had moved to a cottage they had taken for the remainder of the season at Lake Simcoe. But they had sent me word of the change. She knew they had sent me word, and letters had such a way of going astray in those northern parts. It was too late for me to catch the radial car, so I must spend the night in the city. It was not easy to find a room in a hotel, for they were crowded, but one, of which I had never heard, took me in. It was a small hotel convenient to the radial station. The proprietor gave me his own room. But when I tried to lock the door, I found it had no lock!

I made a barricade of the washing-stand and two chairs. There was little bedding, so I laid my coat over me and at last fell asleep. I caught an early train to Lake Simcoe and found the cottage, standing among apple trees. I was greeted by an uproar from the dogs. There followed explanations of letters and telegrams undelivered, of anxious waiting, but all were happy because I was looking so much better. "But, darling, where are your eyebrows?" cried my mother. I gave a lurid account of what had happened and everyone agreed that I had looked better with eyebrows. My mother declared that, had she known what I was to go through in that place, she would never have closed her eyes in sleep.

It was heaven to be home again and to be feeling stronger. I sent off my story to the *Smart Set* magazine and it was shortly accepted. This magazine, I think, was edited by Messrs. Nathan and Mencken. It was the first to publish Somerset Maugham's famous story "Rain" and it also published stories by Lord Dunsany, D. H. Lawrence, Christopher Morley, W. B. Yeats and other famous authors. Not long ago I was sent an anthology of stories from the *Smart Set* and when I discovered this one of mine among them, my mind flew back to Lake Simcoe and the day when the letter of acceptance came. I always was surprised when my stories were accepted. I was equally surprised when they were not. This gift (or weakness) of surprise was born with me and has ever since remained. Nothing has so much surprised me as that I should be writing my autobiography.

The cottage we had rented at Lake Simcoe belonged to a remarkable old farmer named Yates. He and his son George had built it among clover fields, where now are neat rows of cottages, with little well-kept lawns, and a motor car in front of each cottage. Then it was open, free, long-grassed, and the lake had not become the sporting place of week-enders.

My father disliked motor cars, but that summer he bought for Caroline and me a delightful chestnut gelding to take the place of the pair of shaggy Welsh ponies we once had owned. Johnny was a handsome cob with a will of his own. How we loved him! And how we delighted in those drives over the deserted country roads. Now and again a farm wagon, now and again a motor car or a farm labourer driving a cow — nothing more.

Not only Johnny but we two stole from the orchards and devoured the sweet-scented apples as we drove along the peaceful road. Sometimes we sang at the tops of our voices. Once I recklessly let Johnny gallop down a hillside and he stumbled and fell. A shaft broke. Caroline and I were thrown over the dashboard into a ditch. Two hours later we, a bruised trio, limped back to the cottage.

And what of our play in those careless days? Certainly it did not fail us. As the autumn advanced and the lake took on a greenish cast and the maple trees hung out banners of scarlet, so our play became more vivid, more enthralling to us. I gave to it what I might have given to imaginative writing and gave it without a thought to the future. Not a word of it was written — yet nothing was forgotten. Every so often new characters were introduced and took their place in the enthralling gallery of our living cast. When nights became colder and frost descended to crisp the grass, we would take long walks down the road that ran by the shore. Above the road, on a ridge of land, there was a large barn and above it the full moon hung in its splendour, making the road very white and the great elms and cedar clumps that bordered it black as the night that lurked in the woods.

As we walked, linked together, the silhouette of our united shadow etched on the road before us, one character after another came to life and walked with us. Our play, in those nights, became more subtle. Now one sentence might be more pregnant than formerly a complete episode had been. My physical strength was not equal to the force of my teeming imagination. I could write so little without strain to the nerves that our play became the outlet. My written stories were mere cups that were inadequate to contain the stream. The capacity of our play was boundless.

The years were long and the future stretched endlessly, it seemed, before us. We made no plans but took for granted that all would come out well. We were used to being protected, and if there were many things we could not have, we still had much. The world beyond meant little to us. Life was never for a moment dull. Never could it be dull for two imaginative girls growing up — with parents so high-spirited and full of hope, in spite of disappointments they had suffered. My father (more like brother than father) would say to me, "Before long I shall be able to afford a splendid trip for us. We'll see England, France, Ireland together." Always together — together always.

One day he said, "I have missed my vocation. I have tried many things, but I know now that I was meant to be a farmer. I believe there is a great future in farming. A fruit and stock farm is what I should like to own."

My mother agreed that she was meant to be a farmer's wife. Always he was able to inspire her with his own enthusiasms. Caroline and I were eager to live in the country all the year round, instead of just spending the summers there. We began to read advertisements of farms for sale. We made excursions — sometimes my father and I, at others he and Caroline — to view the offered properties. What we sometimes saw would have daunted those less determined to be optimistic. Our very lack of experience gave us confidence. The countryside was so beautiful, the prospect so pleasant.

At last, on the shore of Lake Ontario, between Toronto and Hamilton, we discovered what we felt was the perfect farm for us. My mother had, during her married life, moved a number of times. This last removal she welcomed as the one which would see her happily settled for all time. She herself did not go to view the farm but trusted to our good judgment. It was a peculiarity of hers that she disliked on sight every house into which we moved. Perhaps it was because her fancy had built too bright a picture of it. Be that as it may, we were accustomed to several days of dark foreboding on her part before she settled down.

It was so with the farm.

In the first place, and by far the most difficult for her to endure, was the nearness to the lake. Not a friendly lake like Lake Simcoe but a great stretch of water — impersonal as a sea. It was tumbling in rough waves the day when she arrived, and that less than a hundred feet from the front door. . . . It seemed a monster ready to devour her. And the roar of it! Would that never be out of her ears? She chose a bedroom at the back of the house and retired there in seeming despair. And, though the house was solid and built nearly a century before, with thick walls and deep windows, it was a depressingly ugly colour and the rooms were smaller than she had expected.

But, as was always the case with my mother, her eager spirit triumphed and in a few days she was full of plans for beautifying the house and grounds. Caroline and my father not only fell in with these but added suggestions of their own. It was enough for me to explore the shore, the creek that emptied into the lake, the farm lands, the lovely wood. Here, I thought, we should be happy; should be successful; and I should be able to write.

It was then a lovely spot. A rugged bluff fronted the lake below the house. An old wind-bent tree grew on its highest point. This bluff had withstood so many years of battering by the waves that it seemed invincible, yet when I revisited the farm some years later, it had entirely disappeared and an unimpressive slope had taken its place. The bluff had been formed of a reddish shale that the waves had eaten away. It had looked so permanent and we had felt so permanent when settled there.

This farm had fields for crops and pasturage; it had two fine orchards, an apple orchard and a cherry orchard. It had crops of all the small fruits promising well. Indian pickers would be coming to garner these.

My father, with his sense of the dramatic, appeared at breakfast, on our first morning there, dressed, as he considered, appropriately for a farmer. He wore corduroy breeches, leather leggings and an Irish tweed jacket. He looked magnificent. My mother and Caroline and I agreed that he had created the proper atmosphere. My mother said she would go into the rearing of turkeys. Caroline, for some reason known only to herself, chose pigs, while I decided on Leghorn hens because I had been told they laid many large white eggs. My father was to breed pedigreed stock — to say nothing of enlarging the area that produced fruit.

In the meantime there were the vans at the door unloading the last of our furniture. There were a thousand things to be done. Soon painters appeared and the house was painted an ivory colour,

138

with pale green shutters. Standing immaculate behind the giant elm locust trees it was scarcely to be recognized as the dreary-looking house it had been.

My mother was delighted. She and Caroline set to work on the interior. Painters and paper hangers soon transformed it. Ivory paint took the place of ugly chocolate brown. Cupboard doors in the dining-room were taken off and discovered shelves for china. Every window looked out on a delightful view. The windows of our spirits were thrown open to welcome the new life.

A married couple had been engaged — the man, who had experience of farming, as manager, his wife as cook. Two young Scotsmen as farm labourers. We felt ourselves one with the countryside. It was pleasant to exchange a greeting with someone met by chance on the road. My father was teeming with information he had picked up from meetings with fruit growers. He subscribed to several agricultural journals. As for my mother, she soon had set the two young Scots to work to lay a terrace of flagstones. Years afterward, the then owner of the house showed me the same paved terrace, as a great find — a relic of a century ago which, overgrown by grass, she said her husband had discovered. I think she found it difficult to believe that my mother had had the stones laid just twenty years before.

Only those who have known the pleasure of transforming a grim and ugly house into one inviting and a pleasure to live in can appreciate our gratification. As though to add the final touch, the great elm locust trees put out a mass of sweet-scented bloom, in which the honey bees tumbled all day long; the sound of their happy humming could be heard above the lapping of the lake. Alternate summer showers and warm sunshine ripened the acres of strawberries. They nestled like jewels among their green foliage. One evening a swarthy troop of Indians came down the road and turned in at our gate. We felt that our life as fruit growers had begun in earnest.

My father and I together planted a huge asparagus bed. How carefully I had read the directions! We pictured the great juicy stalks that would grow from it — so succulent and so profitable. I bought an incubator and filled it with fine Leghorn eggs. Twice every night I stole from my bed to see that the lamp was properly set. I shall never forget the night when, peering in through the glass, I saw one of the eggs rocking. I could not tear myself away but remained till a draggled bleak-eyed chick was able to free himself from the shell and survey the pale immobile spheres that were to be his brothers.

But a goodly hatch followed and I proudly installed them in a brooder beyond the apple-house.

My mother had bought turkey hens and set them on clutches of eggs in coops. These brought out large broods upon which the mother hens trampled with the liveliest possible energy. They would scratch in the straw on the bottom of the coop and with each scratch send a poult hurtling against the side, while my mother besought the mother hen to have more care for her offspring. Certainly some of these survived and when they were of adventuring size, the turkey hen would lead them through the most distant berry canes — preferably on a wet day — and lose the half of them. . . . How much more sensible were my little white hens — Leghorn and Wyandot — and the boisterous piglets and the Jersey cows!

Before long the farm was teeming with life. The dark figures of the Indians bent above a munificent strawberry crop. In the evening the sound of a fiddle came from the shacks in the orchard, into which they were crowded with more expediency than decency. But it was not for us to say what was right or wrong for the

Indians. They had occupied these same shacks each summer for many years.

When the strawberry season was at its height, a wild storm came from the lake and blew the sand before it in a cloud that covered all the red berries in a coat of grey — left their leaves withered and dry. There were still the raspberries, the cherries, the blackberries, the Lawton berries, the apples, but this misfortune to the strawberries left us a little subdued, for they were one of the most profitable of the crops.

During that first year on the farm I wrote more short stories. These were very different from my first stories and I was able to sell them to American magazines, which paid well, or — failing that — to Canadian magazines, which paid much less. Sometimes I wrote with little strain to my nerves. At other times I suffered and weeks would pass when I dared not put pencil to paper. At those times I would shrink from the sight of my reflection in the glass, such was my pallor, my look of exhaustion.

Once, when I was suffering in this way and was on the point of laying the story aside, I suddenly made up my mind that I would finish the story, no matter what it cost me. I persisted, day after day, with all the too familiar symptoms of nerve fag — the restless, almost sleepless nights, the exhaustion so extreme that I would stumble as I walked. Yet — it was bearable. I did not reach the point when I could not endure the strain. I finished the story. It was not one of my best.

Our cook was a woman who had had picturesque experience and liked to tell me of her life as cook in a hotel. I wrote two stories based on happenings of which she told me, and sold them to the *Metropolitan* magazine. These two stories were later the basis of my novel *Delight*.

Two of our greatest pleasures at this time were our drives behind our lovely chestnut cob Johnny and our walks to the wood at the back of the farm. The lake on the front — the wood at the back. This wood was a lovely spot, as was the lane leading to it, gay with trilliums and violets in the spring; there were little hollows carpeted by wintergreen. Our first Christmas on the farm was an unusually mild one. In the afternoon Caroline and I walked to the woods. It was mild as an April day. We sat on a moss-grown fallen tree and talked rather pensively of our future. What would our Christmases be, in the years to come? What lay veiled, awaiting us? The birds had forgotten to go south. They twittered about us as we talked. They too spoke in pensive tones.

Chapter 9

The
Changeful Years

MY MOTHER'S sister, Aunt Eva, was now a widow. My grand-mother lived with her in Toronto but sometimes came to stay with us at the farm. Always we were happy to have her. Though she was close to eighty, there was a resolute strength in her bearing. It gave one courage just to be with her. She herself needed all her cheerfulness, for Aunt Eva was greatly given to self-pity and never spared Grandma her outpourings of dissatisfaction. Aunt Eva could be lively and amusing also when she could for a time forget herself.

Both Grandma and Aunt Eva thought it was an ill-advised move for my parents to take two girls into the country where we should be isolated from our friends and have no opportunity to establish ourselves in a life of our own. But Caroline and I looked on the change as a splendid adventure. We left our friends, male and female, without misgiving. How could we ever feel isolated or bored when we had our play? And there was the fitful exhilaration of my writing. When I had a story accepted, my family were happy about it, but never were they fatuously admiring of anything I accomplished. Never was I set apart as a being of different clay, as I have seen some writers set apart by their adoring families. My father's attitude remained what it had been in my school days when once I had shown him my report which placed me second in a form of forty. He read the report with dubious pleasure, then gently asked, "Why was it you didn't come first?"

My mother saw to it that Caroline and I went to Toronto to hear great singers when they appeared at Massey Hall and every so often to see a play. We would spend the night at a guest house and would feel ourselves to be experienced indeed. Looking back on our innocence, our ignorance, we were, it seemed to me, no more than children put into long skirts and with our hair done up.

It was during a visit to Aunt Eva that I met Pierre. He was a young French engineer who was engaged in work with Sir Adam Beck. Pierre had spent several years in the United States before coming to Canada. He spoke English fluently but with a charming foreign accent. He was, at that time, startlingly handsome but thought nothing of his looks. He was serious, absorbed in his work, intensely European. He regarded the New World with indifference and was sure he never could be content here. His arrogance stood out all over him. But, beneath his arrogance, he was sensitive. In company he either talked with great animation or was completely silent.

During that visit we spent many evenings together. He would take me out to dinner and I would drink strong black coffee and not be able to sleep till nearly morning. He was eager to show how extravagantly he was attracted by me. My grandmother declared that she had never seen a man so deeply in love. When I returned home, he wrote to me every day and I thought almost constantly of him. He delighted in sending me odd and charming presents. I talked of him to my mother and Caroline, who were eager to meet him and were prepared to admire and like him. My father seemed not at all sure that he would like him, but I knew he would welcome Pierre to our house with the warmth he showed to all my friends.

In the meantime Pierre returned to France to visit his people. From there he wrote letters telling of his joy in being once more in his own country. He adored his mother. His youngest sister reminded him of me. Even with the ocean between us, his personality stood out almost too vividly. I was writing a story and I did not want to give my thoughts to anyone but those characters of my creation.

This story was one of those which were later to be collected under the title *Explorers of the Dawn* and published by Alfred A. Knopf. I could not today write one of them — not to save my life — but, at that time, I was fascinated by them, and they attracted the attention of Christopher Morley, who was then fiction editor of an American magazine. He wrote asking me for more stories and it was he who interested Mr. Knopf in them. Now, more than twenty years after publication, a new and beautiful edition of this book has lately been published by Plon of Paris. In this edition the title is *Trois Petits Diables.*

Many were the preparations we made for a visit from Pierre on his return from France. I stood looking about the bedroom he was to occupy, with feelings of mingled foreboding and happy anticipation, but never — never — was there tranquility for me in his companionship. I wanted him to give me freedom to be myself without hindrance. He craved freedom to be moody or gay as he chose, without regard for me. Regard, consideration, for each other was something we had not learned. Both were impatient — unwilling to subdue ourselves to learning tolerance, each for each.

Yet when I heard the train's whistle, my heart beat with painful excitement. When I went toward him on the platform and saw his face alight with pleasure, my legs trembled beneath me and he exclaimed at my pallor. He came to meet me with his quick uneven step. He had suffered an attack of polio as a small child and it had left one of his legs slightly shorter than the other. He was extremely sensitive about this defect. To his mind his handsome face and figure weighed little against it.

Now he was laughing in sheer joy at our reunion. All the way along the road to the farm this mood of almost astonished joy in being again together held us. One of the young Scots drove the two-seated vehicle we called "the surrey." The dark bay horse Mike was well-groomed. The countryside beamed in harvest fulfilment. The lake lay tranquil, as though meditating. I was proud to show Pierre our house, shining in its fresh ivory paint among its elms. He was not responsive to any of these (to me) so lovely aspects of my home. His mind was too full of the beauties of France, and the lake was an insipid imitation of the sea.

It was a moment to be remembered when I introduced him to my family. In his impatience to show me the presents he had brought me he was eager to go to his room and unpack. My mother, who like myself was susceptible to good looks in men, found Pierre almost too handsome. I remember her exact words when he had gone up to his room.

"And am I expected," she exclaimed, "to get used to that dazzling beauty about the house?"

He possessed indeed a sculptured beauty of feature. His hair was thick, jet black and very straight; his head well set on a strong neck; his long, amber-coloured eyes beneath clearly marked brows; his lips full and arrogantly curved; his complexion with no trace of olive but almost fair in its fresh good health. I have never seen more perfect teeth. There was only that lameness to mar him, and it he never forgot.

While writing this I have asked Caroline to tell me what were her feelings toward Pierre at that time. She thought a moment and then answered, "I felt both antagonism and fear. . . . I don't know why it was, but that was what I felt."

Pierre's attitude toward her was one of complete lack of understanding. Because she was small and blond and pretty he thought of her as frivolous — ignoring her cool, critical quality. Once, when she picked up a book of essays he had been reading, he took it from her with a curt, "But, my dear, you would not yet understand this," and deeply offended her.

My father and he got on very well, though Pierre took not the slightest interest in the farm or horses. After their first meeting I eagerly awaited what Pierre would have to say of my father, but he dismissed him with the remark, "What French eyebrows he has!"

In fact, he wanted no one but me — to be with me from morning to night — to drive together, to walk, to talk, to read aloud. He would read to me by the hour, in his full rich voice, with that delightful accent. He was genuinely hurt when I would suddenly laugh at his mispronunciation of a word, but when my French moved him to derision, that was a different matter.

He was meticulous in all he did. I was impulsive and careless. When he took photographs of Caroline and me in our canoe, we were quite worn out by paddling round and round till we were in a position to please him. Yet, with no preparation, I made a snapshot of him with my Yorkshire terrier Toutou in his arms which was a pleasure to look at.

Pierre was interested that summer in kite-flying. It was a passing interest, for I think he never again indulged in it. He made himself a kite, with great pains, and spent hours in gazing upward at its soarings. He expected me to be as enthralled as he by this pastime.

Up and down, up and down the field we would travel, ever gazing upward. . . . It was not in me to be the sort of female who knows no boredom, no fatigue, so long as she can trail after the man she fancies.

It was a relief to me when Aunt Eva suddenly appeared on the scene for a visit. Pierre had never given more than a polite consideration to Aunt Eva, but now he discovered in her an enthusiastic audience to his kite-flying. It was amusing to see this trig little middle-aged woman doggedly pursuing the movements of the kite. I opened the drawer of my desk and took out the manuscript of the story I was writing. I was in no mood to write, but I enjoyed holding it in my hands. . . . When Pierre's visit was over, I returned to the story with a tranquility I could not find when he was in the house with me.

But, on my next visit to Toronto we were again happy in each other's company. Theatres, dinners or just talk filled our evenings. He refused to go with me to the homes of my friends. He was unsociable toward any but the odd person, chosen by himself. Aunt Eva was in straitened circumstances, which were a never-ending worry to the family and especially to my Uncle Walter, her brother. The top floor of her large house was not in use and now Pierre suggested that she should let it to him. She agreed and soon his lively presence was installed and charged the atmosphere with a new vitality. He was sympathetic toward Aunt Eva, in his detached way, and when he had an attack of tonsilitis, she nursed him. I was pleased by the arrangement. Pierre now seemed almost one of the family, but I found no promise of permanence in our relations. I did not consciously analyze these. With my customary indolence I was willing to let things — aside from my writing — drift.

As time passed, life on the farm became more complicated, more difficult. It seemed impossible to find married couples who both were efficient and dependable. I remember various couples, as they followed one another in dire procession. The operating of a farm without experience should be a rich man's hobby, not the serious enterprise of a man with small capital, especially a man with other business interests to call him away. I remember only too well the misfortunes which befell the livestock. I wake sometimes at night remembering them.

There was the high-priced pedigreed cow that had just calved, and was given a bucketful of ice-cold water from the stream. I can see her lying in the stableyard, a great black and white mound, dying. There was the bay gelding Mike, turned to pasture in a field where the barbed-wire fencing was hanging loose. He cut an artery in his breast. I went to his stall to see him while we were waiting for the vet. My father was in the city that day engaging a new man. How often he was absent when the catastrophes happened and the bad news must be broken to him on his return. . . . Mike was standing with his legs stiffly planted, his eyes distended, the blood gushing from his deep breast like water from a tap turned on full. He stood in a pool of blood. He was a young and spirited horse. I remembered how one day not long before he had somehow got one of his forelegs caught over the halter that tied him to his stall. He was plunging and rearing in a frightening way when my mother discovered him. All the men were away on business of the farm. The cook, a fine buxom woman, went with us to the stable. We were confident that she would free him, but when she saw his wild rearings, she changed her mind. "I wouldn't go into that stall," she declared, "not for a hundred dollars."

I have always been rather pleased with myself that I did not flinch from it. I went in beside the great lunging body. He crowded me against the side of the stall, but I spoke to him soothingly, got

149

hold of the foreleg, and suddenly he was quiet. I freed him and he nuzzled me.

Now I said, "Good-bye, Mike," and left him, unable to bear the sight of his suffering.

There was the pedigreed young ram, hamstrung by a clumsy man when cutting his tail.

There was the litter of lusty young pigs, overfed till they became paralyzed and died.

There were the turkey poults drowned in their run when there was a flood of the creek. This same flood overran stables and poultry house.

But the greatest grief was the loss of Johnny, the bright chestnut which my father had given to Caroline and me. Many were the lovely drives with Johnny along the lake-shore road, especially in fall and winter — in fall when the trees flaunted their red and gold — in winter when the silver jingle of our sleigh bells hung on the air. My parents enjoyed driving as much as we. When friends visited us in their motor cars, we did not envy them. The horse moved fast enough for us.

But a loved horse could die and could not be replaced, and so it was with Johnny. A stable boy let him out into deep snow, for exercise after a week of inactivity. Johnny, full of joy in the sudden freedom, flung himself on a snowdrift to roll. He rolled — he whinnied in distress — for he could not rise. He had ruptured himself. . . . It was Caroline who went to comfort him as he died. She saw his bright chestnut coat turn black with sweat, and he was lying in the snow! He gave her a look of questioning, of puzzlement, she said — before he died. We seemed to have an endless supply of tears for him.

Of course, these misfortunes were scattered, with happy intervals between — the orchards in a storm of bloom, when every tree bore promise of a crowning crop — the berry canes, heavy with fruit — the apple house, filled to the roof with apples of a fine-fleshed quality never seen on the market today because the fruit growers have been taught how to produce tougher varieties suited for shipping to a distance.

From the day when the Indian pickers arrived, till the last of the fruit was garnered, all was stir and anxious activity on the farm. But when they had gone (that dusky tribe whom I came to know so well — their lively children — their patriarchal head who played the fiddle), then we settled down to enjoy the autumn. The lake became more personally attached to us then, as though observant of our doings. From the moment I opened my eyes in the morning, till I slept at night, I was conscious of it. Even in my dreaming, there it was — sighing, laughing, shouting. Once it achieved a stupendous ice storm. Great hummocks formed and it forgot its boundaries and beat its way over the bluff and showed a new glittering world. I still have the snapshot Caroline took of me in this arctic scene, wearing a grey squirrel coat and white woollen cap.

My paternal grandmother, that tall stately woman, with a gentle heart, died in her eighty-seventh year, when we had been less than a year on the farm. This was the first of the bereavements that followed close after one another. My father was pensive, rather than sorrowing, over the loss of his mother. It had been his grandmother's death which had brought him a greater grief, for they had been alike in temperament, but he told me, when he returned from the funeral, how his brother François, on the motor drive back from the cemetery, had become wildly hysterical and it had been all my father could do to quiet him. This was strange indeed, for Uncle François had, through years of an unhappy, childless marriage, schooled himself to a relentless self-control. Often I had thought of him as a man of little feeling. But — there had been this wild outbreak after his mother's funeral. . . . I remembered the last time I had seen her, some months before her death. I was visiting Uncle Danford and Auntie Ida. Grandmother was then confined to her bed — not ill but suffering a slow disintegration of her splendid constitution. I now think this was caused by boredom, rather than old age — for she had no active part in that house.

So, on this visit, I met the dear old lady in an upstairs passage. The house was large and she, having left her bed when the daily nurse was out of the room, had lost her way. She towered above me, in her long white nightgown and her nightcap tied under her chin. She said, in her pleasant Irish voice:

"Would you be so kind as to direct me to the bathroom? These passages are very confusing."

I led her to the door of the bathroom, which was the size of an ordinary bedroom, and carpeted in Brussels carpet. There I asked, "You do know who I am, don't you?"

She bent to peer at me and then answered, with formal politeness, "I think you are my son's daughter. . . . Yes indeed, he is my second son and you are his only child."

She gave me a little bow, then sailed into the bathroom. She was like a drifting ship — rudderless but still impressive. . . . She had a few curly grey hairs on her chin and I remember how once, when she was visiting us, she had given me a small pair of scissors, requesting me to take them to be sharpened, for she needed them to be sharp to cut those hairs. The man in the shop had run his thumb along the blade of the scissors. He had demanded, "Do you want them sharpened to cut silk or wool? Each requires a different edge."

For a moment I had considered, perplexed. Which were my grandmother's hairs — silk or wool? I chose the latter.

"Wool," I said firmly.

And now she was gone. . . . She had given her love with single-mindedness to a man who — worthy or unworthy — had been the moving power in her life, had fathered her three sons.

Her death was the beginning of four troubled years which reached their climax in financial disaster and the death of my father. I myself had an acute attack of appendicitis, when, for a time, my life was in danger. The young country doctor was eager to rush me off to hospital for an operation, but my mother had a horror of operations, so in the torrid heat of midsummer, starved, ice-packed, delirious, I managed to pull through. I emerged wan and weakened, unable for some months to write, but the lovely autumn weather was tonic and my natural resilience asserted itself.

While I was convalescent, my Yorkshire terrier died. Scarcely did I feel able to bear the grief of his suffering. What we endure in the suffering of our loved dogs! They give us their loyalty, their adoration, their trust — yet we are not the gods they believe us to be. What can we do for them, when their short life comes to its so often tragic close?

Not long before my Yorkshire terrier's death, an Irish terrier named Barney, belonging to my father, had been taken to the mill by one of the farm hands. Barney had followed the waggon over the dusty roads through scorching heat and, on his return, had had an attack of hysterics. He had run wildly over the lawn and kitchen garden, frothing at the mouth. In terror the cook had called to her child at play and dragged it in through a window. I could see Barney bounding, leaping, as though possessed. The manager came running into the house. "The dog is mad!" he cried. "He must be shot!"

My father was in the city. My mother got his gun and, white-lipped, handed it to the man. She pulled down the blinds so that we should not see what was to happen. But the horror, the fascination of it drew me to peer through a crack of the blind. I saw the manager, a figure of doom, standing, gun in hand, the three farm labourers clustered about him, waiting for Barney to reappear. . . . Presently he came, lolloping — panting. The man raised the gun to his shoulder. Scarcely could I bear to watch, but horror held me. Yet the gun was not discharged. The manager for some reason could not fire it. He took a pitchfork from one of the men. Barney ran to him for protection from the evil that pursued him, but he got no protection. The fork was thrust into his side. He fell, and the other men joined in to stab him. A little undersized fellow from Glasgow who had been sheltering behind the others darted forward and when he saw that Barney was dead, again and again pierced the poor body with his fork.

In those last years at the farm ill luck gave us no respite. Fruit crops failed or were burnt up by the sun. It became almost impossible to get responsible help, for it was the time of the First World War and the best men had gone to fight. I remember one season when another fruit grower enticed our Indian pickers from us and there were the berries ripe — and no one to pick them! It was the season of the black currants and Lawton berries. Caroline and I did what we could, desperately picking berries all day long, till we were tanned to the colour of Indians and our arms covered by scratches, but we were only two and a dozen experienced pickers were needed. I remember, in another year, how the price of cherries dropped, till it did not pay to market them, and they hung till they fell from the trees and lay, a bright red carpet, beneath. And that same year, outside investments of my father's failed.

Pierre had gone to New York to better his fortunes there. His letters told of his absorption in his work — how he prospered. He wanted sympathetic understanding, but I had little to give. My mind was occupied by the bereavements, the misfortunes heaped upon us.

My maternal grandmother had died, after a short illness, in midwinter and, less than a year later, her elder son, my mother's brother George. His death was a sorrow, for he had a lively and affectionate nature and he was only fifty. But it was the death of Grandma that left the great blank in our lives. Never again was Christmas the same. The spirit of the day was so bound up in her. Long before it came she was making her preparations. She had not much money to spend, but she gave a great deal of thought to each present. They were carefully wrapped and hidden in her room, and with each addition to that store, the air of happy mystery which she wore like a jaunty halo brightened. She had had a great deal of trouble in her life, but never did I hear her utter a word of self-pity. She had much to complain of but never complained. She had a keen sense of fun, yet was graced with good sense and kindness.

When we heard of her desperate illness, Caroline and my father went to Toronto. My mother and I were left alone but for the farm labourers. As ill luck had it, our married couple had gone on a holiday.

It was midwinter and the weather severe. That first night when we were alone, the lake, as though aware of our isolation and dread, prepared a great storm. It was already heaving and the wind high when at bedtime I went out on the flagged terrace. Out in the chill wildness I hoped to gain calm before I rejoined my mother. Always her security lay in pretending that she had no fear. She dared not give way to grief or apprehension.

I looked up at the brilliant stars. Like a child I said aloud, "I have a grandma — I will not let her die."

The fact that she was old in years meant nothing to me. She was young in spirit and with a power of enjoyment lacking in many of my young friends.

I shall never forget the storm of that night. The lake gathered itself together and hurled its strength against the shore. But its thunder could not drown the shrieking of the wind. At times it seemed that a great army was marching down the road. There was the tramp of soldiers' boots on the frozen ground — the heavy beat of drums — the playing of bugles — the scream of bagpipes. The crackling air vibrated to the blare of wild martial music. . . . The music would cease and in its place the thunder of battle shook the shore. Then came the shrieks of the wounded and, as they died, the keening of mourners. Over and over throughout the night the turmoil of this tragic drama was enacted. There was no respite from it. It seemed that the lake was pounding on our very door. My mother's bedroom was upstairs and mine was on the ground floor. Neither of us, I think, had more than nightmarish snatches of sleep. I have seen storms on the Cornish coast, storms in mid-Atlantic, but never have I heard such sheer madness of tempest — such savage howling and insane forgetting of the rules of decent storms.

But, in the morning, a brilliant calm brought icy stillness to our shore. A few particles of snow floated on the air. Ice hummocks and caverns had been fashioned by the storm and beyond them the waves tumbled in wintry abandon. The bridge across the creek had become massive in ice. Telegraph wires sagged under the weight of a thousand icicles. It was bitterly cold. The soles of shoes which had been damp when I set them on the floor of the coat cupboard were frozen fast there.

My mother and I looked at each other, heavy-eyed. But we were thankful morning had come. That day my father returned to us and we relaxed in the security of his presence. That day

Grandma died. Caroline, who had contracted a bad case of tonsilitis, remained with Aunt Eva.

The seasons progressed and with them our progression toward financial ruin, but never was there any gloomy talk. Never did my parents give up hope that conditions would improve — or so it seemed to me. The hired help came and went — each lot more inefficient than those which had gone before. But some of them were kindly. It was not their fault that they were ignorant of the methods of farming in Canada, but the mistakes they made were endless and costly. The war made our difficulties the greater. But always there was the beauty of the countryside — the wood, the lake. We four would stroll together in the evening talking of all we would do when times were better.

Pierre came from New York to see me and to talk, but though he was there in the flesh — his thick black hair the same; his amber eyes looking contemplatively into mine; his beautiful hands making just a few, very expressive gestures — he still seemed far away, as though that distant American city claimed him. We talked and we talked, but his stay was not long. The night before he left, he said at dinner, out of the blue — leaving us all four speechless, "There are those who say, and it is often said in my country, that a man should marry for convenience — for a housekeeper rather than for love."

There was complete silence for a moment, then my father genially asked Pierre whether he liked his beef underdone. Then we all began to talk.

In a few months Pierre and Aunt Eva were married and she went to New York. She was twenty years his senior but looked much younger than her years. She wore her clothes with a trim, studied style, and, like all her family, was extremely fond of dress. She was exacting in her housekeeping. Everything was orderly, too orderly, and any deviation from this upset her. Always she was quick to show her annoyance. I think she made Pierre comfortable and content for a number of years. He found the strain of life in New York a very different matter from life in Toronto and came home at night tired out.

On my part I think I looked on this marriage with relief. I had nothing to give Pierre at that time. All my thought was for my family; the farm, which, like a doomed ship, was rocking from every new onslaught; my writing that claimed what of me was left over. It was not till years later that we discovered the strength and loyalty of our love.

I wrote at this time a story which I sent to the *Atlantic Monthly*. In accepting it Ellery Sedgwick, the editor, said he would like to have a meeting with me, if I could go to Boston. My parents and Caroline were all for my going, but money was hard to come by. Everything I made was absorbed by the increasing demands of the farm. They were endless, these demands. I was like the boy who put his finger into the leak in the dyke, but I could not stop the flood. . . . I wrote to Mr. Sedgwick saying it was not possible at that time for me to go to Boston. We exchanged a number of letters, in which I addressed him as Miss Ellen Y. Sedgwick (for so his signature looked to me) and he addressed me as Mr. Mazo de la Roche, till the day came when he told me that he was "born to be a man," and I confessed that I was not Mister but Miss.

One day, returning home on the train from Toronto, I discovered that my father was on the same train. I was surprised, for I had expected him to come by a later one. This sudden meeting with him remains vividly in my memory because I was made so abruptly aware of a change in his looks. He entered the carriage where I was already seated and glanced about, looking for a seat. As always when he appeared, people noticed him. I thought,

"What a striking figure of a man," before I realized who he was. He had, without my being conscious of the change, lost his look of supreme good health and well-being. He was pale; he had lost flesh; he looked weary. But when he saw me and smiled and came to sit with me, he seemed the same.

He was not the same, and his decline from strength was obvious before long to us at home. He had never in his life had an illness. Always he had been the protector, the one to guard delicate women. Now he was driven to consult a doctor. The country doctor gave him a tonic. He did not improve and, after a time, he went to a doctor in Toronto — and then another. They could find nothing wrong with him. He had, they said, the healthy organs of a child. That was in the springtime when all the fruit trees were in blossom. He struggled on, in a gallant pretence of improvement, till my Uncle Danford persuaded him to consult a specialist, and accompanied him. The specialist told my uncle that it would be a miracle if my father were alive at Christmas. That was in August, but such was his hold on life that he lived till the following July — eleven months!

My uncle insisted that hope should not be taken from us. All through the winter that followed we lived in hope — otherwise we could not have borne it. Or did we only pretend we hoped? Certainly everything we saw was evidence against hope. We were ruined financially and knew it, but never acknowledged it even to each other.

Once, when I was alone by the lake, I allowed my agony of mind to overcome me. It was autumn. The apple trees were laden with fruit. My father had walked as far as the orchard to see it. My mother was with him and now, he leaning on her arm, they were returning. I stood at the edge of the bluff watching them as they moved slowly toward the house. But — was that really my father?

That gaunt man whose coat hung loosely on his broad shoulders — whose dark eyes looked so large and hollow? . . . I remembered him as we sat side by side in the sleigh on a wintry drive, when he would just flick his horse with the whip and it would speed along the glittering white road, sending clots of snow onto the bearskin rug that covered our knees. I remembered the healthy flush in his cheeks, the vivacity of his well-cut mouth. I remembered the swing of his walk that always had given us confidence in his power to protect. . . . And that was he — leaning on the arm of my fragile mother!

I did not go to meet them as I had meant to do. Instead I stumbled down the side of the bluff to the stony shore. There I was hidden from everyone. There were the tumbling green waves, casting themselves with thunder on the stones. It was the time of the equinox. Their roar was my fastness. I heard someone giving terrible cries — hoarse cries, as though torn from the breast. Surely it could not be I who uttered them. . . . But no matter if it were — there was no one to hear.

After a while I climbed up the bluff and went into the house. Not even when my father died did I again suffer such agony of mind.

He himself was confident that he would recover. Otherwise I think we could not have survived that winter.

My Scottish friend Alastair, with whom I had long corresponded, came that autumn to see me. We never yet had met, but the attachment begun in our letters now blossomed into something warmer. He had always appeared to me as a romantic figure and there was no sense of disappointment in meeting him. Later on I went to Toronto and we spent pleasant evenings together, but pleasant evenings — music, plays — could not make me forget. Always there was the picture of the lonely farm by the lake — the three who were dearest to me — to make all distractions meaning-less. I would not leave them to go to Scotland with Alastair. There had been a time when I might have gone, but not now — not now — when everything lay dead under the doom of winter, and my father — oh, let me fly home to my father. . . .

Shortly before Christmas he said to me, "As you know, nothing would please me quite so much for a Christmas present as a puppy. It would be fun for me to train it. It would amuse me when time hangs heavy on my hands. And I know just where a Scotty could be bought, at a quite reasonable price — from champion stock too." He always knew.

It was wonderful to hear him ask for something. How gladly I sent the order to the breeder — leaving him to choose the prettiest, the sweetest-tempered puppy from the litter. Scarcely could we bear the waiting for its arrival. Our man drove to the station and brought back the small crate and set it down in the kitchen. We all crowded round. Two glowing almond-shaped eyes looked up at us between the slats. The man took off one of them, put his hand into the crate and lifted out a tiny black brindle morsel of life that wobbled when he set her on her feet. This was Bunty.

She became an important member of the family, and during the thirteen years of her life, her understanding of our ways, her loyalty to us, her capricious feminine nature were a wonder and a delight. In *Portrait of a Dog* I have written her history. I wrote it when I was living in Devon, far from the farm by the lake where she came to us as a puppy. John Galsworthy told me that he thought he had never read a more beautiful story of a dog. This pleased me very much, for he himself had written a lovely life of his spaniel in *Memories*. As for his feeling for *Portrait of a Dog*, I share it. I would make a claim for it, in its own place, that I would not for any other book of mine. Unfortunately, my publishers produced it in the same season with a dog story by Rudyard Kipling. I do not see how Mr. Kipling could have brought himself to write of a Scotch terrier in the unreal baby talk in which he indulged himself in *Thy Servant — a Dog*.

As the coming of Bunty is a poignant recollection of those last days on the farm, I should like to quote here the first pages of *Portrait of a Dog*. Better than I could now re-create the atmosphere of that Christmas will these few pages picture it.

It is not easy, here in Devon, to picture the scene which was the setting for my first sight of you. Between it and me the lovely Devon landscape rises, a green and sunlit barrier. The thick rounded clumps of trees, the hedges outlining the curious shapes of the fields, Dartmoor itself rising darkly to High Willhays, all shut me in from that far-off place. The song of the finch, the scent of the moss rose, shut me in.

I close my eyes, put my hand across my forehead, and press my thumb and middle finger against my temples. The red ploughed fields, fields of shining barley, of silvery oats, of fine fair wheat, are darkened. For a space I still hear the bird song, smell the sweet garden scents, then they too fade and slowly, against the darkness, I find the place I am looking for.

I see the grey sky of winter, the square stubborn house facing the grey waters of the lake into which slow snowflakes fall and disappear. The land sleeps, under its covering of snow — not, it seems, in rest after fruitfulness, not awaiting the glad renewal of spring, but in a chill trance of disdain for those whom it has defeated.

Still, it is Christmas. There is a holly wreath upon the door, green club moss and boughs of balsam are above the pictures and the square, small-paned windows. The resinous smell of the boughs, the smell of a pine knot burning, have given us a strange feeling of gaiety, made us forget the shadow that hangs over the house.

We are gathered about you, standing on your uncertain puppy legs in the middle of the room, staring up at the faces surrounding you.

You were courageous then, as always. Pathetically small and soft and round, you stared up at us who must have seemed beings of formidable proportions to you — terrifying, one would think, after the snugness of your kennel, with your brothers and sisters all about you and your mother's side looming warm and protective between you and the world. You had been snatched from that, suffered the cold discomfort of a long railway journey, a long ride in a sleigh over snow-drifted roads, and then, the slats of your box having been wrenched off in the kitchen, you had been carried in to us by the stableman and set down on the rug before the fire. What appalling changes for a tiny being two months old! Yet you turned up your little muzzle, looked from one to another of us out of velvety dark eyes, and, when a saucer of warm milk was set before you, you plunged your nose into it, nor raised it again until the last drop was gone and your eager tongue propelled the empty saucer across the floor.

After the milk you looked even rounder than before — more intrepid; your tail took on a cocky curve; again you raised your muzzle and surveyed us. Each bent toward you with an outstretched, coaxing hand, each longing to feel the baby plumpness of your body. Your nose was wet, a drop of milk hung on your chin, your eyes shone. You looked at us half timidly, half roguishly. There was no fear in you. Then, with a little kick of the hind legs that nearly sent you over, you trotted straight into the hands of the one who was to be your master. Laughing, he picked you up, laid you against the broadness of his chest, and bent his head to you. You were my Christmas present to him, the last Christmas present he was ever to get.

The Scotty was indeed a pleasure to my father and to us all. She romped with Jock, the collie; dared the dignity of Christopher, the big grey cat. Always she could make my father smile. He would

163

be sitting by the window, staring out on the cold grey lake, then she would come and paw his leg and he would bend down to pat her or lift her to his knee.

We used to play cards in the long evenings of that long winter — my parents against Caroline and me. My mother was an erratic player, but my father's play was so brilliant that for a time we younger ones almost always met with defeat. Later he showed weariness at the tenseness of the game and one evening, when in the lamplight I brought out the cards, he said, with the rueful smile that hurt me, "I think I'll not play tonight. Somehow I seem to get tired . . ." So, that was the end of that.

His brothers both paid him visits that winter. Uncle François asked him how he was. Straightening his shoulders he answered, "Better. I feel myself improving every day."

There was a sombre look on my uncle's face which did not lighten at the words. My father threw him a startled glance, then turned to gaze out of the window at the lake.

The winter passed.

In the spring we had a sale.

We saw the crowd thronging the stables, leaving their buggies and motor cars to give the place a strange public air.

An auction sale — livestock and implements bringing low prices because of the war. We had an oddly impersonal feeling about the whole proceeding, as though it mattered little to us. We saw the horses led out, one by one, prancing a little, nervous, restive. All were sold but Molly, the pretty mare; her and the trap we were retaining for our own use. We saw the fine, well-fed cows disappear. The expensive implements — bringing so much less than we had expected. But then — we always hoped for more than drab reality offered. Crates of poultry were carted away. I had had success with them. They were irritating creatures, but

164

they were amusing too. Once I allowed five anxious hens, determined to sit, to take up their abode in an old corn crib — each established on a clutch of eggs, in a clean nest. Exactly three weeks
later, when I came to feed them (it was a sunny Easter morning),
five triumphant mothers clucked their achievement to me. Each
hen had hatched out exactly twelve chicks — sixty downy yellow
chicks on an Easter morning!

I remember when I visited the farm buildings after the sale.
Empty now, save for Molly. So silent now — after all the whin-
nying — the lowing — the clucking. . . . I could hear the murmur
of the stream as it passed on its way to the lake. In the poultry
house I found a single white egg, like a good-bye note. I held the
egg in my hand as I made the rounds of the empty buildings. How
silent it all was!

There was so much to be done that we had little time for painful
regrets. Our furniture must be got ready for storage. We were to
remove to a furnished house, the half of which we had acquired.
It was about two miles away, on the lake shore.

How well I remember leaving the farm. My mother had driven
ahead in the trap with the youth who was to remain with us for a
while to look after Molly and make himself generally handy. We
others followed in a hired car, a wretchedly small one with not
nearly enough space for ourselves and the innumerable small things
we had collected at the last. The three of us on a seat not much too
wide for two, Bunty sitting very upright on my father's knee, and
in front of us a medley of packages, a bundle of treasured walking-
sticks, a hamper, a travelling rug, a branch of cherry blossom, a
bunch of violets from the lane. The house looked squat and lonely
beneath the towering trees. I could not look back at it. The dark
face of my father was all alive with interest in this change, after his
long inaction. If he had regrets, he hid them.

This was a strange house to which we moved, part of it old and weather-beaten, covered by vines and climbing roses. The remainder, a much later addition, was always called "the new wing" by the owners, though it was more than fifty years old. It was like a separate house, for it had its own front door and porch, its own hall and drawing-room, sparsely furnished with some good pieces brought from England by the naval officer who had built the house. His two daughters lived in the old part. A portrait of this officer hung in our living-room and there was a gilt-framed mirror and a marble-topped table. In this room my father's bed was placed, as he was no longer able to climb the stairs. But he took short walks in the neglected but still lovely grounds where daffodils and narcissi lifted their fragrant faces among the tall grass. Wrapped in a heavy plaid travelling rug, he would rest on a rustic seat, while Bunty made her first adventuring, always to return to the protection of his presence. Strangely, though he was now cared for as an invalid, that protective comfort still remained — in the warmth of his deep voice, in his eyes which appeared to grow larger and more brilliant, as his cheeks grew hollow and his colour faded.

As I say, we had retained our mare, Molly, so that Caroline and I were able to drive to the village to shop, or allow Molly to amble along the quiet country road by the lake. Isolated so, and thrusting from our minds the shadows that deepened about us, we would throw ourselves into our play with an almost impassioned eagerness. From my fertile brain a new situation or plot would emerge and we would so sink ourselves in it that our characters took on a most vivid reality. In their imagined suffering we relieved our own. In their pleasure we took deep breaths of reflected pleasure. Three characters in particular became our favourites and so identified with us, regardless of sex, that we indeed became them.

A slight change in the manner of speaking was enough to identify them. Like a fresh wind they came to us.

One day my father, as though he would force himself back into strength, decided he would go for a drive. We could not deny him this, though we feared it would tire him. Tom polished the trap and groomed the mare till they shone. My father gave them a look of approval. We watched him mount the seat and take the reins with a familiar gesture of content — one who loved horses and cared nothing for motor cars. Molly strode out as though she felt the need of exercise. The narrow sloping shoulders of the youth, the broad shoulders of the man disappeared. I lay down on the grass. Bunty touched my neck with her tongue, in a strange, wistful sympathy.

That was a long drive. It seemed that the sound of Molly's hoof-beats would never come. But at last there was the faint, then the imminent clatter. Then the gleam of her chestnut flank between the lilacs. My father alighted and handed the reins to the boy. Never again would he drive.

We waited for what was going to happen in that house of which we occupied half, and in the other half, two elderly gentlewomen, strange, sensitive, neurotic creatures. Never did we acknowledge what we waited for — only lived from day to day. No longer did my father take his walks. When he rose in midmorning, he sat in a chair facing the faded mirror that gave him back his melancholy reflection. Now it might be seen that he had given up all hope.

Looking at him one day, sitting there, unseen by him, I remembered how, in strange foreboding, I had more than once, joyful in his homecoming, thought, "How many more times shall we, united, embrace. . . ."

Now in midsummer he died.

Relatives came to the house. The most deeply affected of these was my father's elder brother. He and I clasped each other and wept together. But not a tear fell from my mother's eyes. In heroic self-forgetfulness she had, single-handed, nursed my father through his long illness. Now, heroically she bore her heartbreak. Caroline, thinking only of others, attended to the things that must be done. Her courage never failed us. It was she who carried the lilies my mother had gathered, and laid them near his folded hands.

This same elder brother of my father's spent that first night, after his death, in the room with him. The next morning he said to me, "It was the worst night of my life. Yes — the very worst night."

Chapter 10

Three
Against the World

CLOSE outside my mother's bedroom window there stood a massive
cedar tree. Its shape was grandly pyramidal and all through that
long wet August it held the rain in its sweet-smelling boughs long
after it had ceased to fall from the sky. This cedar tree was so
close to the window it seemed almost to be in the room. Because of
it the light inside was of a watery greenish tone which imparted a
strange pallor to the faces of my mother and Caroline. For many
hours each day they sat close by the window to catch the light
on their sewing. And always what they sewed was black, black
for mourning. I still remember the sound of rain dripping from the
cedar tree, and their low voices as they sewed.

I would go into the stable, that was half in ruin, and groom
Molly, for we had let the boy go, then wander through the long
grass to the great boulder by the lake and wonder what our future
was to be. Sometimes I harnessed Molly to the trap and we would
drive to the village to shop or along the road by the lake, where of
late we met more motor cars than formerly, and at these Molly
would shy a little.

It was decided that we should move into Toronto. A friend of my father's who was then minister of education promised to do what he could to find a position for Caroline in the civil service. With what she earned and what I made from my writing, combined with what we had salvaged from the wreck of our resources, we hoped to keep our small ship afloat. In visits to Toronto Caroline and I discovered a small house that would just suit us. What must be done now was to prepare for the removal. Our furniture must be taken from storage, our personal belongings packed. A thousand details to be arranged. Molly and the trap went to pay a debt. And always was there the sewing of black material in that upstairs room, with the cedar tree mourning in the rain outside the window.

In the midst of all this I was writing a story.

Strange it was to be writing — stranger still that it should be a humourous story — in the room where so lately my father had died. Strange that I should be sitting in his chair, the tall mirror giving back my reflection instead of his. Sometimes I would find myself smiling at what I had written. Then again, the memories of that room would overcome me and I would put my head down on the marble top of the table, blinded by tears. Then a warning pain would go through my head. I would control myself and again take up my pencil.

The story I was writing was one of the series collected under the title *Explorers of the Dawn*. When it was finished, I sent it to the *Atlantic*, which had published "Buried Treasure," the first of them. However, Mr. Sedgwick, the editor, did not like the subject of the story and rejected it. Later it was published by *Harper's* or *Cosmopolitan*, I forget which. Under the strain of writing it I felt, for the first time, the neuralgic pains in the head which later caused me so much suffering.

170

While we were passing through times of sorrow and preparing again to move, the Scotty, Bunty, was developing in her own sturdy, carefree way. She busied herself in the grounds or explored the neighbouring cornfield. But when I wrote, she would come and lie at my feet and so was the beginning of her share in my work. When I had laid the manuscript aside, she would follow me to the lake. I would kneel by the water and choose two round stones, just the right size. I would hold these, wet and icy, against my temples. She, watching me intently, would select another stone and lay it on my lap.

My mother had been approached by a man who bred West Highland terriers. He was anxious to sell one to her, but Caroline and I hesitated, thinking of the cost. Earnestly had we begun to consider the cost of things. But we could see that my mother longed to buy the puppy, and, in truth, so did we.

So on the day when we set out for Toronto we stopped at the house of the breeder. My mother went in and selected a puppy. She returned with him in her arms. She was elated, flushed, her eyes shining. We had come prepared with a little box to put him in. He was not a pretty puppy but a skinny little fellow, with a horri-fied yellow eye. The Scotty looked him over with smug appraisal. We tucked him into his box and fastened the lid.

Ever since my mother's nervous breakdown of years ago she could not bear the thought of travelling by train. Never again in her lifetime did she enter a train. So we must make the long drive by carriage and pair. Motor cars had already displaced horses, so that it was not easy to hire them. But we discovered a livery where they were available, and so set out. The carriage was piled high with our belongings. A clock in their midst began to strike, its note in the open sounding new and strange.

The puppy would not settle down in his box but yelped distractedly, till we were forced to take him out of it. Then he began to scramble about, in a frantic effort to obliterate himself. He found a place at last on top of the clock, but again it struck and so terrified him that he fell off, down the mountainside of luggage, between the wheels and onto the road. When, fearing the worst, we looked round, we discovered him trotting determinedly after us. He knew that, strange as we were, we belonged to him.

What a contrast in that road, as it then was, to the stream of traffic that rages over it today! Then we stopped at a grassy spot, beneath a chestnut tree, to open our hamper and eat our lunch. The driver fed and watered his horses. We had tea at an inn by the way, and it was almost dark when we stopped in front of the house where our furniture, in chaos, had already been delivered.

And so our new life began. We were three fragile women, with almost invisible means of support. Let me describe us. First there was my mother — five feet three of nervous sensibility and indomitable spirit. She had a tenacious will and an invincible desire to collect beautiful things about her. When she fastened her mind on some object — by hook or by crook, she would acquire it. . . . She was a striking figure in her mourning black, for she was beautifully proportioned, erect, and had clear-cut aquiline features, fair skin and dark blue eyes. She had had a small hat, with a short but wide widow's veil, made for her, and this was most becoming. Her hair, that just showed beneath the brim, was a light, rather gingerish brown. Her hands and feet were beautiful. W. O. Forsyth, who was a musician and teacher of note, gave her piano lessons when she was young. He told me that, all through the lesson, he could not forget her lovely hands. I think she had little or no talent for music. She was demonstrative in her affections and had no understanding of people who were taciturn or phlegmatic, no matter how great their solid worth. They depressed her, as they depress me.

Caroline, even smaller than my mother, had a complexion less fair but hair of platinum blond. She looked on her high cheek-bones as a defect, but, in truth, they have given character to her small face. She faced those difficult days with a gallant resolution which I was not then experienced enough to appreciate. I took it for granted that she should be the principal pillar of our little household. The position in the civil service to which she had looked forward was not for a time forthcoming. In the mean-while she secured one job after another, always bettering herself. She had a talent for appearing to know more than she did, and there was something in her face that inspired confidence. Before a year had passed she was firmly established in a post in the Parliament buildings. There she got on well, for she was conscientious, pleasant to work with and I never have known anyone so completely free from jealousy or envy.

The black shadow of war darkened those days. In the newspapers were the pictures of men who had been killed, among them the faces of friends. At night, in our street, companies of soldiers were being drilled. The tramp of their feet, the shouted commands of the sergeant came to us. Caroline rejected an offer of marriage from an impulsive pilot of the Air Force who had been acquainted with her for only a month. In the first place she could not leave home, she said, and in the second she had no affection for him. But she had a deep platonic affection for another young officer, the handsome Harry Mumford, an attachment they both cherished till his untimely death several years ago.

As for me, the third of the trio, I had written but that one short story in that last house by the lake. My health was greatly impaired. I began to wonder whether I should ever again put pencil to paper. I took Bunty for walks through the quiet streets in their autumn-coloured foliage. We were familiar figures in the ravine park — that park now destroyed, obliterated, by a city council that apparently hated trees and grass. I would look into the faces of passers-by with an expression so interested that sometimes they spoke to me. Sitting on a park bench, I was quite often the recipient of confidences of strangers.

My health by slow degrees improved. I turned again to writing others of the *Explorers of the Dawn* series. I became a member of several literary clubs. I renewed old friendships and made new friends. Every summer we took a cottage on the shore of Lake Simcoe. We would let our house — Caroline retaining a room for herself and coming to us at the week-end and for her holidays. We keenly felt this separation. When the time for her coming drew near, what preparations would be made! Everything in the cottage must be bright and shining. The dogs must be groomed. Well they knew what was afoot as they gambolled beside me along the lake shore to the radial stop where she would alight, carrying her suitcase and a load of packages. Bunty and Hamish would fairly devour her in the ecstasy of reunion. The radial tram would toddle off on its leisurely progress through the fields. Clear in my mind remain our trips on it to the lake — the dogs restrained by harness and lead, my mother, flushed by excitement, sitting very erect, knitting socks for the soldiers. These socks must always be of white wool (so much kinder to their feet), but I wondered how long they would last in Flanders mud.

The week-end passed so quickly. Caroline always spent the first evening relaxed in the hammock on the verandah, and my mother would light the Chinese lanterns in her honour. The happy time was when her holidays came. Then there were weeks when life was tranquil — but for the dogs.

174

Other people seem able to make their dogs behave. Not we.
Our dogs are invariably intelligent, terribly affectionate, full of
charm, but just as surely they are disobedient and born to fight
other dogs. Up and down the road Bunty and Hamish raged,
fighting, chasing boys on bicycles, motor cars, waggonloads of
hay, even perambulators. Then off to the woods to chase rabbits.
There seemed no end to their mischief. Bunty would trot to the
neighbouring farm and return swaggering with a chick in her
mouth. With a prideful air she would set it on the floor in our
midst. She was doing her best, it appeared, to add to the family
larder. Not once was a chick injured. Simply it stood there looking
dazed. But at night Caroline and I would steal through the darkness to the farm, fearfully search till we discovered the mother
hen, then return the chick to the comfort of her wing.

The dogs slept in a small room off the kitchen. In it was an old-
fashioned rocking-chair. All through the summer night they took
turns in the rocking-chair. It creaked as they rocked, and that
creaking was a not unpleasant accompaniment to our slumber.

The summer cottage was a luxury indeed and it was an unfore-
seen shock when the nice young couple to whom we had let our
house in town made off secretly, without paying their rent. We
had depended on that rent.

When, feeling much subdued, we returned to Toronto and
opened our front door, we found a number of letters left by the
postman. Among them was one from an American magazine enclosing a cheque for the story I had submitted. So — always we
were lucky. So almost always something turned up which saved
the day. The cheque was for an amount rather more than the
rental of the cottage.

In our second summer in the cottage Hamish was killed by the
train. Bunty returned without him, which had never before hap-

175

pened. Two days of anxious search passed. Two nights of waiting for the sound of his feet on the verandah. Then on the third day I saw my mother coming across the fields, carrying his rigid white body in her arms. We shed many tears for him. He had given me such adoration (this is the only word for it) as I have never had from any other dog. He would sit at my feet gazing up at me, as though I were the most wonderful being in the world — and so I was to him.

I well remember how the paper boy said of Hamish, when digging his grave, "He was bound to come to a bad end."

Chapter 11

We Two Left

THE war was over. In the years immediately following we began to feel a security in life which we had not experienced in a long while. Caroline had had a rise in her salary. Every so often I sold a short story. Each summer we took the cottage on the shore of Lake Simcoe. In the winter we had our friends. We were out of debt. My mother regained much of her old gaiety. She succeeded in making the house attractive with the furniture we had been able to retain. She had much to live for. I have known no one with a greater zest for life — no one to whom the acquiring of some longed-for object (even though it might be no more than a coloured-glass goblet or a collar of lace) gave so much joy. To me possessions have meant little.

Her death, after an illness of only a few weeks, again shook our little world, left us shattered.

It was at the time of a serious influenza epidemic. Caroline was the first to contract the disease. Her fever was so high that my mother and I were frightened — but not for ourselves. "I am not in the least nervous," said my mother, when we had been told by the doctor that Caroline had flu. In those days it was a dangerous illness. But — "I'm not in the least nervous," said my mother. "I think I am immune. I shall nurse Caroline myself."

The following day I went down with the sickness and the day after that, my mother. All three were very ill. In my mother's case pneumonia developed. . . . How unreal was the small house — filled with the comings and goings in which we had no part. We could not read — we could not eat — but lay dumbly waiting. Friends sent us flowers and tempting dishes but could not come to see us because of the infection.

At the first it had been difficult to get a doctor. All were over-worked because of the epidemic. But we were fortunate in finding Dr. Leonard Murray, a Haligonian, newly come to Toronto. Handsome, warm-hearted, he was our staunch support through all that time of trouble.

It was difficult to get a doctor, it was in the first ten days of our illness impossible to find a nurse. It was then that my mother's brother Walter came to our rescue. He was happily married; he was absorbed in his profession; but he put all aside and came and nursed the three of us with unswerving devotion. He had no time for sleep. I think he did not take off his clothes but went from bedroom to bedroom, a mask over the lower part of his face, do-ing everything for us. At last a nurse was found — a kindly soul — ecstatic in the religious sect to which she belonged. On her first day, when she was bathing me, she asked me whether I should like to be "saved." I said that I should very much. From that moment my baths were times of religious revival and the nurse had great hopes for me. In contrast, Caroline showed no desire to be saved but lay with her face turned coldly away.

I remember how, when my mother's illness became critical, we hung on Dr. Murray, one clinging to either shoulder, and begged him not to let her die. He showed how deeply he was moved, but he could not stay the progress of the disease; nor could the other doctors who filed solemnly up the stairway, whose steps I could hear moving overhead.

One night, when all was over and our nurse was on another case, she sought out Dr. Murray, struggling through a blizzard to his house. Standing there in the hall, her head and shoulders white with snow, she tried, in her simple way, to lead him to her God — to tell him how to be "saved."

"No one ever did such a thing for me — never before!" he exclaimed. "To come all that way through the cold and snow . . . to 'save my soul.' " He was deeply touched.

Often in those days my thoughts turned backward to the past summer by Lake Simcoe, the last summer we were to spend there. It had been a cold autumn, yet we stayed late at the cottage. In the corner of the field where Hamish lay buried, there grew a clump of goldenrod, of a darker gold than the stubble fields. The haze from northern forest fires would drift down to us, smelling just pleasantly acrid. Unknowingly we clung to this, our last time alone together. We were enthralled by books. My mother read aloud *Don Quixote,* from a very old copy, with a strange print and stranger illustrations. It had belonged to my grandfather de la Roche. There were nearly a thousand pages of it.

The thought of that reading comes back to me and with it the picture of Bunty, sitting on a chair near-by, as though listening. She had grown more gentle. Her eyes had a look of puzzlement in them and by degrees their brilliance was clouded. Repeatedly I had taken her to the veterinarian, who seemed hopeful of curing them, but in those days of our illness her sight had completely failed. She was totally blind.

My mother had been anxious about Bunty's eyes. Once she had said to me, "If her sight should go, I think it would be better if we . . . I think we couldn't bear to keep her, could we?"

But now, clasping her active young body in my arms, the thought of parting with her was unbearable. She should have her life, regain her courage, as I must regain mine.

It was arranged that we should let our house furnished for the summer. The early part of the season I was to spend in New York with Aunt Eva and Pierre, while Caroline was to visit friends. Later we were to go to Lake Joseph, in Muskoka, where we had taken a flat above a launch house.

It was cruelly hard for Caroline and me to part at this time when, above all things, we needed to be together, but we had had those invitations and the flat in Muskoka was not yet available. It would be a benefit to rent our house, for expenses had been heavy. I was fortunate in being able to sell second rights in ten short stories to the editor of the *Canadian Home Journal*. These all had been previously published in American magazines, so I considered myself lucky to get a thousand dollars for them. With heavy hearts we got our house ready for letting and ourselves for leaving it.

I took Bunty with me to New York. It was a trying experience for a little blind dog to be tied to a towering pile of trunks in the noise and confusion of the baggage car, but there was no alternative, and she had developed a sturdy courage in her days of darkness, combined with an appealing charm. Even the men in the train were moved by this and were kind to her.

It was strange to be in Aunt Eva's house in that Long Island suburb, with Pierre as her husband. I thought of it as her house, for she was the prevailing figure there. Everything must be as she would have it. She talked a great deal about trivialities. Pierre and I had little to say. When we found ourselves alone together, we had still less. We would exchange a few desultory thoughts on the music we had heard over the radio or he might recall some incident of his boyhood in France. Our spontaneous pleasure in the company of each other was gone. Yet, when Aunt Eva came suddenly into the room, we had a feeling of guilt, like two children plotting mischief.

I longed above all things to return home.

Looking back over my life, it is borne in on me how much I have walked. Walk — walk — walk — usually with a dog beside me — over city pavements — along country roads. And in New York that summer, the miles covered by Bunty and me! I learned to know those streets about Aunt Eva's house better than ever did she or Pierre. They had bought it, a house far too large, because of its view across a golf course toward the sea, but soon it was "developed" and rows of houses sprang up where the golf course had been.

We (Bunty and I) left New York at a time of torrid heat, but in Toronto a cool breeze was blowing. Caroline met me at the Union Station.

As the train drew in, it was easy to distinguish her in the crowd on the platform, slim and straight in her black and white dress, a wing of bright hair against her little black hat. How pale her face was and how blue her eyes!

After the sorrow, after the separation, it was an almost unbearable happiness to be together again. Almost at once we left for the flat in Muskoka. It was, as I have said, above a launch house, beside a sheltered bay and surrounded by dense woods and undergrowth. The owner, Dr. Sinclair, and his sister lived in a cottage on a hillside above. He was a professor in a department of the university that had to do with the education of young children. He had intelligence tests for children of every age and had implicit belief in these tests. If a child failed in the test for his age, he

181

sank at once to a lower age group. I discovered that, according to ability, I was about four years old.

The Sinclairs wore private smiles on their plain faces, as though they cherished a secret joke. They used to twit each other in Latin and Greek. They were proud of the terrific electrical storms in the district and I twice sat with them on their verandah during such a storm. At each brilliant rending of the heavens, they would smile at each other as if they had had part in its production, while I cowered in terror.

The Sinclairs kept bees and poultry. From them we were able to buy honey and eggs. Unfortunately, there were many more hens than customers and, as Miss Sinclair's rule was to sell the oldest eggs first, we never had fresh ones. That is, till we hit on a scheme to frustrate this. . . . When we saw the Sinclairs depart in their launch, we would go up the hill to their cottage, steal down into the cellar where the eggs were stored, and exchange our stale ones for fresh. It was a nerve-racking experience, but the eggs were worth it.

In the launch house beneath our flat several barrels full of gasoline were stored, and when there was an electrical storm, it was a frightening thought that the building might be struck by lightning and we blown up. Still, it was a time of return to physical vitality. From the moment when we alighted from the train (we had been the only passengers for that "stop") and found Bunty tied to a telegraph pole, where the brakeman had secured her, there was something interesting to do. We had at our disposal a rowing boat and a canoe. Bunty delighted to sit in the bow of the rowing boat sniffing the watery scents on the breeze. We would not risk her presence in the canoe, though she could swim and we could not. Her cries echoed from the launch house as we paddled across the lake for our supplies of food. At night we sat on our little verandah and she would prick her ears at the mournful laughter of the loon.

My health wonderfully improved, in spite of a severe attack of whooping cough which I contracted from the young son of a friend. I coughed my way, whooping like a crane, through the autumn. In spite of it, or possibly in part because of the isolation it brought me, I began to conceive the earliest thoughts of my first novel — *Possession*. The scene of it was to be our farm on the lake shore. That bit of land, the Indian fruit pickers I knew so well were to be pictured in it. In the meantime I was interested in writing one-act plays. These were later successfully produced in the Hart House Theatre. *Low Life, Come True* and *The Return of the Emigrant* were collected in book form by the Macmillan Company. *Low Life* has been performed many times and has its own little history. Its story was first poured out to me by a charwoman who came in regularly to work for me. She had a worthless husband and I sympathized with her. At that time the Daughters of the Empire had a competition for a one-act play. The prize was one hundred dollars. I sent *Low Life* to this competition and it won the prize. The play was printed in the I.O.D.E. magazine and there was an announcement in the daily press, with a picture of me. About the same time the Authors' Association of Montreal held a similar competition. I had sent a copy of *Low Life* to both competitions. Caroline and I were delighted when I was notified that the play had also been successful there. Another hundred dollars in prize money! I remember how we clasped each other and danced through the house. That was before the day of stupendous prizes on TV quiz programmes. In any case, there is something remarkable in an author's winning two prizes with the same play. . . . But our triumph was shaken when the secretary of the Montreal Authors' Association wrote me

183

a scathing letter demanding the return of their prize money and questioning my right to submit a play that also was entered in another competition. But I could not have returned the prize money, if I would. Already it had been spent.

In the meantime I had became acquainted with Hugh Eayrs, the young president in Canada of Macmillan of New York. At a meeting of the Heliconian Club someone had remarked to me, "The man who is most interested in your writing is Hugh Eayrs and he is here to-day." We were introduced, I never guessing the influence he was to have in various decisions I made. Indeed, the influence he exerted in literary and publishing circles in Canada was remarkable, as he himself was remarkable. Born in Yorkshire, he had come to Canada as a youth but retained the sturdy qualities of the Yorkshireman. He was short, inclined to stoutness, blond, with quite beautiful eyes of a changeful colour. He had a fine speaking voice, was a talented amateur actor, an irresistible mimic. He was an odd combination of sweet good humour and ruthlessness. His early death brought sorrow to more widely different people than any other I can recall. He was a most loyal friend.

I have reason to remember my first visit to his office. He had invited me to have tea with him. I was excited, partly because he was he, partly because it was my first visit to a publisher's office. It was winter and before I left the house I went down to the basement to have a look at the coal furnace, to make sure that all was well there. Remembering those days, it surprises me how doggedly Caroline and I clung to the responsibility and expense of a house, when we might have been snug in an apartment.

Before I went down to the basement I drew over the pretty dress that I wore for the occasion a grey sweater, for its protection. The sad thing was that I forgot, in my excitement, to take the sweater off. On top of it I put my muskrat coat and set out. Hugh Eayrs made me welcome in his private office. A typist brought in the tea things and left us.

Hugh was about to help me off with my coat when he was suddenly called from the room. "I shall be back in a moment," he said and hurried away. I was left alone and thought I would myself take off my coat. What was my shock to discover that I still wore the sweater, old, shabby, with a hole in one elbow! I decided that I must refuse to part with my coat. I would say I had had a chill. But the room was hot. I should surely faint in a fur coat. I was in a panic. Then I discovered that a window was open onto the street. I did not hesitate. I threw off my coat, I tore off the sweater, rolled it up and cast it out of the window.

Hugh briskly returned. "What a pretty dress!" he exclaimed. Then, "Will you pour tea?" But I could not forget the sweater, lying in the street. I expected, at any moment, that it would be returned to me, but never did I see it again.

It was Hugh who replied to the letter from Montreal and the affair ended in an apology from the president of the Montreal branch of the C.A.A.

I have mentioned before that it was Christopher Morley who interested the publisher Alfred Knopf in my writing. Mr. Knopf came to see me and offered to publish *Explorers of the Dawn*. He was handsome, agreeable. So ignorant was I of the publishing of books that I did not realize that usually it was the author who sought out publishers, not the reverse. Mr. Knopf was generous in sending me copies of the books published by him. I had only to mention them and they would arrive. I remember a complete set of de Maupassant and many others. I thought of myself as lucky to have such a publisher and my imagination turned to the writing of a novel.

Ringing the Changes

I shall not forget the first Christmas Caroline and I spent without my mother. Christmas always had been a great day with us. Now how were we to spend it? We thought with foreboding of a day under the shadow of past happy times. As it turned out, we were invited to stay with the Garvins in their delightful house in Russell Hill Road.

John Garvin was a lively, exuberant man, intensely interested in Canadian writing, sometimes to the neglect of his own business of stockbroking. He spent large sums in publishing expensively bound editions of early Canadian books. His wife, "Katherine Hale," was a member of the Galt family of Warnocks, long friends of my family. When my first short stories were published, I looked up to her as a writer of experience. Indeed she was and has been connected with literary life in Toronto for the greater part of her life, book critic for the *Mail*, a sensitive poet, and author of a number of books on Canada. So, with them our Christmas was spent — in play-acting and parties. Bunty too was included in the invitation and so cleverly had she trained her other senses that those who were not informed of it did not realize that she was blind. Soon she knew the Garvins' house from end to end.

Again, in the following summer she journeyed with us to Muskoka, but that summer was not a success. As always with us we expected things to turn out well. We are incorrigibly unconcerned with details. We knew that the coal oil stove, by which we did our cooking, was derelict in the previous summer, yet we risked using it again. Indeed, Miss Sinclair had promised us a new one, but it did not materialize. Now when the stove had been burning for only a short while, it suddenly would send up flames in a terrifying way. Expecting an explosion, I would remove the oil container and carry it to the verandah, ready, when the explosion came, to

186

throw it into the lake below. The Coxes, who had a cottage down the shore, told me that every morning their first act on awaking was to look out the window to discover whether we still were there or had been either blown up or burned out. We survived.

We survived the savage heat of that summer, to which there has since been nothing comparable — not till this summer, more than thirty years later, and it is much less torrid. The dense woods shut out all movement of air. The lake lay like molten brass and in its murky depths could be seen the dark shapes of moss-grown fallen trees. The thermometer would register ninety-eight degrees when we crept from under our mosquito netting in the morning and before noon it would rise to well over a hundred degrees. Mosquitoes, black flies were our torment. Immense black spiders became bolder every week. Bunty sat panting, ceaselessly snapping at the flies that buzzed about her eyes. In the evening we would go out on the lake in our rowboat to eat our evening meal, while Bunty sat in the stern, greedy for tidbits, in spite of the heat. We had no ice and I remember dribbling the butter from a spoon onto our bread. In spite of all this discomfort we often were gay. Our laughter would mingle with the laughter of the loon, as we dipped our oars into the dark water and saw the great red moon rise out of the wood. Even then there was no lapping of the lake on the shore — just a breathless tropic stillness.

The worst times were the days when we must go to the "supply boat" for our supplies. We would set out in the canoe, leaving Bunty shut in the flat. This was the hottest time of the day. The sullenly shining lake reflected the blazing heat of the sky. After the long paddle across the lake came the long walk over the dusty road, sweat dripping from our faces — then the return, laden with our supplies. Deer flies plagued us on this walk. Whoever says that the north is never hot has not experienced such an ordeal.

Once Bunty escaped from the flat and swam out into the lake after us. It was unbelievable that she could have found her way through the forest, where there was no scent to follow, and emerged on the shore exactly opposite us. Yet that she did and gallantly swam out to us, her face lifted to the glare of the sun. She could see nothing, but she gave a sharp yelp of joy at the sound of our voices. There was nothing for it but to turn back. By the time we had her safe in the flat and had made our second trip across the lake we were sunburned wrecks of what we once had been.

When Caroline's holidays were over, I remained in Muskoka and it was there I wrote the first chapter of my first novel, *Possession*.

The weather had changed. It was cool at night for sleeping. The lake was rough and the boats, knocking gently together in the launch house below, were the accompaniment to my imagination set free. It was fervently unloosed in *Possession*, in my memories of the years spent on the farm.

Caroline and I decided to let a part of our house and agreeable tenants presented themselves in the persons of a newspaper woman, Jean Graham, and her mother. Jean Graham contributed regularly to *Saturday Night*. She was a jolly, stout woman who was a friend of the Sinclairs and had not been long in our house before she suggested that we might let our top floor, which was not in use, to them. Quite soon Dr. Sinclair and his sister were installed there and we could hear them as they passed in and out cracking jokes in the dead languages. They also had a dog, an irascible Yorkshire terrier, Toots, between whom and Bunty there was no more than an armed truce. Toots was a woman-hater and

Bunty a man-hater. This arrangement with the Sinclairs worked very well till its rather comic denouement.

If we had been fairly roasted alive in the Sinclairs' flat above the launch house, they, in their turn, were chilly in our flat beneath the roof. The house was heated by a hot-air furnace and when our backs were turned, Miss Sinclair would shut the heat off from our part of the house and turn it to theirs — just as we had exchanged stale eggs for fresh in her basement. The upshot of it was that, when a year had passed, Dr. Sinclair took a house in the same street and lured Jean Graham and her mother away from us. He offered her a signed agreement whereby it was promised that her apartment would never fall below seventy degrees, no matter how cold the weather. It was a wonderful promise and the Grahams departed.

But less than a month had passed when (while the Sinclairs were out) the Grahams fled with all their belongings. They never had, they declared, been so cold in their lives as in that house. Strangely, the Sinclairs turned to us for sympathy. It was I whom Miss Sinclair called up by telephone when Toots was killed in the street and poured out her grief over the wires.

Caroline and I talked of taking an apartment, but there was all our furniture, much of it too massive for a smaller space. There was Bunty, who needed a yard for her activities. What seemed to us the right house was offered. We prepared for a removal. This was necessary because the house where we were living had been sold. Looking back over my life, I seem to have spent a great part of it in packing up, in the exhausting experience of moving from one house to another.

Before this removal was accomplished, Knopf had published *Explorers of the Dawn*. It was highly praised by the critics and sold moderately well. Christopher Morley wrote of it: "There will be readers who will look through it, as through an open window, into a land of clear gusty winds and March sunshine and volleying church bells on Sunday mornings, into a land of terrible contradictions, a land whose émigrés look back to tenderly, yet without too poignant regret — the almost forgotten land of childhood."

For a time it was on the list of best sellers in America and I think it is not without interest to give the titles and names of the authors of the four books which preceded it on that list. They were, and this was in 1922: *The Secret Places of the Heart,* by H. G. Wells; *Gentle Julia,* by Booth Tarkington; *Memoirs of a Midget,* by Walter de la Mare; *Adrienne Toner,* by Anne Douglas Sedgwick.

My novel *Possession* was finished. I was under contract for its publication by Knopf. But Hugh Eayrs was anxious that it should be published by Macmillan of New York. I always have had the feeling that in breaking away from Knopf I behaved rather badly. Mr. Alfred Knopf was admirably patient. He agreed to one demand after another till there was nothing for it but to let me go. He did not realize that my letters to him were written for me.

Possession was published simultaneously in England, Canada and America. In England and America it had excellent reviews that were most heartening. The Canadian reviews were mixed. *Possession* was a very different kind of Canadian novel and some of the critics bitterly disliked it.

One paragraph from this novel was quoted in many reviews, as though the feeling in it had indeed struck home. This is it: "What a strange thing was possession. You thought you were the possessor when in truth you were the thing possessed."

We were now established in another house, but because of the removal and the writing of *Possession* I was very tired. Dr. Murray said the sea air would do me good. Conveniently I was offered a pass on the railway to Halifax, and in return for this I was to stop off at several places on the Nova Scotian coast and was to write a brochure on their attractions. I was in that province for more than a month and liked it so well that I was eager to go there to live. But there have been so many places where I should like to live. It was the same with my parents. If, when they were out walking, they came across an attractive house for sale, they would scrutinize it with the keenest interest, compete with each other in plans for its improvement, regardless of expense, though they well knew they had no intention of buying it and probably could not have afforded to do so.

It was at about this time when I began to have a certain dream. At first this dream came at fairly frequent intervals, but of late, less often. I write of it because it was so vivid, so beautiful — a contrast to the wild and nightmarish dreams to which I have been subject since childhood.

In this dream I am walking alone across a wide stretch of sandy beach by the sea. Beyond the beach stretches a sunny moorland and, at its edge, facing the sea, stands a house, with all its doors and windows open. The house has a cheerful and welcoming air and I can see that it is sparsely furnished. One room has nothing in it but a refectory table and a chair or two. There are no curtains, no pictures, no one living in the house, yet it is not desolate. A most beautiful and comforting radiance emanates from it — a luminosity from the sands of the shore and the very shells that lie there. Yet there is nothing ethereal about the house. It is very real and I am terribly eager to go into it — to live there. Yet always, as I reach the doorsill, it fades and is gone.

While I was in Nova Scotia, Carolina had taken Bunty with

her to her office in the Parliament buildings every day. There the little dog was everybody's favourite, but it was a dull life for her and when Caroline's holidays came, it was with glad relief that they went to spend them on the lake shore at the Blue Dragon guest house kept by a Mrs. Fairbairn and her daughter. It was a charming place in the seclusion of woods and gardens and near the tiny village of Clarkson. Grace Fairbairn is now the proprietor of the Clarkson Antique Market.

It was while staying at the Blue Dragon that Caroline had a (to us) stupendous idea. A part of the land belonging to the Harris family was being sold by a daughter, Anne Sayers, to a few people who, she hoped, would form an agreeable neighbourhood. This estate had belonged to an Irish gentleman, the Reverend James Magrath, who, with his family, had emigrated to Canada in 1827. He became rector of the church in the near-by village of Erindale, named after his estate, and remained there till his death. His sons took to the new country with zest. One of them, Thomas William, became a quite notable figure in the new land. He wrote excellent articles on Canadian field sports for the New York *Spirit of the Times* and for the London *Sportsman*. It is amusing to read that William Lyon McKenzie wrote in his newspaper of one of these articles — "It is from the pen of one of the Messrs. Magrath who, whatever you may think of their politics and their rectories, are clever writers and have given some admirable descriptions of rural life in their adopted country." It is certain that the Magraths would have despised not only the politics of Mr. McKenzie but his cowardly escape, dressed in woman's clothes, to the United States, when, after instigating a rebellion, he fled, leaving the men he had persuaded to join him to bear the punishment of banishment or hanging.

The remainder of this estate of the Magraths was a charming

little community that still cherished the traditions of its early days. Anne Sayers, a descendant of the Magraths, and her husband, Beverley Sayers, were selling small parcels of woodland at a price within reach of people of moderate means. Certainly our means were moderate, but Caroline's nimble mind caught at the idea of a small house in the woods where we could spend our summers. Eagerly I caught the fever (what a place for writing!) and before long we had visited the Sayers and arranged to buy enough land to insure us privacy. Beverley Sayers engaged a carpenter to build a cottage for us. I was thrilled. I thought of little else — outside the new novel I had in mind to write. If I could not find that house by the sea, of which I had dreamed, at least I might have a cottage in a woodland.

The carpenter drew plans and that very fall began building.

In town I wrote several short stories and a one-act play, then settled down to write my novel. I had great hopes for it.

My visit to a certain foggy, out-of-the-way spot in Nova Scotia had inspired it. I felt that it was going to be a more interesting novel than *Possession*. Nothing I ever had written would equal it. Assuredly nothing I have written can compare with it in failure and disappointment. But — when for the first time I re-read it, this summer, thirty years later, I thought it a remarkable book. Yet I saw where I had gone terribly wrong. I had been so struck by that place in Nova Scotia, the strangeness of it to me, an Ontarian, that I had crammed all sorts of irrelevant guide-bookish descriptions into the story, which was quite able to stand on its own legs. Re-reading it, I thought — "What a film it would make!"

When the novel had been typed, I sent it to Hugh Eayrs of Macmillan and waited, full of eager hope, for his opinion. He was to take tea with me and, in honour of the occasion, I brought out the teapot of a beautiful blue lustre tea set that had belonged to my grandmother.

Shortly before the tea hour my aunt by marriage, "Auntie Ida," dropped in quite unexpectedly. She had chosen an unfortunate time. I was excited, tense. When she left, the first thing I did was to knock over the teapot, shattering it into fragments. The tea lay in an amber pool on the floor. I was aghast. It was a bad omen. All the Celtic superstition, the dark side of my nature, reared itself. I was not surprised when Hugh told me he did not think the novel a worthy successor to *Possession*. He would publish it — yes, he would publish it — but he counselled me to read it — to think about it — possibly rewrite it.

But I had had enough of it. I flung the manuscript into a drawer and tried to forget it. I took long walks. The weather was very cold that winter. Snow was heaped so high on either side of the street that one walked between walls of pure whiteness. Bunty scampered safely, free of the lead, because she could not pursue the cars in the road. Though she could not see them, still she would, if she had the chance, joyously chase them, returning with jaunty tail after each hairbreadth escape.

With the purchase of land and the building of a cottage on our hands, to say nothing of the expenses of a removal, it was a serious matter that my work of more than a year should be fruitless. I read manuscripts for Macmillan. I did some book reviewing for Eaton's. These brief reviews, appearing above their advertisements in the morning paper, greatly influenced buyers of books. Ivor Brown had written them the previous year.

At this time the head of Eaton's book department was a charming and sympathetic woman, Norah Thompson. Associated with her was a genial Irishman whose name escapes me. She had an excellent taste in books. He was a good business man, so they made

a capital combination. Together they combined in a business enterprise greatly to my advantage. Eaton's had advertised a sale of
handsome fur-trimmed coats. Caroline and I went out a good deal
and badly did I need a handsome new coat. The sale opened at
eight o'clock in the morning — an appalling hour for me. But
Norah Thompson and the Irishman were on hand at the urgent
moment. They chose the very best of the coats, and very becoming
it was to me. Clothes were quite a problem to us. Caroline could
always get amazing bargains in shoes because of her tiny feet —
not I!

Eagerly we strained toward the day when the cottage would be
completed. Trail Cottage I named it, because an Indian trail of
some bygone days lay in the midst of its aspens, oaks and gleaming
white birches. Over it the moccasined feet of Indians had passed
as they made their unhurried way to the Credit River, where they
met the traders who, in exchange for the fine furs they brought,
gave them pots and pans, the hatchets, calico and beads they
prized. The Credit River was a placid stream, with a few boats at
anchor where it emptied into the great expanse of the lake. But
once the salmon had sought it out, coming all the way up the St.
Lawrence from the sea, to spawn there.

Before Trail Cottage was completed, friends would motor us
out to see it. With a grand gesture we would welcome them to its
windowless magnificence. It smelt of the clean new pine wood.
Trees crowded all about. From the virgin soil sprang trilliums,
bloodroot, columbines, rare fringed gentian, trailing arbutus, and
where there was no flower or fern, the wintergreen spread its
glossy carpet, showed its scarlet berries. Oh, but the air was sweet
with scent of flowers and unspoilt countryside!

On these visits with our friends we picnicked in the living-
room of the cottage. Already Caroline was planning its furnishing.

Already Bunty was exploring the woods. We expected everyone to admire the cottage as much as we did. Especially for the fireplace did we expect, even demand, admiration. Its proportions, its chimney, the way it would devour either a pine cone or part of a stump were to us a miracle. Caroline especially demanded appreciation for the fireplace. She, usually restrained, inclined to understatement, really let herself go when it came to the fireplace.

Beverley Sayers had discovered the very right carpenter for us — a new man, anxious to establish himself — and his work was good. Our little roof never leaked, our two verandahs, one front and one back, behaved just as verandahs should. Our casements opened and shut with never a squeak of protest. We had no plumbing problems, for a well was dug, a spring discovered, and a pump installed, convenient to the kitchen. A rain-water barrel was sunk at the corner nearest the well and into it the eaves gushed, dripped or trickled rain water for bathing or dish-washing. To be sure, you had to go down and up several steps from the kitchen door every time you wanted fresh water, but we thought nothing of that. A drink of pure spring water out of a tin dipper — what a pleasure! Its coolness touches the lips; it is balm to the tongue; bliss to the palate; a blessing to the throat; a benefit to the stomach. What a contrast to the evil-flavoured liquid that goes by the name of water in this city. We had a little lavatory, a kitchen, the large living-room with two divans. What more could we want? Every second day ice was brought to us. We had a faithful gardener and woodcutter, John Bird, a "character" if ever there was one. Every morning he clumped through the woods from his home two miles away, his axe over his shoulder. Each morning he would lay on the doorstep a little nosegay of wild flowers for me, tied with grey yarn.

From the village across the ravine came a willing little woman,

Mrs. Roland, to do the washing and cleaning. Together Bunty and I went along the sandy road to get the delicious milk and butter from a near by farm.

It was a great day when we took possession of Trail Cottage. It was the month of May, the weather was fair, we could not bear to wait another day. Our friend Harry Mumford was early at our house in town to drive us out. He was almost as excited as we. Gay, companionable, charming, was there ever better friend than he! Nothing was too much trouble. His car was mounded to the roof with our belongings. A mover's van had already taken the furniture. There scarcely was room for us three to get into the car. Bunty indeed was in the seventh heaven, her face turned to the breeze, her nostrils sniffing the countryside.

How we three worked! By evening we were fairly settled in. All was so clean, so new, so sweet-smelling of the pine wood of which the cottage was built. We had not been able to wait till windows and doors were put in, consequently the trees crowding close were almost in the room with us, were conscious of all our doings. . . . Oh, I pity the millionaires who never have had the experience of building a *little* house!

Beverley Sayers was rather anxious about our lack of protection in this woodland place. That very first evening he strode to our doorway, bringing a handsome inlaid pistol to lend us. From that night, through all the summer, I slept with this on a chair at the head of my bed. It is a wonder, as I was subject to realistic dreams and nightmares, that I did no harm with it. In truth I became quite attached to it.

We woke early on that first morning, the sunshine making even greener the leaves just beyond the room. Squirrels and chipmunks scampered over the roof, astonished to discover us. Then came the clump clump of the approach of the gardener, John Bird, along the Indian trail. Next the blows of his axe as he attacked the undergrowth. And there was Bunty running out to bark at him, for there was no door to restrain her.

Caroline had made curtains of blue and gold for the casements. There were blue and gold covers and cushions for the divans. There was matting on the floor. There was blue china in the old walnut dresser, and shelves with shining copper and brass. We had robbed our house in town for some of these things, but curtains and covers were new and the whole was to Caroline and me a creation of breath-taking beauty.

We had our excitements there.

In the ravine near-by there were not only primeval pines, but now and again one saw a snake. Unlike most women I am not alarmed by them or by mice, but to Caroline a snake is a thing of terror. Once we encountered a puff adder, as large around as a man's arm. He lay coiled on our path, decorated and lacquered in his sinister beauty. He uncoiled a little, just enough to raise his head, and emitted something yellow through his dark lips, then he loosed all his length and slid, in leisurely retreat, out of sight.

That night Caroline woke me with a penetrating whisper so full of panic that I sat up straight on my divan.

"It's the snake," she said. "It's in the basket at the head of my bed."

A colourful Mexican basket hung there against the wall.

"How do you know?" I whispered back.

"I can hear him moving."

"But he's too big. He couldn't possibly get into that basket."

"Then it's some other snake. I tell you I'm positive. You must get up and carry the basket outdoors."

"I can't."

"You must. Oh, I'm so terribly frightened!"

It was seldom that Caroline showed fear. I knew that there was nothing for it but to get rid of the adder.

"Quick — quick — it's moving," she moaned, and shudderingly drew the bedclothes over her head.

Gingerly I got out of bed. I lighted a candle and tiptoed to the basket. I took it from its peg and carried it at arm's length to the door. Outside I hurled basket and contents into the woods. I flew back into the room banging the door after me. At that instant, from the raftered ceiling, something fell on my head — a soft, strange something that touched my face and lay on my shoulders. I uttered a shriek that brought Caroline from her bed. Wildly I sought to disengage myself from what clung to me. Then an excited chattering came from above and I discovered a little red squirrel peering down at us from a beam. He had built his nest there (apparently from the filling of a pillow) and the slamming of the door had jolted it down. The noises heard by Caroline had been the squirrel's nocturnal activities and he was as distraught as we by the tumult.

Our nearest neighbours were the Livesays, who had already spent several summers in the woodland. They had built a comfortable house and surrounded it by lovely gardens. J. F. B. Livesay was president of the Canadian press. He had been a Canadian war correspondent and had written what was acknowledged to be the best book on Canada's part in the First World War. He came from the Isle of Wight and, though no more than a youth when he left home, he was always and most noticeably an Englishman. He was sensitive, irritable, fastidious. Although he worked much in his garden, he always looked immaculate. He had a slight stammer, which did not at all detract from the lively and mobile impression he made. He built for his own privacy a tiny log cabin in his garden. It was kept by him in Spartan neatness. Its outlook was a tennis court and a thousand daffodils waving among the silver birches. He and his daughter Dorothy were cherished companions. Now one of Canada's most interesting poets, she has written a "Lament" for him, than which I think I have read no more beautiful tribute to a father.

The younger daughter, Sophie, with her elfin dark locks and grey eyes, was a wistful, elusive child devoted to their Irish terrier Sukey, who was seldom without a litter of puppies. She was also devoted to her mother. Mrs. Livesay was a poet and was fervently interested in mushrooms. She might be seen, a picturesque figure, wandering through the woods, twirling a new-found specimen in her fingers. The Livesays had a rather erratic maid with the romantic name of Flavia and when Mrs. Livesay was in doubt as to the quality of certain mushrooms, always she had Flavia make a tempting dish of them. She could not bring herself to sample a new variety, but "Live," as he was called, blithely devoured all that were offered him, and survived. Our woods blossomed with many varieties, dark red, purple and pink, even the beautiful and terrible "destroying angel." I remember how one evening Mrs. Livesay dropped in as Caroline and I were enjoying a dish of mushrooms. "You're not afraid of them?" she enquired. "Indeed no," I said, "for you gave them to us." "Read this," she said, and laid a copy of the *Geographic* magazine on the table. In it was an article telling of the agonies suffered in death from eating the "destroying angel"— even the tiniest particle. "It is so easy," she said, "for a little poisonous mushroom to get into the dish unnoticed" — and she drifted away.

In the middle of the night I spoke to Caroline, from my divan to hers. "If I live till morning," I said, "I will never eat another mushroom!"

I lay listening to the cry of the whippoorwill. I counted. One hundred and ninety times he gave his mournful cry. I slept. I woke. I survived.

We too must have a garden. We planted a flower border and flowering shrubs. The wild flowers surrounding us were not enough. Another and most necessary thing was a compost heap. John Bird made a magnificent one for us. Rich loam, dead leaves — I read that you might put almost anything that would rot into it, from tea leaves to an old pair of shoes. "Nothing need be wasted," I said to Caroline and she agreed.

Not long after I discovered a pair of shoes standing on the bottom step of the back verandah. "Aha," I thought. "The very thing! Caroline has left these here for the enrichment of the compost heap." Immediately I set to work. I buried the shoes deep so they might have plenty of time to rot before needed.

Time passed. It was the hour of departure for our daily "help." She came to me, her ruddy face troubled. "Pardon mé," she said, "but has anybody seen my good shoes?"

"Your . . . shoes?" I stammered.

"Yes," she said firmly, "my *good* shoes. I left them on the verandah steps and put on my old ones to work in. I can't find them. I'm sorry to trouble you."

Well — we dug and we dug. All three of us, armed with spade, trowel and rake, delved into the compost heap — surely the most massive, inextricable, uliginous compost heap on record. Upside down, inside out we turned it before we unearthed the shoes. We laughed as we dug and none so heartily as Mrs. Roland. She laughed as though to have her good shoes buried were the greatest joke on earth. After all, when they had been given a thorough cleaning, they looked almost as good as new.

Early, five days of the week, Caroline set off along the woodland path to the little railway station. On her way there she passed between two rows of the most magnificent pines I have ever seen. They were noble survivors of the primeval forest. So dense, so luxuriant their foliage, so sweet their scent, so buoyant a carpet their needles made, that to walk that way was a delight.

Later, on a pretext of making the road safer for motorists, and to give a contract to some villain, the pines were cut down. It was a heart-breaking sight to see them butchered. Yet, at the same time, those in authority ignored a near-by level railway crossing, where Hugh Eayrs and I barely escaped with our lives and his car was completely wrecked.

Left to ourselves, Bunty and I settled to the day's work — she to sit close beside me while I wrote, then to explore the woods, to press her way into distant undergrowth, wild blackberry bush, to snuffle into the burrow of rabbit and mole. It was not long before I began a new novel. Not only did I write in the delicious privacy of this tiny birch-embowered cottage, but I sat while writing in a chair which had swayed (for it was a cane-seated rocking-chair) beneath the majestic weight of my father's mother. Never before had I owned a rocking-chair. They had not been popular in our family, and how this one now came into my possession I cannot remember. But there it was, slender and graceful in shape, not one of those rocking-chairs that give a protesting thump each time they are tilted backward, but it swayed, with a smooth noiseless sweep, like the rocking of a bird on a bough. How many years had my tranquil grandmother rocked in it? Probably each in turn of her three baby boys had been soothed by its movement; first the lusty, red-haired, pink-cheeked Danford; next the curly-haired Richmond, with his luminous brown eyes; last the pale, black-haired François.

Sitting in that chair, I began my third novel. At that time I had not heard how often is a second novel a failure and I was astonished and humiliated that this should have happened to me.

But this third novel, *Delight*, would be different. In it I would write of Ontario, the province I knew so well. I have already said that the basis for the novel was two short stories, published some years before. But other characters were introduced, characters which had impressed me — the fishmonger, for instance, and the Scot, "Fine Nicht."

My drawing-board on my knee, I sat upright when I was writing, but when I was at a loss for a word, or triumphant in the finding of the right one, violently would rock. And so, something invincibly childlike in me was satisfied. As for books of reference, I had only one source. That was Dr. Johnson's *Dictionary* in two bulky volumes. They lay on the floor beside me and each time I wanted to look up a word I heaved up one of the books and often became so fascinated by other words that I quite forgot the one of which I was in search.

Summer passed, in fair weather with the exception of a hurricane that uprooted the finest trees of the ravine — and so bent a young oak near Trail Cottage that never again did the trunk stand upright. Otherwise it flourished, put forth green boughs and glossy acorns. Birds nested in it, but it remained bent, like a man stricken in his youth. This storm was gathering as Caroline walked through the woods on her return from the city. It broke as she entered the cottage and we secured the doors and windows. The roar of the hurricane, the saffron colour of the sky, the sight of uprooted trees terrified us. The storm found its outlet in the ravine, then suddenly there was calm. Birds broke into song.

Summer passed. Then, just after our return to town, came the dire news that the family from whom we leased our house must themselves live in it; so we were forced once more to go house-hunting. It appeared to us as very hard luck, as we had thought of ourselves as settled in that house for some winters to come.

Now another upheaval took place. Once again the moving van stopped outside our door. Once again the removers trampled through our house. The things my mother had cherished stood forlornly in the street. Into a barrel went the *Three Graces* in marble. Swathed in an old blanket were the silver candelabra. Her mahogany sewing table, the antique oak chest, the old Bristol glass that had been a wedding present. Even the little trunk that held a few of her clothes with which we could not bear to part. One thing which did not accompany us was the piano. We had sold it, for living was becoming more and more expensive and my royalties were smaller than we had hoped for.

At the last moment Bunty was not to be found. After distraught searching we discovered her, smugly sitting on the driver's seat in the van, making certain that she would not be left behind. Full of courage, despite her blindness she had clambered there. Surely never was greater spirit than hers. She had all the best traits of the Scottish.

We had made a great mistake in taking this last house. An unconscionable amount of coal was required to make it livable. The expenses weighed more and more heavily on us. Then suddenly, aware of the number of unused rooms, it dawned on us that, like many of our friends, we might be more comfortable, might save money by living in a flat or apartment. So, after a stay of only one winter, we stored the greater part of our furniture and moved into a flat in a large house which once had belonged to Auntie Ida's family.

This flat was on the top floor and under its sloping roof we felt almost Bohemian. The westward windows had a good view over fine gardens and the sunset. The sunset was the only warm thing about that flat. If we had been chilly in our last house, almost we froze in the flat. And the stairs! Two steep flights to descend and climb each time Bunty was taken to the yard, and she demanded to be taken to the yard every half-hour, or so it seemed to me.

The steps leading into the yard were sheathed in ice. Added to this, Bunty had to undergo a serious operation and the complications of her convalescence, which she bore with the most spirited fortitude, were indeed a trial. The owner of the house was a broker and he persuaded me to invest the few hundreds I had at my disposal in some sort of mine, which effectually swallowed them.

In midwinter my father's elder brother died. This red-haired, hot-tempered man, of brilliant initiative and bad judgment, of generous impulses and always trusting the wrong people, had plunged from one fruitless enterprise to another, till lying on his deathbed he was a ruined man. Shortly before he died Caroline and I went to see him. It was an attack of bronchitis that was his end. He was in bed, very ill, but he still had plenty of flesh and his fine speaking voice was strong. When he and I were alone he said:

"Mazo, I want you to go to your aunt and see if you can persuade her to let me be baptized into the Catholic Church before I die. You know that I have for long been a Catholic at heart and it would make me very happy if I might be received into the Church and have its last rites. Will you do this for me?"

I went straight to Auntie Ida. She was preparing some food for him. She was doing it with exactness, almost matter-of-factness, but when I told her of his request, she began to tremble in unhappy anger. Her light eyes filled with tears.

"He can't do it," she said vehemently. "I won't allow it. I've been a Presbyterian all my life. My people were Protestants always. He used to go to church with me."

"But he hasn't — not for a long time. This would make him so happy."

"I won't allow it," she repeated.

I persisted. "It seems to me, Auntie Ida, that if I had loved someone for many years, at a time like this I'd agree to anything that would make him happier — even if he wanted to become a Mohammedan."

"I won't allow it," she cried. "I couldn't bear it. I'd feel disgraced."

So I was forced to go back to the dear man, lying there on his deathbed, and give him the sad news.

He was calm. "Very well," he said. "I understand. And I believe in our Lord Jesus Christ and that he gave his life to redeem us. Perhaps that is all that matters."

A little later he looked toward the ceiling and said, "I see the most beautiful lilies there, and the antlered heads of deer among them."

After his death my aunt wrote to me and asked me if I would like to have my grandfather's books, which had been stored in a room above the stable ever since his death. I very much wanted to possess those books, that is, to possess what was left of them, for my Uncle François had years ago taken those which he wanted. Also I was eager to own the portrait of my great-grandmother brought by her in a sailing vessel from Ireland, which had hung in Uncle Danford's dining-room. This he had promised should be mine.

One wintry day Caroline and I, and of course Bunty also, set out to visit Auntie Ida and to choose what books we wanted. We wore our oldest clothes and Auntie Ida enveloped us in large pinafores. We mounted the steep stairs above the carriage house where all was shrouded in dust and cobwebs and bats hung from the ceiling. Up there it was cold and the light was dim, but

we were so excited we did not mind. Thirty large packing cases of
books stood before us. With characteristic carelessness Uncle François had, after going through the books, not troubled to close the
cases properly, so that the top layers were deep in the accumulated
dust of decades.

Three days we spent in sorting over the books. With grimy
hands and aching backs we bent over the packing cases. Sometimes we uttered an exclamation of delight at the beauty of a hand-
tooled leather binding, the strange and sometimes grotesque illustrations. But our exclamations were more often of dismay at the
havoc wrought by rot and mildew. Some of the most beautifully
bound literally fell to pieces in our hands. Dozens upon dozens we
were forced to throw away. It was heart-breaking to see them, and
there were the bookmarks to show where my grandfather had left
off reading, and there were passages he had marked! What charmed
me most, and it was in good condition, was an ancient volume of
natural history with fabulous pictured beasts. Almost all the books
were in Latin, Greek or French, the poetry and drama of the
classics. Did my grandfather, demanded Caroline, never relax with
a thriller? Why, yes, there was a book by Edgar Allan Poe — and
in English, too!

I knew that many of these books were valuable. Among them I
found letters to my grandfather from dealers in London and Paris
telling of their search for certain books which they would forward
to him as soon as possible. Some enclosed accounts that amazed
me. It was easy to see where a large part of his money had gone.
With the help of Mr. Percy Robinson, the headmaster of St.
Andrew's College, the most interesting were selected. From the
thirty cases, four large ones were filled. The remainder I sent to a
Catholic college in the West. The fate of the chosen ones can be
all too briefly told. They were put into store and, seven years

later, when I again brought them to light (being on a visit to Canada from England, where I was then living), intending at last to give them a proper setting in my library, they (all four cases) were stolen by the removal men. I had made the mistake of leaving the closing of the cases to the men. The worst was that I did not discover the theft for several weeks, when it was too late to do anything about it, especially as I was at that time setting out for London, where the production of my play *Whiteoaks* demanded my presence. So ended my last link with the grandfather whose very name had always held a fascination for me — never the warm, glowing affection I had felt toward my maternal grandfather, but still a provocative and stimulating influence.

My novel *Delight* was published simultaneously in London, Toronto and New York. Its reception was more varied than that of any other book of mine. To say that it was disliked by some Canadian reviewers is to put it mildly. One Toronto critic in particular was so violent that his review was almost a classic in abuse. I wish I had it by me that I might quote from it, but I sent it to a friend in London who did not return it. His comment was: "Reading this review I feel like an old lady who, having spent all her life in a cathedral town, is suddenly brought face to face with life in the raw."

The reception of *Delight* abroad was unanimously good.

The reviews of *Possession* and *Delight* meant a great deal to me. At that time reviews had the power to depress me or to give me confidence. They helped to bring out the mettle in me — to give me heart of grace in the writing of my next novel.

Chapter 12

Jalna

WITH my nature, easily downcast, but healthily resilient, the mixed reception of *Delight* kept my mind for a time in a state of turmoil. Alternately wounded and praised, I varied between a desire to hide myself in a distant place, never to write another line, and a proud resolve to go ahead regardless of abuse and write the novels that I knew lay waiting in my fancy. Through all these ups and downs Hugh Eayrs was my steadfast friend. To every situation he brought his swift invention, his wit, his magnetic charm and affectionate encouragement.

The truth was that I had, the previous summer (before the publication of *Delight*), begun a new novel. Two of the characters in this had been half formed some years earlier and were to have been characters in a play that never was written. They had no names, but later they were to emerge as Meg and Renny Whiteoak in the novel *Jalna*.

Jalna was inspired by the traditions of that part of southern Ontario on the fringe of which we had built Trail Cottage. The descendants of the retired military and naval officers who had settled there stoutly clung to British traditions. No house in particular was pictured; no family portrayed. From the very first the characters created themselves. They leaped from my imagination and from memories of my own family. The grandmother, Adeline Whiteoak, refused to remain a minor character but arrogantly, supported on either side by a son, marched to the centre of the stage.

The name Jalna was suggested to me in this way: a member of the civil service, in the same department as Caroline, had spent many years in India. When she told him that I was in search of names of military stations there, he sent me a list of quite a number. I pored over them and chose Jalna because it was the shortest, it was easy to remember and looked well in print. When I wrote it at the top of my first page of manuscript, it never entered my head that one day it would become well known to quite a number of people.

That summer I lived with the Whiteoaks, completely absorbed by them. In fancy I opened the door of Jalna, passed inside, listened to what was going on. Except for Bunty I was isolated in my woodland till Caroline's return in the evening. As the chapters were finished she read them aloud.

The months passed.

In the fall of the year we removed to still another flat, for we could not face a second winter of such discomfort as the last. Now we had found a place really to our liking — convenient to Queen's Park and Caroline's work, in a street which then was quiet. It was in the house of Gertrude Pringle, whose father, the Chevalier Enoch Thompson, was once Canada's representative in Spain, and a brother of Ernest Seton-Thompson, writer of animal stories. We (I should say Caroline) made a very attractive apartment for us. Our favourite pieces of furniture and rugs were arranged to the best advantage. The *Three Graces* in marble, so cherished by my mother, had a cabinet to themselves. Above the mantelpiece the portrait of Great-grandmother, dark-eyed, smiling and young. The chimney drew well and we and our friends sat in front of many a good fire. The hearth rug was Bunty's.

Gertrude Pringle was always charming to us. Once only during our stay in her house did she criticize me and that was the question of my good taste in the use of a certain word. She had been reading my novel *Delight*. "I greatly enjoyed it," she said, "but I was surprised and rather shocked when, in speaking of a teapot, you used that word in describing its shape."

"What word?" I asked anxiously.

"It was" — and she lowered her voice — "the word *belly*."

Mrs. Pringle has since written a book on etiquette so excellent that I see no reason why any other should ever be written.

Besides ourselves there were two other people who rented rooms in the house. These were a stalwart man whose name I never knew and a little Englishwoman, Miss Turner. This man was of a very retiring nature, possibly his defence in a household of women. My glimpses of him were in early morning when I took Bunty down to the yard. Then, from the stairway, I would see him through the transom above his door, kneeling at prayer. One glimpse I had, then went on down the stairs, feeling more serene because a business man was occupied with things spiritual early in the morning.

Miss Turner was as friendly as he was reticent. She had come out from England to care for her brother's children, left motherless in Saskatchewan. When they were reared, she set about the precarious task of making a new life for herself. How was she, with no training, to earn a living?

She invested in an enormous Newfoundland loom and learned to weave. She had artistic talent. The scarves, the curtains, the dress materials that came from her loom were a pleasure to the eye, as well as being wonderfully durable. As an accompaniment to my writing the steady hum of her loom came from the room above.

Ringing the Changes

Never insistently loud, not starting and stopping, but humming on and on. She had a beautiful young tortoise-shell cat that used to sit on the loom watching Miss Turner out of amused amber eyes. This little cat had a savage, untamed streak in her. She had as lief scratch you as look at you. She was a dainty feeder and usually left a part of her meal in the dish. Bunty, listening in our living-room below, would be conscious that the dish was not being propelled across the floor and, with an indescribably furtive air, would creep up the stairs to finish the fish.

Some years later Miss Turner moved to the country, where she lived in a very small cottage and kept several cats. Never would she turn away a stray and, though she might deny herself, the cats never went without their tinned salmon. One of the best short stories I have written was about Miss Turner and her cats. It is "Electric Storm." It is rather odd that I, a dog lover, and merely tolerant of cats, should find them so fascinating to write of. Surely I have written no better short story than "The Ninth Life," which has found its way into a number of anthologies, the latest a collection by Pamela and James Mason.

I must not leave Miss Turner without telling of her end. Things were difficult for her. During the war people did not buy very much hand-weaving. She added to her income by giving painting lessons to young people at twenty-five cents a lesson. Her father had been an artist in Yorkshire. And still the cats had their salmon! One spring day she went alone to paint in an orchard and there she was found, dying, in front of her easel, with all the flowering trees about her, her thick white hair on the new grass, her beautiful blue eyes unseeing. One of the nephews she had brought up came from western Ontario to bury her. With true devotion he collected all her cats and took them back with him to his home.

At the time when I was writing *Jalna* there were a number of lit-

erary clubs active in Toronto. There were the Men's and Women's
Press Clubs, the Writers' Club, the Canadian Authors' Association,
the P. E. N. Club. The Authors' Association was by far the most
active of these, its flame fanned by the enthusiasm and selflessness
of William Arthur Deacon. The P. E. N. Club, a much more elegant but less virile affair, was evoked by Professor Pelham Edgar
but, for some reason, did not long flourish. Its chief ornament was
Professor George Wrong, Canada's greatest historian. There were
stirrings in the hearts of those who would have liked to produce a
new magazine devoted to the arts. Raymond Knister, Morley Cal-
laghan and I decided that we three would found such a one. Others
had failed but we would succeed. However, we were promptly dis-
couraged by Hugh Eayrs. "Not one of you," he declared, "knows
the first thing about publishing a magazine. You have no capital.
You are bound to fail." And so we gave up the idea.

In time *Jalna* was finished and the typed manuscript sent to
Macmillan of New York. Hugh Eayrs had already expressed great
hopes for it. The New York house agreed and were to publish it in
a few months. Preparations were on the way. Then, in a chance
copy of the *Atlantic Monthly* I came upon the notice of a competition the editors were holding for "the most interesting novel" by any
author from any part of the world. The prize was large. Very much
I should have liked to enter *Jalna* in this competition, but there it
was — bound by contract to the New York Macmillan!

The more I thought of it, the more I wanted to enter that competition. "I don't see how you possibly can," said Caroline.

Neither could I see how I could, but still I mused on the possibility.

Then brightly came the thought that as my chances of winning
were slight, it would do no harm to anyone and would be a satisfaction to me just to send *Jalna* to the *Atlantic* and discover if it

made any impression. I could not resist the temptation. The bulky manuscript (a carbon copy) was posted and when Caroline returned that evening, I confessed what I had done.

"Now," she said, "you may be in for trouble."

Weeks passed and more weeks.

Between the *Atlantic* on the one hand and New York Macmillan on the other I began to get really nervous. Then came a letter from Harold Latham, fiction editor of Macmillan, setting the time of publication and speaking of proofs to be corrected. This sort of double life could not go on. I decided that I must retrieve my manuscript from the competition. How terrible it would be, I thought, if I should win the competition during the full tide of preparation for publication by Macmillan. Why, I might end in prison!

I wrote to the editors of the *Atlantic* asking them to return *Jalna* to me, as I had a publisher for it. They replied that my manuscript was being held, with two others, for further consideration. I should hear from them soon.

A flood of excitement shook me, but I was not submerged. I had promised myself that I would be henceforth honourable and aboveboard with publishers, and so must I be. I wrote to Mr. Latham telling him that I had entered a second copy of *Jalna* in the *Atlantic* competition. I asked him if, in the event of my winning, Macmillan would release me from my contract with them. He replied (I suppose that in his wildest imaginings he did not consider this a possibility) that they would release me. There was kindness indeed. I settled down to wait.

Oh, the cruel suspense of that waiting! Each morning after breakfast I perched on the window seat to watch for the postman. Each morning I flew down the stairs to get the mail. There was nothing from the *Atlantic*. I made up my mind that one of the other manuscripts had been chosen. *Jalna* had been thrust aside and forgotten. . . . Again I wrote demanding the return of the manuscript. "How I wish you never had gone into that dreadful competition," exclaimed Caroline. "You grow paler every day. It is killing you."

Next a telegram came from the *Atlantic*. It was signed T. Fitzpatrick and was to this effect: "Have patience. Happy news awaits you."

But it was difficult to have patience. If I had won — why, in God's name, why did they not tell me so? As days passed I sank into one of my darkest moods — I was the victim, I told myself, of some ghastly joke. I did not reply to that telegram. Then came a long-distance call from Boston. The voice at that end was the voice of T. Fitzpatrick — not the voice of a man — not the voice of Thomas or Terence — but the voice of Theresa, secretary to Ellery Sedgwick, editor of the *Atlantic*. She was charming but still told me nothing definite. She counselled patience.

It turned out that Mr. Sedgwick was ill in bed at the time — and wanted no one but himself to give me the good news. He and I had had some very friendly correspondence — confidential on my part, warmly sympathetic on his. He had remarked of me to a visitor from Toronto, "She has a far better friend in me than she guesses."

It was he then who wrote to me of the judges' final decision.

When Caroline came home from the office, I told her that *Jalna* had won the *Atlantic* competition, but she was past rejoicing. Too long had she suffered suspense. She simply said, "Oh," and sat down and looked at me. The fount of our enthusiasm had dried. We sat silent, unable to rejoice.

After a little I said, "It is a large prize I have won."

"Yes, it is large," she agreed.

"Now we can travel."

"We can never leave Bunty," Caroline objected.

Bunty, hearing her name, rose and came to me. She placed her forepaws on my knee and, raising her face to mine, gave a gruff, protesting little bark, as though to say, "I will go anywhere you go."

What emotion we felt was dammed within us, for the editors had begged me to preserve complete silence on the subject of my triumph till they had sent proper notice to the press. It was not easy to mingle with one's friends — to appear nonchalant when they asked me if I had had any news of the competition, to look subdued when they implied that I had better give up hoping.

The *Atlantic* was to publish *Jalna* in collaboration with Little, Brown of Boston, and in Canada by the firm with which they were affiliated, of whom a Mr. Gundy was head.

Nothing appeared impossible to Hugh Eayrs. Nothing really surprised him. When I told him that I had entered the *Atlantic Monthly* competition, he at once considered the probability of my winning. He wrote to Mr. Gundy (word of mouth would not suffice) and asked him if, in the event of my being successful, he would agree to the book's being published in Canada by Macmillan. Mr. Gundy cheerfully agreed, in writing. Therefore, when the newspaper headlines filled those in his office with joy, he could only ruefully admit that he had promised the rights of *Jalna* to a rival house.

In the period of waiting, the ten days or so of secrecy, Caroline and I decided it would be easier for us if we were out of town. Removed from all that was familiar, we could rest, collect ourselves, prepare for the ordeal of publicity to come. Always have I hated publicity, and if all those "in the news" were as unco-operative as I, the newspapers would require fewer pages.

We went to a small guest house in Niagara Falls, Bunty of course accompanying us. Never had I known Bunty to like less any situation in which she found herself. She was restless. She was demanding. When we left her in our bedroom while we went to meals, she yelped, as though in acute suffering. When we brought her down to the dining-room, she sat up and begged with insistent barking or tried to climb into our laps. But her barking was as nothing to my barking. Somehow, perhaps because I was tired, I had contracted a very bad cold. I coughed and I coughed. Scarcely a meal passed that I was not obliged to leave the table and go upstairs to cough.

I lay on the bed coughing. When a questionnaire came from Little, Brown for use in publicity, I felt too ill to answer the questions. Caroline filled in the form as best she could, with only a few mistakes. Two days before the date when a notice was to be given to the press we returned to town. At two o'clock in the morning we were woken by the telephone. It was a call from a newspaper office to ask whether it were true that I had won the *Atlantic Monthly* prize. The secret had somehow leaked out.

There followed exciting times for us. Our first lack of emotion when we heard the news was followed by a period of sheer excitement that was at once delightful, stimulating and exhausting. Though the press was less demanding than it is to-day, still newspaper reporters crowded into our living-room; there were interviews and articles. Telegrams, flowers, letters of congratulation deluged us. The warmth, the feeling of goodwill toward me, was, as I remember, universal. Even critics who had not been very kind to my books joined in the praise. The general feeling seemed to be that of rejoicing that a Canadian (not this Canadian in particular) had achieved distinction in the United States, a country which heretofore could scarcely have shown less interest in Canadian letters. Thomas Raddall, that fine Nova Scotian novelist, has written to me: "You cannot imagine what your winning of the *Atlantic*

217

Monthly prize meant to us other Canadian writers. It was as though you opened a door that had been inexorably shut against us."

The *Canadian Forum*, in an editorial, said: *"Jalna* opened the eyes of Canadians to the fact that Mazo de la Roche possesses distinctive qualities as a writer. Now they are applauding her, not because her earlier books possess subtle merits, but because the Boston literati have decided that *Jalna* is worth $10,000. Mazo de la Roche was writing just as well a year ago as now, but only now are her countrymen commencing to realize that she has style. . . . Her case might be pressed upon the attention of the log-rolling fraternity who prefer self-advertisement in public places to concentration in the privacy of their attics."

A really splendid dinner was given for me by combined literary societies. Speeches by the Lieutenant-Governor and other dignitaries — a handsome silver tea service presented to me by the City of Toronto — I making a small, rather tremulous speech of thanks, and wearing a French evening gown, long-waisted, short-skirted in the extraordinary fashion of the day. This dinner was held in the Queen's Hotel, a house of dignity and fine traditions, quite unlike the seething anthills of business conventions and heartless high-pressure traffic which the hotels of to-day have become.

The Arts and Letters Club were to give a dinner for me. It was, I believe, the only time in the history of the club when they gave a dinner for a woman. For this occasion there came from Boston the assistant editor of the *Atlantic Monthly*, Edward Weeks.

He came dashing up the stairs to our apartment, long-legged, thin, with large blue eyes and a friendly smile. We met — with rather guarded appraisal on my side — with beaming benignity on his. It was the beginning of a lasting, a rewarding friendship.

Delightfully he spoke after the Arts and Letters dinner. Hugh

Eayrs read an extract from the yet unpublished *Jalna*. It was the "Death of the Foal" and he read it feelingly. He had a beautiful speaking voice and this particular scene was his favourite in the book.

I remember that above the tables in the banquet hall there hung a life-size cut-out drawing of Bunty by an artist member of the club. After the dinner it was given to me and I cherished it for years. More than the baskets of flowers, almost more than the silver tea service, I valued it. Coming upon it in some dim cupboard, I could see again that gay company, feel the surge of wonder, of exhilaration that then enveloped me.

In these pressing and almost breathless days was our play forgotten? Were our people cast aside? Never. Returning to our flat after a reception — my throat almost too tired for speech — we would turn to the pleasure, the relaxation, of our make-believe world, so much more satisfying than the material world. Our thoughts would turn from overcrowded rooms to a quiet house by the sea, or possibly a ship in mid-ocean, where two of our, by now, very large "cast" were absorbed in the most fascinating problems. Our last words before sleep overtook us would be, not a bit of amusing gossip we had heard that day, not speculation on what our future might be, but words spoken from the mouths of actors in our play.

It was in that spring Uncle François, the last of my father's family, died. In the midst of so much which was exciting and exhausting I was anxiously trying to arrange his affairs for him before he left to visit his relations-in-law in the United States. He was a sick man, his nervous system wrecked, so his doctor told me, by terrible years of strain with his morbid and exacting wife. He had suffered an overpowering breakdown. He had been a man of fine physique, a barrister, well thought of in his profession, who should have been successful, but life had defeated him. I remembered hearing how when the time of his marriage approached he had shown great reluctance to prepare for it. His elder brother Danford had been horrified to discover that, at the last moment, the prospective bridegroom had neither proper shoes nor gloves, had not even bought the wedding-ring. The brothers went together to buy these things, and so the reluctant bridegroom set out, prepared for his grievous destiny.

It was a delight to settle down in Trail Cottage, with the woodland fluttering in new green leaves, the flowers of May drawing strength from the virgin soil — a delight to walk to the farmhouse for milk, to gather watercress from the stream, to drink tea beneath the graceful white birches. But we were not to spend the summer there. We had taken a house in Rockport on the Massachusetts coast and to it we journeyed, with much anxiety on Bunty's account, for we had to change trains at Boston. With us went Mrs. Hugh Eayrs and her Airedale terrier Danny, and a singularly plump and good-natured maid.

To live by the sea was a new experience for us. The house was in true New England style, furnished with authentic colonial pieces, a spinning wheel, old blue china, "rag" carpets and an attic with a steep sloping roof, remote from any sound but the movements of the tides. It was in this attic, the window overlooking the harbour, that I wrote the first chapters of *Whiteoaks,* a sequel to *Jalna.* I sat in my attic revelling in the fishy smell left by the receding tide and renewed my intimacy with the Whiteoaks.

Almost every day we had a picnic lunch on the shore and bathed in the cold, clear water. After all the publicity, this was a free, a devil-may-care existence. Slacks for women were becoming fashionable and we each bought a pair in Gloucester. They were rather warm and woolly, but we delighted in them. When we went in bathing, we left the lunch basket to be guarded by Bunty. Small, full of importance, she sat close beside it. People smiled, observing her air of consequence, little guessing that she could not see. She would have starved rather than touch her tuna fish sandwich which she knew was inside the basket. She flew in a fury at any dog that came near our belongings.

One day I swam almost a dozen strokes. I was triumphant. I stood up and shouted, "I swam! I swam!"

"If you can do it, I can," said Caroline, and she too swam.

We enjoyed lovely weather on that coast and when our holiday was over, refreshed and with a healthy coat of tan, we went to Boston. But in the excitement I forgot my manuscript, left in the attic. Weeks later it was sent to me to Canada. I had not yet missed it! In Boston I met Alfred McIntyre, president of Little, Brown, who published *Jalna* in affiliation with the Atlantic Monthly Press. Alfred McIntyre was so much more than a good business man. There was no free and easy geniality about him. His friendship was not lightly won, but when it once was given, how loyal, how truly valuable it was! During that visit to Boston he and his lovely wife became friends indeed. The McIntyres and the Weekses gave delightful dinner parties for us. Fritzie Weeks was a tactful and easy hostess who made one feel at home in her house. There I recall an interesting evening when Robert Frost, the poet, was a guest. We also went to Cambridge to lunch with Basil King, the novelist. I spoke at several luncheon clubs. But literary gatherings and famous people have never, in themselves, had the power to hold my interest. With a sense of almost voluptuous relief I escape from them.

From Boston we went to New York. Aunt Eva was very happy over my success. She had first discovered it at her breakfast table in the *New York Times*. To sit down to breakfast, casually to glance over the headlines, to see her niece's name there was enough to make her jump up from the table and dance about the room. As for Pierre, he was deeply happy for me. But the space already between us had somehow widened. When by chance we were for a few moments alone together, we found little to say. In these moments there was an unhappy silence, excepting when he talked of his work in engineering. More and more was he immersed in that work. He came home at night tired out. His beautiful colouring had faded a little. His complexion was now more of a pale olive. In his manner he was quieter. He seemed less French — more American. Neither he nor Aunt Eva had the gift of making new friends. They lived isolated in that great city. Their house was large, she delighted in buying new things for it, but almost no one came into it. She bought expensive clothes but wore them only when she went out with him, to a restaurant or a play. Both took a genuine pleasure in the lively comings and goings of Caroline and me, for we had many invitations.

What had Pierre become? No longer an arrogant critical Frenchman. A patient American husband listening by the hour to his wife's prattle, with his own thoughts far, far away? I did not know. I did not ask myself. My mind was too occupied by my own fascinating doings. He would turn on the radio and sit quietly listening to the music of Beethoven or Schubert while Aunt Eva talked on and on. By an effort of will he seemed to detach himself from the sound of her voice, to listen, unperturbed by it, to the music he loved.

Chapter 13

Whiteoaks

Our visit over, we returned to Trail Cottage. I felt an almost pagan joy in the reunion with our trees. In the interval they seemed to have grown, their boughs stretched out to touch the cottage, to shield us from the world outside. Our health was greatly improved. The weather was October and every morning the gardener made a fresh bonfire of brushwood and dead leaves. The air was full of the acrid smell of wood smoke. Bushes were heavy with sweet overripe blackberries. A few birds had forgotten to leave us and sang dreamily in the reddening trees. Bunty spent these days in a state of bliss.

When the leaves fell from the trees and the flowers froze, we were forced to return to our flat in town. We settled down comfortably enough, with fires burning in our living-room and the hum of Miss Turner's loom coming from overhead. I intended to do some good work on my new novel, *Whiteoaks*, but I had weakly promised to speak to quite a number of clubs, both in Toronto and in other cities. I am sure there are many writers who could have undertaken these engagements without undue fatigue, but public speaking took, and still takes, an oppressive toll of my nervous vitality. For days before a speech I am in a state of gloom. As the time approaches when I must rise to my feet, my heart begins to beat with painful rapidity. The strange thing is that, once on my feet, my nerves become steady and I enjoy speaking.

My work on the new novel was interrupted not only by the making of speeches but by the demands of society. There were a great many parties, late hours in smoke-filled rooms. But no matter how I had spent the evening before, no matter how tired I was, the next morning found me, writing-board on knee, zestful for the further doings of the family at Jalna.

Our Christmas that year, which should have been merry indeed, was the reverse. One evening, some weeks before the holiday, Bunty had a violent seizure. She fell from the sofa to the floor, then, as though demented, she tried to climb up the wall. On the seashore the summer before she had picked up something that had poisoned her. She would have died but for the skill of a veterinarian from Gloucester. "In three days," he had said, "there is going to be either a funeral or a rejoicing here." It was a rejoicing we had, but the time came when we almost wished it had been the funeral, and that she had not lived for this suffering.

After several weeks at the vet's she came home to us, supposedly cured, but she was only a shadow of the sturdy little dog she had been. So thin she was she seemed to float as she walked. A continual excitement burned in her brain. And so — the day after Christmas — she died. We took her body to Trail Cottage and John Bird dug a grave for her beneath the snow, under the trees where she had hunted, sniffed the scents she relished. We set a little stone there in her memory and for it I borrowed a line from Byron's epitaph for Boatswain: "Virtue of man, without his vices." The bodies of two other dogs lie there, a Scotty and an Irish terrier which belonged to a friend, Madge Parkhill. Twice attempts have been made to steal this little stone, and it seems to me it is a mean person indeed who would do such a thing.

That winter was a disappointing one. I had expected to do much work on my new novel, *Whiteoaks*. Instead I spent six weeks or more in acute suffering from pain in the head. I had an engagement to speak in Montreal when the attack came on. Crawling, insidious pains moved with dreadful regularity over my temples, down the back of my neck. To write a postcard was beyond me. I lived and had my being in pain. I consulted Dr. Murray and told him of the coming engagement in Montreal. "Overstrain," he said, and comforted me. "We'll soon have you able to go to Montreal," he said, and told me to rest and drink a glass of Scotch and hot water each night before going to bed.

But I could not rest. The drink of Scotch seemed to aggravate rather than help the misery I endured. The visit to Montreal was cancelled. Again I consulted Dr. Murray. Now he looked serious. "You must go to the hospital," he said, "for electrical treatments." He made the appointment for me. I went — rattling along on the tram, every metallic vibration stirring up the rage in the nerves of my head. The hospital seemed almost peaceful after the tram. I lay on a cot in a small cubicle. The nurse began the treatment. After a little the doctor in attendance came in and with him Dr. Murray. They were very kind and looked down at me rather as though I were a sick child.

"Are you sure this is not neuritis?" the hospital doctor asked doubtfully.

"Positive," returned Dr. Murray.

Several times I went there for electrical treatments. I cannot remember how many. Pain dulled my memory. But I do remember that after each treatment I was worse. I could not be still but walked in the streets, looking into other people's faces — wondering what it would be like to be free of pain. I felt myself to be almost an outcast from the normal world. A pain in the head is like no other pain — it cannot be ignored, no matter how great the victim's courage. The days seemed endless.

One morning at the hospital the nurse said to me, "I am sure these treatments are bad for you. Do you find yourself in more pain all the time?"

I said I did.

"Then," she said earnestly, "don't come any more. I'm sure I'm right. But please do not tell them I said so."

So that was the end of the treatments.

But now Caroline left the civil service. The extraordinarily good sales of *Jalna* had given us the longed-for independence. Caroline was liked and admired in her department of the service and when she left, they presented her with a quite lovely wrist watch.

Her being at home with me did me good. She read to me. Gently she massaged my temples and neck. The attack lessened. By slow degrees it passed. But the demands on me did not lessen. Invitations, requests to speak, letters, letters. Ambitious writers sent me bundles of manuscript to read and criticize. Sometimes they themselves brought their manuscripts and did not know when to leave. Interviewers came from newspapers. It was a marvel that my head continued to improve.

We made up our minds that there was nothing for it but to go away somewhere and hide. If *Jalna* had given us independence, just as certainly it had, for the time being, stolen our privacy. Above all things we longed to relax, to be unknown. We chose a small guest house in the Niagara peninsula. The thousands of peach trees were showing their first shy buds, but there were wild flowers in every sheltered spot, the lovely trilliums, the bloodroot and hepatica. What a refuge it seemed — with breakfast in bed and the dozen other guests neither speaking to us nor we to them.

I remember Caroline's digging the roots of a number of wild flowers to plant at Trail Cottage and at last, much refreshed, we took train for Oakville. It was toward midnight when the train arrived and we were obliged to take a taxi from there. Those who know Oakville as it is today can have little idea of the great charm of the village it then was. While we waited for the taxi the only sound to break the stillness of the night was the croaking of frogs from a swampy spot near the station. The frogs had been silenced by the coming of the train, but when it moved into the darkness, they threw themselves with fresh ardour into their serenade of spring.

The taxi came and into it were stowed our travelling bags and the heavy basket of wild-flower roots. Unfortunately the driver had no idea of how to find Trail Cottage. Neither could we clearly direct him. One side road after another we tried before we turned, after long search, into our little sandy road that ran down into a ravine, climbed up the other side and found itself on the old Indian trail. I think the driver was as thankful as we to discover the cottage. He carried everything indoors for us. We paid him and heard his car bumping over the sandy path toward the road. We heard the hoot of an owl as it flitted among the trees. The moon came from behind a cloud and it was no longer dark. Moonlight flickered on the boles of the birches making them white as marble. Here was heavenly privacy. Now I should be able to write, to finish my novel *Whiteoaks*. We lay down thankfully on our two cot beds and quickly fell asleep.

Refreshed and hungry in the morning, we found that there was nothing for breakfast but one orange and coffee. So we divided the orange and stayed our hunger with clear coffee, till we walked through the wood for supplies. Grass had covered Bunty's grave and close beside it a meadow lark had built her nest, there on the ground, her eggs exposed to the mercy of any who discovered them. Every morning I went to see if they were safe. One morning the nest was empty. Snake or squirrel or other vandal had taken them.

While staying at the guest house, I had, when walking on a country road, discovered something I very much wanted. This was a wayside booth or stall. There was a sign on it FOR SALE. What a delightful little workroom I could make of it, I thought, if it were set down in our woodland. In it I might achieve the very zenith of privacy, outside a desert island. To be sure, Trail Cottage was very small. It was in a wood, but it was not small enough. A path led to the door. At the moment the great longing of my life was for seclusion. If I could achieve that, I could write. . . .

One day a large truck made its bumbling way along the quiet road to our bit of woodland. On the truck loomed the booth and three men were there to put it in place. Several small trees must be felled and I sorrowed to see them go, but after much heaving and grunting there stood my retreat, looking somehow less inviting than I had pictured it. Still I was enthusiastic. I had shelves made for books. I tacked a few pictures to the walls. I laid a strip of matting on the floor. A small table and a wicker chair completed it. The final touch was a root of Virginia creeper planted at the front, and this I expected would soon grow into a luxuriant vine covering my retreat with rich foliage. But the trees kept the sunshine away and, struggle as it would, the creeper grew no more than a foot high.

On a June morning I installed myself, with the few chapters of *Whiteoaks* already written. There was clean manuscript paper. There was a new pencil. There was my father's penknife for sharpening it. There was my grandfather's Johnson's *Dictionary*.

There was seclusion. All I had to do was to put pencil to paper — to write!

Only a writer who has suffered an attack of nerves, such as I had passed through, can quite understand the effort of beginning, the tremendous eagerness to put down the first words, the fear of defeat, of breakdown.

I knew what I wanted to write. The words were at my hand. But could I write them?

One line I wrote. Then a strange rigidity struck my nerves. The pencil would not move. I could not budge it. Helpless I stared at the paper. One line! One line of ten words. And I could not — not to save my life — write another.

It might have been expected that I should have been depressed. Not so. I had written — after those long months. I had written! And though it was just one line, it was a beginning. I could scarcely bear to wait till tomorrow when I might write again. All the rest of the day my spirit sang. I walked on air, counting the tardy hours.

The following day I wrote another line. The day after that I wrote six lines. The next day, half a page. In a week I had written a page. I was in full swing!

These Whiteoaks, of whom I had written in *Jalna*, now came to be on a different footing with me. I had found them an interesting, a colourful family. Their doings had fascinated me. Now they possessed me. I was one with Finch, for he and I had much in common. I was (at times) one with Renny, for he and I had much in common. At other times I was against him. Never have I been completely at one with any female characters of mine. I might love them, suffer with them, but always they were they and I was I. The closest to me were the two Adelines.

A spell of extraordinarily hot weather set in. The "Folly," as

Caroline had named my retreat, turned out to be a place of suffo-
cating heat. With half its front open to the woods there was no
way of keeping out the mosquitoes. Half-naked I sat writing in it.
Then back along the narrow path my own feet had made, to the
cottage for a cold drink from our well. The water from this well
was pure and of good flavour. That is, it was usually so. But, as
the weather grew hotter, a new and peculiar flavour invaded it.
We tried to ignore this. We said that, owing to the heat, the water
was low in the well, that it was flavoured by its own walls. We
put ice in it. We made lemonade of it. Then one night we both
were very sick. We sent for John Bird and he removed the pump
and set about investigating the well. Then — "Come and see!" he
shouted. "Come and see what you've been drinking off!" He held
up, on the prongs of his rake, the decomposed body of a yard-long
snake. . . . Then we felt sick indeed. I came to the conclusion
that people are not so easily poisoned as one would think.

On a particularly hot day, when I had just returned from writing in the "Folly," Caroline said to me, "You are getting along so
slowly in writing this book, I am wondering if it would be possible
for you to dictate a little of it every morning to me. Even if it were
only half a page, it would be something to help you till your
nerves are quite well again."

That morning I was particularly conscious of the little I could
write, when my imagination was teeming with things to put on
paper. After the heat of the "Folly" the cottage felt comparatively
cool. I laid a sheet of manuscript paper in front of Caroline. She
drew a chair to the table. I sat close beside her and waited for the
words to come. They came, with hesitancy at the first, then as
fast as she could write.

A closely written page was done.

Caroline was the only one to whom I could have dictated. Not only did this working together help me to accomplish much more, but it gave me confidence in myself. No longer did I think — "How much shall I be able to write to-day? Shall I suffer for it?" No — I wrote what I could, then hastened to where Caroline was waiting, eager to put on paper what was in my mind. I should perhaps write two pages, while she would write three or four. And so the novel *Whiteoaks* moved toward its finish. We stayed late that year at Trail Cottage. The leaves turned from green to the gay colours of fall and still we stayed on.

The "Folly" had been given to John Bird as a place for storing his gardening tools. I admitted that, as a workroom, it was a failure. But now, in the stillness of our woodland, we were enamoured of life, of the drifting mysterious atmosphere of the autumn, the cold frosty nights, the golden days. At last, in early October, the novel was finished. I was triumphant that it was finished with no nervous relapse on my part.

The American magazine *Cosmopolitan* had paid me two thousand dollars for an option on *Whiteoaks* for publishing as a serial. Therefore, as soon as I had got it typed, I sent the manuscript to the editor, Ray Long. He read it at once and then from New York there came to Trail Cottage an intelligent assistant to the editor. They would, I was told, accept the novel for serialization if I would write a new ending. She spent the day with us, enjoying, as she said, the peace and quiet. But there was no peace or quiet in my mind. I was at the end of long and arduous work. I had endured considerable physical and mental suffering to accomplish it. As always, I longed to be told what to do.

Caroline looked me firmly in the eyes. "You are not to attempt it," she said. "It would ruin the story. It would be madness."

"But it would change the ending only for the magazine," I insisted, wishing really to rouse her. "It would not affect the book."

"It will affect you," she declared. "I won't see you ruin your health."

"But twenty-five thousand dollars . . ."

"What is twenty-five thousand dollars?" she demanded scornfully in a rags-to-riches tone. "I won't let you do it."

We decided that I should promise to write to the editor when I had had time to consider the proposal. This I did and *Whiteoaks* was serialized instead in the *Atlantic Monthly*.

Now Indian summer was past. We felt that a chapter in our lives was closed. A new world was opening up. We thought we should like to take a trip right round it. Before coming to Trail Cottage that year we had given up our apartment and stored our furniture. Now we were to close the cottage for perhaps a long while. Suddenly it looked very small and rather forlorn. On our last morning I stood contemplating it, how it had suddenly appeared in that woodland, a mushroom growth, unbeautiful, but our creation, our very own, how we had planned, striven, for every improvement, how when accomplished we had exulted. From its chimney had curled the smoke from sweet birch logs. Its roof had protected us from the heaviest storms. Never had it leaked. Now all about it were the flowering shrubs we had planted, and beneath a young pine was Bunty's grave. I stood looking down at it. I kept my morbid fancy from what now lay there and made myself remember what she had been in life, what her sturdy companionship had meant to us. Surely there is to each of us one human being loved above all others, one house, one horse, one dog. Never could another dog be what Bunty had been. She had sat close beside me when I put my imaginings to paper, patient with me yet so thankful when I laid down the pencil and stretched and was ready for a walk. Then she too would stretch, wave her tail and utter her gruff little bark of approval. She had been close beside me when I was in agony of spirit. She would press closer still, as though she sought, with all the power in her, to understand and to make me conscious of her understanding.

She had possessed the most expressive, the most luminous eyes I ever saw in a dog's head. Too large, breeders said, for a Scotch terrier, but just right they were for her. It was hard to see their beauty veiled by the film that began to cover them when she was but five years old. By the end of that year she was totally blind. That was many years ago, but how poignant to me is the recollection of the moment when I discovered that this was so. My mother had died only a few days before. I was myself barely convalescent from the same illness. Bunty came to me, raised herself against my knee, as though to look into my face. I struck a match and held it in front of her eyes. She did not flinch but drew nearer to sniff. I realized that she was in impenetrable darkness.

How she overcame this handicap was amazing. Never had her spirits failed her. Always she was full of play and equally full of fight. She would tackle a dog three times her size and, after an imaginary victory, swagger away with waving tail, ready for what life brought to her.

Yesterday I met a man walking with a Yorkshire terrier on a lead. He told me it was quite blind. I could tell by its sad, uncertain movements that it was utterly without spirit. I remembered Bunty and her courage and I felt that we had accepted all she had been to us with too little appreciation. But we had loved her, and now, standing by her grave beneath a young pine, there were tears on my cheeks. I should like to quote here a few sentences from Arthur Bryant's lovely essay "A Dog That Chose":

> A dog's supreme charm to a man, I suppose, is that, sharing human life, he transcends it. He "outsoars the shadow of our night." The world may be breaking, war or invasion at hand, ruin staring one

in the face, one's life work broken, one's nearest and dearest faithless, but a dog's capacity for happiness, love and zest for living remains unchanged. . . . Unhappiness is an individual thing that passes with the individual; joy and life are eternal and the law of the universe. Whoever knows that has found a clue to existence. A dog — and this is perhaps his supreme service — can help a man to understand it. A philosopher has said that to have a dog is like having the Absolute come to one's table and feed from one's hand.

Chapter 14

Setting Sail

IT IS a risky thing to go to a place recommended by a friend. It is risky to recommend a place to a friend. How true it is that one man's meat is another man's poison. A friend had praised that house in Quebec where we now went for a holiday. He said we would be happy there. It was true that the French family were kind. They were indeed charming. But it was not a restful change. Never was there respite from noise. All day it was church bells, drowning for a time the noises of the cobbled street. At night, if there were not a wedding party, with the participants parading the street and singing, there was a fire. Never have I known firemen who dashed into the street with such a clanging of bells, such unrestrained zest, at the first tinkle of alarm. In the house the old mother said her prayers aloud at six in the morning at a little shrine outside her bedroom door. The grandson played the piano with the loud pedal always down. The bed was lumpy and the quilt like a particularly heavy carpet. There were long black hairs in the bath.

It was rest indeed when we escaped, after a week, to the quiet of the Château Frontenac. There we talked of and planned for our trip round the world. Brightly coloured brochures littered our bedroom. Nothing but a trip round the world would satisfy us. That was, until another friend persuaded us that this might be very disappointing. We might, he said, be bored almost to death. He had known people, he said, who had been so bored by the company in which they found themselves, that they would have chosen to sit forever on their own back porch rather than endure another trip round the world.

This friend was Pelham Edgar, professor of English at the University of Toronto, a man whose opinions could not be ignored. He was a distinguished-looking man. His cultivated manner, his voice left you in no doubt as to his attainments. Therefore, when he said, "You cannot possibly go on a trip round the world. The place for you is Italy," we at once gave up our cherished plan and procured coloured booklets about Italy, though I still had a hankering to see Japan, gay with cherry blossoms.

We were at this time comfortably settled in a pension owned by Mrs. Billings. It was in Bloor Street and has lately been demolished to make room for shops. I doubt if its like could be found in this city today, with an atmosphere of such personal warmth and kindness, and delicious meals. Mrs. Billings had inherited the place from her mother. She had inherited the cook, John, from her mother. She had inherited many of the guests from her mother. The guests seldom left Mrs. Billings. They just stayed comfortably on, till they died of old age. Not that the house was filled by decrepit people. Far from it. They were a hale and vigorous lot, entertaining their friends, eating largely of the tempting food, playing at bridge and mahjong. Later I wrote a dog story, "Peter — a Rock," with the scene at Mrs. Billings's.

Looking back on the two months we spent in that house, they appear pleasant indeed. We gave little dinner parties, we went out a great deal, we were free from care. We belonged to a dancing

club. We had many preparations for our trip abroad. It was pleasant to buy clothes without worry over their cost.

Before we set forth I made my will. Fancy my having something to will, who, by my writing, had earned such a precarious
livelihood! I remember feeling really important when I went to
the lawyer's office early one January morning. The grim buildings
were beautiful in a covering of hoar frost, but the hoar-laden air
was bad for the bronchial cough I had contracted. This cough I
took with me to New York, where I had a round of engagements.
I remember how I sat coughing in a house in Fifty-third Street
while an artist from the *Bookman* made a drawing of me. That
night we went under the Hudson to a theatre in Hoboken where an
old melodrama was being revived by Christopher Morley. We
reached our ship just as the gangway was about to be drawn in.
She was the *Vulcania* and this was her maiden voyage. She was
commanded by a Captain Cosulich. A luncheon had been given
for me on board by my publishers, where without preparation I had
had to make a short speech. Afterward I was photographed on
deck surrounded by sixteen men in the book business. I still have
the photograph, in which, wearing a great bunch of violets, I
look dreadfully like a movie star. That night, casting myself on
my berth completely exhausted, I burst into tears. I thought I
knew what movie stars felt when they took an overdose of sleeping
tablets and ended all publicity.

But I needed no sleeping tablets. I slept like a log, lulled by
the gentle rocking of the *Vulcania*. On her we made our first, our
most thrilling voyage. Surely the Mediterranean never appeared
more brilliantly beckoning than on the morning when we moved
past the coast of Spain. I was early on deck, sniffing the sweet
scents that came from the land. The islands of the Mediterranean
had cliffs of gold and amethyst. Surely Vesuvius never showed

with better effect or Naples appeared more entrancing. Six weeks we stayed there, I coughing more and more; then went on to Taormina. We stayed in a hotel kept by the widow of an English doctor, a Mrs. Dashwood. In the first twenty-four hours my cough left me. I lay sunbathing on the floor of our bedroom, a French window opening on a balcony draped in wisteria, and, lying there, dictated two short stories — "The Broken Fan," suggested by a strange couple on board the *Vulcania,* and "Quartette," a story of Americans in Naples. I was pleased indeed when the sale of these two stories paid the expenses of our voyage and stay abroad. About this same time I wrote a story called "Baby Girl" which Sir John Squire bought for the *London Mercury.* This was the beginning of a pleasant association with him.

We remained in Taormina till May. I think few could be less efficient as sightseers. People who spent a week in our hotel saw more of the island than ever we did. We ignored guidebooks, mosaics and ancient ruins. We were content to amble down the fishermen's path to the sea, to bathe, to climb the path to Mola, to walk on the Corso at twilight and watch the goats being milked. One saw few motor cars on the Corso in those days. We made friends with some of the residents; the most interesting were Percival Campbell and Miles Wood, who lived and still live in a lovely villa, full of treasures to delight the artist. On the roof was a theatre and many a play was in it professionally produced by Miles Wood, who not only is an actor but a painter of talent.

Back once more to Naples, then the voyage to England on an Orient liner. The Bay of Biscay was smooth as silk, though Caroline had done our packing the day before, in preparation for sea-sickness. She is a poor sailor but a happy voyager, who forgets past miseries the moment a new journey by sea is in prospect. Many voyages have we made since then but never a smoother or one in better company. In mid-May we passed Sardinia, Corsica and Elba. The harbour of Toulon was full of battleships and destroyers, magnificent, warlike in the crimson sunset, yet we thought of war as something of the troubled past. In the Bay of Biscay a service was held in memory of the wife of one of the passengers who had been drowned at that spot when a vessel was torpedoed during the war. We saw her husband drop a wreath of flowers overboard. What experiences we were having! What experience to sail up the Thames to Tilbury!

It was blazing hot — as hot as Canada. By the time we were settled in the private hotel in Portman Square we were very tired. But we were in London. In England, where we had longed to be since we were children. Where — in our play — we had spent many a happy time. We had piled up so many expectations of London, and there we were, in warm sunny weather, all its vastness about us. And there was Hugh Eayrs to enjoy it with us.

But it was not long before we had another plan and that was to take a house in Devon. I had seen one advertised in the morning paper. It was to be let for two months furnished. This advertisement was irresistible. A cottage on the edge of Dartmoor, we decided, was just what we wanted. There I should have quiet for writing the book I had in mind. Somehow, somewhere, the galley proofs for *Whiteoaks* had been corrected. Somehow, somewhere, five hundred fly-leafs for a special edition of the same book had been autographed. I cannot remember. But now our single occupation was the acquiring of the cottage. We wrote to the advertiser and Mrs. Acland, the wife of Captain Acland, the owner, came to see us. It was a case of mutual liking. She appeared to look on us as the right sort of tenants; so, without any tiresome formalities, everything was arranged for our occupancy. The maid was to remain, but it would be necessary for us to supply the linen. Hap-

239

pily Caroline set forth to buy sheets, pillow-cases and all the other necessaries. In June we arrived at the cottage. To us it did not look at all like a cottage but like a rather small stone house set in a lovely garden.

There was late-afternoon sunshine when we arrived. The cottage stood on a rise of ground and before us was spread the panorama of the moors, in the foreground the oddly shaped fields with their flowery hedges, then the moors rising darkly to the sunlit tor that was called High Willhays. We explored house and garden, sniffed the moss roses, could scarcely bear to tear ourselves away from the view, but there was the maid announcing dinner. She was a girl with a complexion the loveliest I ever had seen, and a sweet nature. There was just one thing she disliked and that was work. Work of all sorts but particularly work connected with the building of fires. Soon after our arrival a cool damp spell set in. The dining-room was the least comfortable room in the house, but when we suggested a fire should be laid, Susie told us that a pair of swallows had built their nest there and wouldn't it be a pity to smoke out the poor little creatures? Of course we agreed. From that time on we ate our meals in a depressing chill. No matter how warm the outdoors, the dining-room was always cold. We hoped, as weeks passed, that the eggs would be hatched, the fledglings fly away, but no —"I heard them cheeping only this morning up in the chimney," Susie would say. So we resigned ourselves to chill. Later the Aclands told us that no bird ever had built a nest in the chimney, that it was impossible.

Captain and Mrs. Acland were a delightful couple. Her two sisters and their husbands lived near-by and all became our friendly neighbours. Vice-Admiral and Adria Radcliffe indeed became close friends.

The Aclands owned a fox terrier named Ben. As they were

going some place where a dog could not be taken, they asked us if we would mind keeping Ben for them. He would be in his own home and they did hope he would not be a trouble. Ben settled down with us as though he had known us all his life.

Never have I seen a dog in such a hurry. If he looked out of the window and discovered a cat in the garden, he could not endure waiting to be let out, but while we opened the door he would fly at it in a rage of haste. He would bite the door, tear splinters off it, spitting them out as he pursued the cat.

We used to have tea in the garden under a rose-covered trellis, Ben sharing the bread and butter, and the delicious white fruit cake. Near the tea table was a fig tree and one day Ben, replete with bread and butter, did a curious thing. He sprang up and caught one of the smallest branches in his teeth. It lifted him from his feet. Again his weight pulled it down. Rebounding again and again, he continued till the branch broke. He managed then to get hold of another. Like a dancer infatuated by his own art and with a wild delight in his eyes, he never stopped till the lowest branches had beeen snapped off. I think he longed to demolish the fig tree, we being helpless with laughter. At each bound he would roll his eyes toward us — a comedian craving applause.

But soon we had to take tea in the walled kitchen garden among the onions and potatoes, for a small bird was teaching her young to fly on the lawn. Ben would have made short work of them.

He accompanied us on all our walks. In terror we would watch him put a large flock of sheep to rout. With him we were lost for one entire morning in water meadows and bog where lovely iris grew.

We had not long been settled when I began to write the

story of Bunty's life — *Portrait of a Dog.* I had felt myself to be wrapped round by Devon, a willing, happy prisoner. But, as I recalled those scenes in Canada, all else faded. That was the reality.

As to the physical strain of writing, I had not yet recovered the nervous stamina required for the day-after-day concentration. At times the pains in my head and neck were hard to bear. At times I suffered from nervous exhaustion. In Italy I had severely strained my eyes and the trouble from them made writing difficult. Then Caroline would take over. Her quick-moving pencil would be my comfort and my prop. The book progressed but was not nearly finished when the term of our stay at the cottage expired. We were in love with Devon and wanted above all things to live there.

Just beyond the village of Winkleigh there was to let a five-hundred-year-old farmhouse. With it went fields and orchard. "What a wonderful place to live," said Caroline, "almost at the edge of the moor, and always we have loved the country. We really are country people, you know," she said, fixing me with a look from her clear blue eyes, "and if we took this house, it would solve the problem of what to do with all the bed linen and so forth that we bought for the cottage." . . . I had never before heard of taking a house just for the protection of a dozen sheets, but when Caroline says a thing, it always sounds so reasonable. I, on the contrary, may make a profoundly sensible remark, but I make it in such a manner that people only laugh.

The upshot was that we went to a sale at Sticklepath, near Belstone, and bought quite a lot of furniture. We then took a furnished house for a month on the Cornish coast, then another in the village of Willersy for September and spent a month in Oxford. By this time the ancient farmhouse would be available.

Chapter 15

Seckington

REALLY, as Caroline said, we were country folk and now we were firmly established in a farmhouse, built of that ancient but enduring material "cob," a house with a long avenue of oaks and a rose-covered lodge at the gate. Really it was perfect. We should stay here forever. The furniture, the china, the silver we had bought in Sticklepath looked so well, it seemed they had been there always. To be sure, the huge fireplace in the kitchen badly smoked when the wind was off the moors, and the wind usually was off the moors. There was no bathroom, but there was a downstairs lavatory with a green baize swinging door to it. The stairs were the steepest, the most irregular I ever have climbed and unexpectedly ran from a corner of the dining-room. There was no central heating. Caroline and I, however, were not the sort to be balked by a little discomfort. With happy expectation we settled into Seckington.

We could look back on a summer of many pleasures and some fatigue. In Cornwall we had climbed cliffs and bathed in warm sea pools. We had picnicked in the sun. We had been drenched by cold rains. From Willersy we had explored the lovely near-by villages, Broadway and Saintbury and Chipping Campden. Caroline had bought an oak settle from the inn. It was in Willersy that the harvest moon rose night after night, full and round, above our chimney, the most persistent full moon I ever have seen. It was in Willersy that a little Belgian "daily" made us the best salad I ever had eaten. Friends motored us to Stratford-on-Avon to see *Romeo and Juliet*. It all would have been delightful had I not constantly suffered from the pain in my head — nightmarish dreams.

Amid all these distractions I wrote and while still in Willersy I finished *Portrait of a Dog*. I was relieved when I was done with it, for many painful memories were woven into it. The very next day I wrote the first page of *Finch's Fortune*. Again I was one with the family at Jalna.

Harold Macmillan, now Chancellor of the Exchequer, had written to tell me that my novel *Whiteoaks* had been chosen by the Book Society for October. It had already been published in America, its reception even warmer than was given to *Jalna*. Ellery Sedgwick wrote to tell me of his pleasure in the idea of still another sequel.

Caroline rejoiced in this success, but she had other things on her mind as well. We must choose wall paper for the decorating of Seckington. The landlord would do nothing. His mother, past ninety, had not long before died there. At her funeral he had wept into a handkerchief with an inch-wide black border. As to improvements at Seckington, he considered that what was good enough for her was good enough for tenants.

The wall paper we chose for the dining-room was the prettiest I ever have seen. It was a design of apples, with the bloom of autumn on their redness and half hidden among their leaves. Always there was an open fire in this room. It was the most comfortable room in the house. Here I wrote in the morning. Here, in the afternoon, Caroline typed my manuscript. She had bought a typewriter in London. Several years before she had taught herself to type. Now she was typing *Portrait of a Dog.* Later she made an admirable condensed version of it for an American magazine. But she had other activities that kept her busy from morning to night. She had a friend named "Jarge," a dealer in bicycles, queer junk, and occasionally good antiques. Once a week a red-faced, jolly Devon man named Sam Chambers would drive her to the village on the moors, where she had a happy time exploring Jarge's shop. Some queer things she bought and some very good — among these a handsome sideboard and a Chippendale grandfather clock. Sam Chambers had native good manners and politeness. He had a brother, a farmer who used to ride about his fields on a nice-looking cob, with a rose on the lapel of his jacket. Both these brothers, if they met you before noon, said "Good-morning." If it were but a few minutes past noon, it was "Good-afternoon." If the clock in the church tower had struck six, their greeting was "Good-evening," though the sun brightly shone. These niceties come back to me now, living as I do on a continent where greeting is fast degenerating into — "Hi!" The Chamberses had a married sister who kept the principal village shop. I cannot think of anything less like a "super-market." We were astonished when we settled our account at Christmas to receive a present from her. In a pretty basket were arranged a plump pheasant, shining in his bright plumage, a box of figs and a great cluster of hothouse grapes. For the cook there was a bottle of port wine and a large piece of Gorgonzola cheese.

This little cook, Mrs. Bird, was a character. I never have known a greater spirit, and that in a tiny body, no more than five feet tall, and she had bright blue eyes and pink cheeks. She had been widowed when her two children were young. She had kept a small sweetshop in Exeter and brought them up nicely. Her boy had emigrated to Canada, had enlisted in the Canadian Army and been killed in the war. Her daughter was married. So she packed up her belongings and went to Canada to live with her son's widow. They two, she had thought, working together, might live well. But the daughter-in-law was a hussy who took all without gratitude, who had not been a faithful wife. The cook had a sharp tongue, so between them there was nothing but unhappiness. Seven years passed before the cook, having taken a situation, saved enough to bring her back to England and buy her a tiny cottage in Winkleigh. To it she always went on her day off and planned finally to retire there. In Canada she had quite lost her soft Devon voice and had a shrill edge to her speech.

But the housemaid, Ada, had a voice like velvet and the Devon singsong tone to it. These two worked hard in a most inconvenient house for what today would be considered ridiculously low wages. Each morning before we were up Ada came to our bedroom and lighted a fire for us. As the flames grew stronger her shadow, crouching, would be thrown on the ceiling. The Staffordshire cottage china on the mantelpiece would seem to welcome the morning — the shepherd and shepherdess, the black-haired girl on the pink pony, the dog holding a basket of flowers in his mouth. The windows of the bedroom were framed in the sweet-scented Cape jasmine. At Christmas Caroline decorated the house with holly and ivy.

We could hear the clump-clump of the postman's boots on the long driveway while we still were in bed. Sometimes he made that long walk with no more than a postcard. But as Christmas drew near, the mail grew more and more heavy. It was delightful opening the packages from overseas. My uncle sent us a box of scarlet maple leaves to remind us of Canada.

That winter I sometimes rose early to look out of window. I would see the red sunshine over the meadows white with rime. I would see the shepherd going toward his withy hut with a new-born lamb in his arms. Beyond the great beech tree there would be a glimpse of the moors.

One day the hunt passed in full cry, right through our meadows. On January the eighth I wrote in my diary — "The air is full of bird song, light and mild." By mid-January there were daffodils in the orchard. Those old trees all had grown a covering of moss on the side of the trunk farthest from the moor. They were sadly bent, and when there came a gale from Dartmoor, a number of them surrendered and fell flat among the daffodils. It was one of the most destructive gales in years. In its rage it uprooted three tall fir trees in front of the house and a corner of the roof was blown in quite near to the cook's bed. We remembered the hurricane that tore up the pine trees in the ravine when we were just settling into Trail Cottage. It is the same wherever we go — storms, floods, drought or killing heat herald our coming. . . . Weather is definitely against us.

But when the weather was fair, our front door stood open all day long. I would stand there, drinking in the sweet smells and sounds, thinking that there was nowhere on the face of the earth I had rather be.

The pains in my head were much less frequent. The third novel in the Whiteoak chronicles was coming on well. I thought of these as a trilogy. The new one was to be called *Finch's Fortune*. It was strongly coloured by my experiences in Devon. The manner of my conception of Sarah Court was odd. We had been sitting at lunch at our hotel in Oxford when two women entered the dining-room. One was old, one young. The younger so fascinated me that I could hardly keep my eyes off her. The convolutions of her black hair, the marble pallor of her skin, the strange, gliding rigidity of her walk, her secret smile. "Don't stare so," said Caroline, but how could I help staring? There glided, there smiled, there sat Sarah Court, one of the principal characters in my next novel.

A strange thing was that, a little later, I was passing Mortlock's fine china shop in North Audley Street, and I saw in the window a china figure of a young woman which was the very image of the young woman in Oxford — hair, complexion, smile, even clothes, though the figure in the china shop did wear a bustle. I went in and priced it. Too expensive, I thought, and ever since have regretted it. Certainly neither my mother nor Caroline would have been put off by the cost had they wanted it.

We went up to London several times that autumn and winter. Walter Allward, the Canadian sculptor, was then working on the memorial for Vimy Ridge. At the battle there sixty thousand Canadians had been killed and a hundred and forty thousand wounded. Walter Allward had a studio in St. John's Wood. He and his wife, warm-hearted, hospitable Margaret Allward, gave delightful parties where one met interesting people. We met a good many writers — Sir John Squire, Robert and Sylvia Lynd, Charles Morgan, Hugh Walpole, who had written a glowing review of *Whiteoaks* in the *Graphic*, Clemence Dane, who had done the same in the *Bystander*. Tea in Walpole's flat was always a pleasure. He had beautiful things in it. I remember looking down at a small rug and admiring it. "Yes," he agreed, trying hard to smile, "but it's not really meant to be *stood* on."

At this time I met Rache Lovat Dickson, a young publisher who had married a beautiful Montreal girl. Later he joined the Macmillan firm and our friendship, casually begun, has ripened into one of the most rewarding of my life. Himself a writer of moving prose, he bends his sensitive powers to the skilful editing of the work of other authors.

248

Two of the most interesting people we met were Ethel Colburn Mayne and Violet Hunt, who was an odd woman, with a strange weary, pre-Raphaelite air, a sweet smile and hair that looked ready to leap into a halo. There were bright red doors in her living-room and a portrait of her lover, Ford Madox Hueffer, as a small child, with a red apple in his hand. To sit talking with those two women was to feel that you were on the verge of a revelation — awful, soul-shaking, yet it never came and I did not know whether to be relieved or disappointed. They were on the committee of the Femina Vie Heureuse award. They told me that my novel *Whiteoaks* was considered for it but that it was customary to give it to a younger writer. "But don't mind," said Ethel Colburn Mayne, "for it is an award for promise, rather than achievement."

Not long afterward I attended the presentation of this award to Richard Hughes for his delightful book *High Wind in Jamaica*. In accepting, he spoke apologetically of the beard he was wearing and declared that, in spite of it, he was only thirty-two.

Gay dinner parties that passed smoothly, and without apparent effort, were given by Daniel and Betty Macmillan in their house in Chesham Place. There one met the most interesting people. One night we went with them to see Raymond Massey in *The Man in Possession*. I tremendously enjoyed the scallywag part he played in this — much more than his Abraham Lincoln, though I am sure he would not approve the choice.

I was invited to supper, soon after this, by Raymond Massey to meet a few actors at the Savoy. They all were enthusiastic about *Jalna* — its potentialities as a play. They urged me to dramatize it, and talked of Raymond Massey as Finch and Gerald du Maurier as Renny. I have since regretted a little that I did not attempt this. Sometime later Raymond Massey had a success in *The Shining*

Hour, a play with a considerable resemblance to *Jalna,* in plot and setting.

But, whatever our pleasures we always were glad to return to our home on the edge of the moors. Spring came early there, in lovely sunshine, in sudden storm. The rain clouds came from Dartmoor and Exmoor to meet above Seckington and empty themselves in a deluge. Never had we experienced such gales and rain. Always a lover of the sun, I now sometimes suffered from depression. I asked myself why we had not remained in Italy. Yet in fair weather I was content.

How lovely the walled garden — how lovely the flowering meadow beyond the garden, where one had the best view of the sunset, where the voice of the cuckoo was calling in the springtime — and yet, I was not satisfied. Something in me cried out for Canada, the hot sunshine, the light thin air, the high-up blue sky, the voices of old friends. And so, closing the house and establishing cook in her cottage with the two kittens, we set out. No one was surprised by our going. Nothing we did surprised our Devon friends. "What surprised us," declared Admiral Radcliffe, "was your coming to this remote place."

We had our visit to Toronto, a short stay by the Georgian Bay, a glimpse of Trail Cottage; yet somehow this returning was not so pleasurable as we had expected. We had few regrets when we embarked on the *France* from New York. Aunt Eva and Pierre came to say good-bye. She was beautifully dressed, but she was not well. She still talked a great deal, but she had become vague and constantly repeated herself.

And what of Pierre? His quick animation, his fire were strangely subdued. A new gentleness had tempered the brilliance of his smile. But there was something else, a resigned cynicism, patience toward Aunt Eva and, toward me, an air of something like reproach, as though he would say — "You have done this to me. . . ." But it was not till later that our feelings found expression, when to say good-bye, after each reunion, was a heart-break. I would have made these partings swift, decisive, had the pain over quickly; not so Pierre. He would leave me — he would return, his face lighted by a smile — again the parting — again the return, but this time it would be the last. Now, in this time of departure, there was that unreality, when one is suspended, as it were, between two worlds.

I suppose it was because my mind was disturbed that I left my grey squirrel coat in the hotel lobby. We were well on the way to the pier when suddenly I remembered it. In panic we hastened back to the hotel, and found the coat just where I had thrown it down. Once more we were on our way!

When we had almost reached the ship, I asked the taxi driver for the manuscript of *Finch's Fortune*, which had not yet been typed. It was a heavy manuscript and I had given it to a porter to carry downstairs and put into the hands of the driver. He looked at me blankly. It had not been given to him. We found a telephone and begged the hotel clerk to send the manuscript to the ship with all speed. This second mishap was too much. Our hearts in our mouths, we waited at the gangway. The sailors held it when they saw the porter running. He was full of apologies. Thankfully I tipped him. I clutched my manuscript and we were off. . . .

The *France* was a tall, narrow ship and she carried little cargo to steady her. We moved straight out into bad weather. Seventeen sea voyages have we made since then but none to compare with it in wild winds and mountainous seas. For five days the *France* rolled, threatening at each roll never to right herself. Then, when our insides, after a tumult of nausea, had begun to accommodate themselves to the motion, she decided to pitch. We were nearing the coast of Africa. As we turned a corner, at dead of night, it seemed that the ship had had a furious kick in the stern. She reeled, then literally bounded. She was like a bucking horse. Our wardrobe trunk was hurled from one side of the cabin to the other. Back and forth it hurtled. The cupboard door swung wide, then shut with a bang. Its mirror, in passing, threw us our miserable reflections. All through the voyage it had done this. Caroline was sure that she was more seasick than I, though I could not see how that was possible. Now and again she would say, "You must get up and shut that cupboard door. Shut it tight." I would stagger, a bundle of wretchedness, from my bed, shut and secure the door, but it would not stay so.

Outside in the passage that night we could hear a passenger having hysterics. He screamed, "Stop the ship! Let me off! Stop the ship!" Every so often we would hear the crash of a tray, as a reeling steward dropped it. I would look up at the picture of a French road bordered by poplars, and say to myself, "If ever I set foot on land once more, never again shall I go on the sea." But seasickness, like the pains of childbirth, is agony while it lasts but soon forgotten.

The ship's doctor and the nurse were almost run off their feet. Twice a day the handsome doctor would visit us. He was not in the least troubled by Caroline's sickness but interested only in my cough. "Sit down, please," he would say, when he meant to say sit up, and he would apply his stethoscope to my back. Twice a day the little nurse came to apply a mustard plaster to my chest. She was like a sweet young nun. I felt that nothing would better become her than to cross my hands and lay me out, ready for burial.

Through all this agony our steward and stewardess were our sympathetic props. Prijean was his name. Day and night, you would hear it called through the passages — "Prijean! Prijean!" If he was tired, never did he show it. I wonder where he is now? Cherie, the stewardess, was handsome, cheerful and firm. One day she said, "Never will you recover here. It is time for you to go on deck."

We were positive that it would be the end of us to leave our safe retreat, but Cherie insisted and somehow got us into clothes and herded us on deck. Caroline looked like one recovering from jaundice. I really was ashamed of her, till I saw the faces about us. They all were of the same yellow hue. Cherie installed us in deck chairs, wrapped us in rugs. We shrank from our neighbours, but we need not have worried. At my first bout of coughing they shifted their chairs as far away as possible, evidently convinced that I had a bad case of tuberculosis.

The navy blue sea, the splendid breeze soon completed our cure. By the time we reached the Canary Islands we were quite ready to go ashore. Casablanca, Algiers, Majorca, Naples, Taormina, Rome, Fiesole, Paris — we continued to be lazy sight-seers, and yet we felt glutted. Walking along a street in the Latin Quarter of Paris, Caroline remarked in a whining voice, most unusual to her, "I want to be under my own roof again."

"What's that you say?" I demanded.

"I want to be under my own roof again," she repeated, "and I should like to have seven dogs."

"What breed?" I asked.

Seated at a small table in front of a restaurant, we discussed the breeds. She was not certain, but she rather thought two Scotties, a white West Highland, two Pekes, a Cairn terrier and a poodle. . . .

It was some time before we had acquired even one dog and we did not yet return to our own roof. We took a small house in

Ringing the Changes

Gayfere Street, off Smith Square in London, belonging to Miss Picton-Turberville, a member of Parliament. It was furnished and with it was included the cook, a large, strange creature, half Cockney, half French, who later appeared in one of my books. This was a narrow house, rather chill and dingy, but near to many fascinating places. I remember our first evening there. Our good friend Kathleen Bowker, who lived near-by, sent her son John with an armful of flowers and a bundle of faggots to light a fire for us. A slender boy, he knelt by the grate, the fresh firelight touching his hair to gold. I hold this picture in tender remembrance because later he lost his life in the war.

During those months of absence from England I had written some short stories and I had it in mind to begin a new novel, something quite different from the Whiteoak novels — for I thought I had done with them, when *Finch's Fortune* was finished. The scene of this new novel was to open in New England, then move on to Sicily. When I told Ellery Sedgwick of this, he implored me to stick to the country I knew — to write of Canada, not of New England. But I persisted and when he read the completed manuscript, he said he very much liked it. Certainly it had a good title — *Lark Ascending*.

But when we returned to England, when we lived in Gayfere Street, my mind was filled with a matter very different from the writing of a novel. It was the taking of two tiny children into our life and hearts. Because of bereavement and adversity, the two lovely infants came to us. It was a tremendous responsibility, yet I shouldered it without undue consideration. Our little family of two suddenly had become four. Infant innocence was now mine to protect, to nourish beneath a maternal wing. As for Caroline, there never was a more generous and loving aunt!

Now there was much shopping to be done, a perambulator to

be bought, and a beauty it was! There were the proofs of *Finch's Fortune* to be corrected. Almost every night we went to the theatre or a party. We were happy in London, yet I longed, as Caroline had, to be under our own roof — to be once again in the country.

It was a confused and rather exhausting departure in the cold rain, but when we arrived in Devon, there was sunshine. The house was in bright order, the kittens wore bells, and there was the cook's special scone for tea, with blackberry jam and clotted cream.

What a family we had become, and now a nurse for the babies must be added to it! Like many another brother and sister they were very unlike. Her eyes were a greyish blue, with dark lashes and brows, her fine hair honey pale. He had as yet not much hair, but what there was, reddish gold. His eyes brown and brilliant. Yet it was in disposition that they most differed, for she was lively, a little overbearing and quite undemonstrative in affection, while already, in his baby way, he showed gentleness and a desire to express his goodwill.

I have said earlier in this book that I am always eager for advice, to be told what to do. That, it seems to me, is often a characteristic of women. But to follow that advice, how different a thing! I have friends who lap advice as cats lap cream but never, never follow it. I, on the contrary, fairly fly to do as I have been advised. Yet — in the important things of life, I seem to have followed my impulses, sometimes recklessly but seldom to regret. I try to write of myself objectively, as of a character in a novel.

Now, with my enlarged family about me, I worked somewhat erratically on *Lark Ascending.* Ellery Sedgwick's disapproval of the setting of the story had affected me. Sometimes I could not write for depression. The weather that year was said to be the worst in forty years. Seldom did we take a walk when we were not caught in the drizzle. We swung along the leafy lanes, carrying walking-sticks, our shoes caked with mud. Often Admiral Radcliffe walked with us. Sometimes I wrote with exhilaration, feeling I was back once more in Sicily.

Not always were we walking, for I had bought a car and a young man from Exeter came to give me driving lessons. He was an exacting instructor, I an anxious and nervous pupil. I, who was not afraid to drive any sort of horse, was terrified of the car. The narrow Devon roads with their sudden twists and turns, the little bridges lay in wait to trap me. After a driving lesson I sometimes could not sleep at night. The very smell of the car excited me. Yet bit by bit I mastered it and proud I was when we took a picnic to the moor. Relaxed on the heath, our hamper before us, the breeze-blown white clouds sailing above the dark tor, I would exclaim, "Oh, to live on the moors! Oh, never to leave the silence of the moors!"

By this time I had a considerable mail to cope with. I corresponded with my friends and relatives in Canada. Every so often a fresh batch of reviews of *Finch's Fortune* would arrive. They were almost uniformly favourable. The book was selling in numbers pleasing to my publishers on both sides of the Atlantic. I was writing a new novel. Life pressed in on me from many sides — the result, I longed for the silence of the moors. . . .

But instead of that, another removal lay ahead of us. There was no doubt about it, Seckington was too small, too inconvenient for the household I now had under my roof! There were no proper nurseries for the children. No English nanny could be satisfied there. It was far from London. Yet we wanted to remain in Devon. We thought we should go to South Devon if we could find a suitable house. We consulted agents. Caroline, with Sam Chambers to drive her, inspected a number and before long found one.

Chapter 16

The Rectory

LOOKING backward, how often I see us in the act of leaving a house where we had lived, rejoiced, possibly suffered, a house to which we had gone in hope, believing that our stay there would be long. Yesterday, receiving a letter from a distant friend, I thought with surprise, "Why, he has had that same address for almost ten years. What must one's feelings be — having lived so long in one house?"

As the car moved down the driveway between the tall trees, I had my last look at Seckington, that ancient house with the mas sive copper beech near the door. On that same doorsill, one morning long ago, a shepherd who had been lost on the moors had lain down exhausted and been discovered dead by the maid who opened the door. I gave a thought to him and then had a glimpse of the high meadow beyond the house, a flowery meadow where one had a view of the sunset on the moors. . . . David, the Persian kitten, now quite grown up, was in a basket on cook's lap. His sister had been given to the Radcliffes. Cook was in a state of hilarity. She was going to a larger, more convenient (she hoped) house. She held her beloved pet on her knee. All the way she kept on sucking toffee drops. She sat beside Sam Chambers, who was driving, but he took no notice of her. Wisps of hair blew on her nape. His neck was sunburnt and florid.

As we drove from Winkleigh to Hawkchurch, I was full of hope. A new chapter in our lives was opening. What happiness, what contentment might it not bring forth? We had lost the moors, but here we should have the sea, at Lyme Regis, at Charmouth, just a few miles away. The countryside was lovely. The children thriving. My new novel was going without pain.

Well might a family be content in that house, I thought, as the car passed through the laurels and the rectory was revealed, massive and with many gables and chimneys. About it spread its lawns and gardens, beyond lay the verdant valley of the Axe. It stood on the village street behind a high stone wall. There was a well of good drinking water outside the wall and it was the object of a daily visit by the rector. He would fill his bucket, then return to his house, a stalwart figure, wearing a cassock. He found the rectory too large for himself and his wife, now that his three children had left home, and so he let it to us. The old church stood between the two houses, its graveyard about it. In the springtime this was awave with daffodils. Never, at any time, was it a gloomy spot. There was a squat oak gate between it and our garden and I used to loiter there alone on warm evenings. Our housemaid's father owned the inn across the road, which was called the New Inn though the date above the door was 17 — something. One night the pink-cheeked healthy girl was returning from a visit to her parents. I was alone in the churchyard. It was dark, but the moon was rising behind the church tower. I could barely make out the figure hurrying past the graves toward the little gate. From behind a gravestone I asked in a low voice:

"Is that you, Cissie?"

From a fine buxom girl Cissie was changed by those four words

into a figure of terror. She fled screaming, through the churchyard, through the gate along the drive, into the house. Darting in
front of her was the ghostly form of David, the Persian cat, his
breast as white as the newest tombstone.

On our first night at the rectory he had wandered away exploring. Caroline had not yet arrived. It would be upsetting for her to
find him missing, so I went forth in search of him. It was an evening of muggy heat. To begin with, I had a sore throat. Though
I found David and carried him back, happily purring, I went
down with a bad attack of tonsilitis. My throat, always my weakness, continued, after we were settled, to trouble me. I could not
understand it. One after another the various members of the
household were attacked by some infection. Right down to the
children we were attacked. I asked the rector whether he thought
the drains could be at fault. "Oh, no," he said, "for they were put
in order only twenty-eight years ago."

But Caroline insisted on calling in a plumber. The drains were
found to be in terrible condition. The sewage was seeping through
beneath the scullery. For days three plumbers worked, with masks
over their faces. When the work was done, we all recovered our
health.

What a cellar that was! Arched in stone like the crypt of a
cathedral, its passages were mysterious, its wine cellar, its rooms
for the domestic help, wrapped in dim memories, unused. Above
it was the comfortable kitchen, with its great range, its windows
framed in wisteria, its hooks from the ceiling for the hanging of
sides of bacon or hams. About it the servants' hall, the boot room,
the larder, the scullery. From the dining-room what a view over
the valley of the Axe! But the windows of my study looked into the
massive boughs of the largest deodar I ever have seen. The stone
house, with its Gothic windows, was fairly smothered in ivy.

Ringing the Changes

When the moving vans arrived, it was night. The men carried in the furniture by candlelight. It looked rather sparse when set out in the lofty rooms. We thought of the furniture we had stored in Canada and wished it were here. All those belongings so dear to us and so far, far away! But Caroline made the house look handsome. The panelled walls were a good background for pictures and tapestry. Not that we set about acquiring rare and expensive objects. My obligations were too heavy for that. I had now become the sole support of Auntie Ida, in Toronto, who had during the financial slump lost all her resources. I had a quite large establishment to maintain. In those days in England a cook must have her kitchen maid; a nurse, her nursemaid, who also assisted the parlourmaid; the gardener, his boy. This gardener, Charles Chant, was one of the kindest men I ever have known. He gave my children a devotion that they long remembered. No trouble was too much to take for them. He had been wounded in the war and had a rather disfiguring scar on his face, but never did they notice it. They would be seated on either of his shoulders, clasping his head, while he marched along the garden paths. One of the first words acquired by my small son was "Cha," for Chant. He loved the cook also, whom he called "Coo-coo." He would come from his outing in the pram, in the chill December days, and establish himself on a tiny stool near to the range, while she knitted or cut up runner beans.

How cook Bird and the babies' nurse hated one another! At last, when Caroline and I were on a visit to London, they had a terrible row. The nurse was a Eurasian, absolutely white, but cook, enraged by sneers at her cooking, did not hesitate to call her black.

"You can't cook," nurse had said. "You're only fit to work in the scullery."

"And you're not fit to look after gentlefolk's children," cook had cried. "I wish I knew your back history. 'Tis clear to me that 'ee comes of strange stock. I do believe you're naught but a black woman."

Nurse snatched up a carving knife. "Take the children upstairs," she said to the kitchen maid. "I'll run this knife into the old woman."

Chant came in from the garage just in time to hear this interchange. He took the knife from the nurse's hand. His calm presence restored order.

We found a pretty kettle of fish when we returned from London. This could not go on. For a time we were at our wits' end. Then there appeared on the scene Nanny Bowerman, well-recommended, completely capable, who took the Infants to her heart, as they happily accepted her. Shrieks of laughter now came from the bathroom. Squeals of joy woke us in the morning. In place of oily black hair, staring grey eyes and rather a flat nose, this new nurse had copper-coloured hair twisted into a firm knot at her nape, twinkling eyes to match, and a longish, sharp nose. Her thinlipped humourous mouth spoke gay and tender words to the children. My diary became replete with the doings of the people about me. A novelist, lately, writing his autobiography, says he has always tended to be attracted by people who have made a success of life, have left their mark on the world. To me such figures before long are dim — with the exception of those whom I should have cherished, successful or not. When I consider the people who have made their mark on me — how many of them would be counted by the world as failures, who had no possible way of making their mark except by their own essence.

The year moved on. My novel *Lark Ascending* was finished and once again I was with the Whiteoaks. I had begun *The Master of Jalna*. Our days were pleasant. My study was remote from noise.

My one complaint of it was that it got a small share of sunshine. Early in the afternoon, the deodar tree received the sun into her bosom and held him there till he slept.

The Christmas parcels from Canada brought yearning thoughts to me — never to Caroline. She had given her heart to England. A friend had sent us a box of Mackintosh reds. My uncle, as always, had sent a sheaf of scarlet maple leaves. We joined hands and sang "The Maple Leaf For Ever."

Twice on Christmas Day we went to church. Ah, what has become of my church-going? That same afternoon I took my tiny Esmée to the children's service. She did not in the least understand what it was all about but was delighted to go anywhere with me, especially where the baby could not go.

Although the children were so small, we had a Christmas tree for them that towered inside the windows of the dining-room and had for a background the valley of the Axe. One of their presents was a gramophone. From that time on we four used to dance to lively records at the children's hour in my study after tea. Tiny Esmée and I danced together, but Caroline would put the baby on her shoulder and to the tune of "The Teddy Bears' Picnic" sail round and round.

All the church choir marched through the village that Christmas Eve. It was late and the full moon was high in the sky when they came down our drive, singing "Nowell, Nowell." It was a contrast to our last Christmas Eve at Seckington when the waits had appeared in a gale that had fairly torn the notes from their mouths.

The rector was an odd sort of man. His parishioners did not very much like him and he liked them not at all. He did not in the least care whether they came to church or no. Indeed, I think he preferred to have the church to himself. He used to tell me that I was the only one who understood him, that I was his only friend.

But the love of his life was Paris. There he spent his holidays and yearned toward all the rest of the year. He liked to pick up odd acquaintances and liked the poor much better than the well-to-do. I remember once finding him in the church, the Sunday's collection tied up in a duster. This he kept throwing over the rafters to frighten away small birds that had flown about and twittered during his sermon. He was very pleased by this invention. A boyish smile lighted his melancholy face.

We were kept busy returning calls made on us. It was an agreeable neighbourhood. Our best friends lived in Seaton. These were the St. John Ervines, whom already we had met in London. They lived and still live in a lovely white house with a garden sloping down toward the sea. At that time they possessed six white West Highland terriers — parents and four offspring. They were enchanting but mischievous little creatures and once, when St. John and Leonora were away and they were left behind, they tore the handsome Spanish leather covering of the dining-room chairs to bits.

The Ervines were delightful hosts. Long before I met St. John I had had a great admiration for his plays and his dramatic criticism. In my novel *Whiteoaks,* young Finch had played the part of Cloutie John in Ervine's *John Ferguson.* I was eager to meet St. John Ervine, yet afraid I should be disappointed in him. I need not have feared that, for he is more like his books and plays than any author has a right to be.

On our second Christmas at the rectory we were invited to dinner with the Ervines. There was a white sea fog; Chant was a nervous driver. The nearer we drew to the sea, the denser, the woollier became the fog. We fairly crawled along the road, but arrive we did and had the warmest sort of welcome from the Ervines, their six dogs, and some guests from London. The dinner was delicious, beautifully served, but unfortunately one of the guests (not I) introduced the subject of tinned foods. The other guests, joining in, extolled the excellence of tinned foods they had enjoyed. They became lyrical on the subject of tinned foods. Finally St. John could bear it no longer. He exclaimed, "I have provided fresh lobster for you — turkey for you — wine for you — and you rave over *tinned* food! Never again shall I invite you to another Christmas dinner!"

Of course, we knew he did not mean it. He is a man violent in his words — gentle in his life. But we were properly ashamed of ourselves. St. John Ervine desires to worship woman on a pedestal, but when she gets down off the pedestal and puts on slacks, shorts, blue jeans or any other masculine nether garments, he fairly hates her and enjoys telling her so.

We went now and again to London. There we met a number of writers. The most striking in looks was John Galsworthy, who somehow resembled a bishop on holiday. There were Robert and Sylvia Lynd, who entertained you with heart-warming kindness, though physically you were frozen in their draughty house. There was Charles Morgan with his air of chill distinction. There were the Priestleys in their lovely house in Highgate, with *her* children, *his* children and *their* children, very happy and jolly together. Priestley said to me, "I like your books about the Whiteoaks. You should be compelled by law to write a new one every year. But — let us hear no more about Renny Whiteoak. I hate thin, horsy men!"

Here his wife interrupted: "Don't mind what Jack says. He's just jealous of Renny Whiteoak. Already we've quarrelled over him."

At this time the Priestleys were spending their winters in Arizona, for the sake of Jane's health. It was there he wrote the admirable *Midnight in the Desert,* my favourite among his books.

From Devon we made our first visit to Scotland and again went to France and Italy, but till I had finished *The Master of Jalna* I stuck pretty closely to home. We took the children to picnic on the sands of Lyme Regis and Charmouth.

Is it a small tragedy when a pet animal dies of poisoning? We did not think of it as small when in that cruel fashion we lost our beautiful cat. A keeper at Wyld Court had put out poison for a fox that was stealing his hens, but it was our pet which found it. Cook Bird had gone to spend the week-end in her cottage at Winkleigh. When she returned, she found him dying. The sad thing was that he had climbed up the ivy into her room and laid his suffering body on her bed. He was sure she would protect him from his agony. There she found him and the poor little woman was heart-broken.

Time passed. Sometimes we were content. Sometimes the urge for another change possessed me. Oh, to be in Italy! Oh, to be in London! Oh, to be in Canada! At the end of each novel comes that urge. I had finished *The Master of Jalna,* which has in its pages some of my best work. I was very tired. We both longed for a life more vivid than the Devon countryside. We decided to go to town for a time and, after much searching, found a delightful furnished house. There was an epidemic of influenza in London. In some of the houses we went through, the entire family were prostrate. Two thousand people had died of flu in that week. Yet I do not think it occurred to either of us to remain in the safety of the countryside.

The house we had taken belonged to Mrs. Temple Godman. It stands in Stafford Place, just round the corner from Buckingham Palace, and was one of five houses built for Queen Victoria's ladies-in-waiting. We brought our Devon maid Cissie with us. When she opened the door to visitors, they fairly swooned at sight of so much rural beauty. "What a divine complexion! Wherever did you get her?" Cissie gave a little inscrutable smile, unaware of their admiration. . . . Almost the first thing she did was to go down with a mild attack of influenza. She lay on her bed miserable and desperately homesick. We feared that we should be forced to send her back to Devon when she was able to go. But, when she was able, the good-humoured cook took her out to see London. In no time Cissie wondered how ever again would she be able to endure life in the country.

The delight of the children in London was almost as great as Cissie's. There was so much for them to see, and that near at hand. Nannie would take them to see the changing of the guard at the palace. Once as they waited there the Queen passed through the gates. Nannie showed the baby how to doff his cap and the Queen bowed and smiled at the children. She might well notice them, for they were as pretty a pair as you would see in a day's walk in London. Pushing the mail-cart, I would take them to St. James's Park to feed the water birds. Like many another doting parent, I made note of their infant doings and later I wove them into a book called *Beside a Norman Tower*. It was necessary for me to have a respite from the exacting Whiteoaks. Yet write I must.

I might turn from novels of them, but their demands on me did not cease. I had, in the past months, written a play based not on the first volume of the series, as Raymond Massey had suggested, but on the second, *Whiteoaks*. I sent the manuscript to him hoping he might like to act in it, but I was disappointed in this. I forget whether it was that he had other commitments or felt, after the lapse of five years, that he could no longer act the part of the schoolboy Finch. However that may be, he wrote a most encouraging letter. "This could be," he wrote, "a magnificent play. . . ."

I sent the manuscript to St. John Ervine, who answered, "I am in seventeen minds about it. . . ." He gave it stern criticism and warm praise.

I wish I had these letters by me, but they are in a battered old trunk which has many times crossed the ocean. When, once in a blue moon, I lift its lid and peer into the mass beneath, I quickly shut it again. All my life I have sought for system, for order, but never have achieved it. How many nicely bound notebooks I have acquired, written in them a paragraph, made a note or two of things I wanted to remember for future use, then discarded them. Sometimes I make notes on scraps of paper, which I invariably lose or mislay. I feel a rather resentful admiration for novelists who make bulky notes, so many that they cannot use all of them in their books and sometimes publish them separately. Volumes of this sort I find quite fascinating, just as I find quite fascinating volumes of reminiscence by authors who have met so many of the great. I have met so few. Either the great have eluded me or I have eluded them, to (I feel) our mutual advantage.

Our visit to London over, we returned to Devon. We had seen many plays. Now I was again at work on my own. It was March. The garden was blazing in golden daffodils, primroses and blue-bells. The baby's head was a mass of red-gold curls. The children, so delighted by the sights of London, shrieked with joy at finding themselves in the country again.

We were happy — yet the urge for change was troubling me. I must not include Caroline in this. I think she would have been satisfied to remain in Devon, but I longed for Canada and our friends there. This was a yearning that could not be denied. Caroline agreed to go to Canada for the summer and on our return to find a house more convenient to town. It was hard to leave the rectory, where our belongings looked so permanent. It was hard to part from neighbours, the Greenshields, the Braggs, the Charlesworths. Always we seemed to be saying good-bye and promising not to forget. Never could we forget the rectory. When, a few years ago, we revisited it, we found it strangely altered. The massive oriel window above the front door had been taken away. The cloak of ivy and wisteria that mantled the house had been ruthlessly demolished. The tulip tree, the sun-embracing deodar tree had died. The house stood bare and unfriendly.

But on those spring mornings, when we were preparing to leave, it was beautiful. From four o'clock in the morning the birds sang. Caroline, in spite of heart-ache, took time to fill the house with flowers. The weather was superb, in those last days at the rectory. On Easter Day we went through our little gate to the church for early communion. We drove to Honey Ditches for lunch with the St. John Ervines. Both were ardent gardeners and their garden was a delight.

It was hard to believe that our time in Devon was so soon to be over. Only when Thomas Cook's men, five in two vans, appeared at the door, could we believe in our departure from the loved spot. But the men began to carry out the furniture and place it in the van. As I watched I thought of how often I had seen this miserable business — this tearing up of roots. Now we were exhausted by packing.

We had taken rooms in a small comfortable hotel in Lyme Regis, at the top of that tremendous hill. Our dear "Nanny B.," as the children called her, could not come with us to Canada, so we were obliged to engage a new nanny. She was a pleasant round-faced woman with rather a florid complexion, and I can still see her, crimson in the face, labouring up the hill, pushing the pram filled with an assortment of spades, buckets and lunch boxes, as well as the baby boy,

There were still things to be done at the rectory. Every morning Chant would motor Caroline there and in the late afternoon bring her back, carrying flowers and a heavy heart. Chant would creak up the back stairs of the hotel to the bathroom, where the nurse was bathing the children. She would sit with the baby, pink from his bath, wrapped in a towel; the nurse proudly possessive, Chant tenderly worshipping.

At the last we had a sale of the heavier pieces of furniture and all of the kitchen things and garden tools. These brought much less than we had expected. Our good wireless set brought only five pounds. We were shocked to discover that we had only one hundred and fifty pounds in Lloyd's Bank instead of the one thousand pounds I had thought was deposited there. However, there was actually nothing serious to worry over, as the removal had already been paid for and our passage to Canada also. My short stories were selling well.

On the twentieth of May we sailed from Southampton. The voyage was made in continuous fair weather.

Chapter 17

Canada

I<small>T</small> <small>WAS</small> a joy to be again united with our friends in Canada. After many excursions we at last found a house to suit us. It belonged to Colonel Ponton Armour and was at Erindale, just a few miles from Trail Cottage. It stood high above a river and the lands surrounding it were let to a farmer. We might have enjoyed life there had it not been for two things — the unusually exhausting heat and a motor accident in which Caroline was seriously injured. We were giving a party and she had gone to Oakville to buy provisions. We had brought our car from England with us — an Austin, twelve-six, at that time something of a curiosity on the roads. Caroline was driven to Oakville by a neighbouring youth called Vincent. As they were leaving the village, they were facing several cars going in the opposite direction. One of them, in haste to pass the others, came in head-on collision with our car. Vincent was unhurt, but Caroline had a shattered wrist, injuries to her head, back and leg. A local doctor gave her first aid. While she sat in his surgery waiting, the owner of the car which had run into ours came to the door of the surgery.

"I hear," he said to Caroline, with an ingratiating smile, "that you are Miss de la Roche, the novelist. I am pleased to meet you."

She assured him that she was no such person.

"How disappointing!" he exclaimed; then, without uttering another word, he walked away.

Our car had been wrecked. A pleasant Irishman drove Caroline to the hospital but first brought her in his car to Springfield Farm to tell me of the accident.

My little Esmée and I were on our way to the gate to meet her. When we saw her, white-faced, with bandaged head and arm in a sling, Esmée tugged at my hand.

"Mummy, Mummy," she implored, "let's go away and hide."

Nanny went with Caroline at once to the hospital and I, after collecting necessary things, followed. With Spartan self-control she climbed onto the operating table. She had no preparatory sedative.

The days that followed were spent at the hospital by me. They were days of great anxiety. At last Caroline was able to return to Springfield Farm, accompanied by a nurse. It was now late August. There was no question of our returning to England before the autumn. All four of us had felt the effect of the heat, but September was truly lovely. Stone steps led down to the river and on either bank were sumachs and soft maples that showed red and gold in the misty sunlight. There were a few apple trees and the bright red apples lay in the long grass. Two old horses ambled about, neglected, carefree, munching apples. Down there the children and we spent hours at childish play. It seemed that all our troubles of the summer were over.

But no! One afternoon Esmée came running to me. "Mummy," she said, in an excited important voice, "Auntie Cara has stepped into a hole and broken her leg. We know it's broken because we heard it crack. Come quickly and see."

I sped over the rough ground to where she was sitting with an expression the most doleful. "Oh, how could I do this to you," she cried, "when you've had so much worry already!"

How often I had begged her not to venture down by the river while she was still on crutches! Now one of the crutches, going into a hole, had been the cause of her falling. Nanny and the maid carried her slight weight up the steps and into the house. The local doctor set the leg in splints, the children, enthralled, squatting close, I walking the floor.

I am sure the ankle would have mended properly as it was set, but no — she must (after a sleepless night of apprehension) be taken to the hospital to have X rays, an anaesthetic and the bone reset, the leg put into a cast. Only the week before had the cast been taken from her arm and three doctors had tried to persuade us to have the wrist broken again and a better job made of the setting. We refused, feeling that we had been through all we could bear.

So — once again there was convalescence at Springfield Farm, plans for the coming months, for we had decided to spend the winter in Toronto. There were many things to be done. The house we occupied had been only partly furnished. We had got some of our furniture out of store and also brought from Trail Cottage a mahogany dining-table and dresser we had bought from the Fairbairns of Clarkson. From storage we had got the cases containing what was left of my grandfather de la Roche's library. Of the original thirty cases there were now a half-dozen. But they were large — there were hundreds of books. With aching back I put myself to the task of sorting them. Caroline did what she could to help me, but she still could not use her left arm and her left leg was in a cast. Yet her spirits were good. She would execute a sort of dance on her crutches to the great enjoyment of the children. What she had taken very hard was the destruction of our car. She, who had not shed a tear for her own pain, broke into sobs when I told her that the car had been wrecked.

Our friend Pelham Edgar had found a furnished house for us in Toronto. It belonged to Walter Kingsmill and was in Castle Frank Road. Three hired cars and a truck conveyed us there. The packing cases and furniture were stored in the garage. We disposed ourselves in the house. It was a charmingly furnished house but extraordinarily cold. The room I had chosen for the nursery was too cold for the children, so they lived in and out of our rooms, which pleased them very well. Nanny was adaptable. She had spent years in Japan, as nurse to the little son of a Japanese official, from early infancy till he was whisked off at eight years into a military academy. She had endured the torrid heat of the past summer without complaint. Now with stolid composure she faced the bitter cold. The children enjoyed the snow. With their toboggan they gambolled in the snowdrifts on the lawn. I taught them to make a snowman. Caroline taught them Christmas carols. For playmates they had Hugh Eayrs's fine little sons.

The Master of Jalna had been published, and in November I began a new novel of the Whiteoaks which I called *Cousin Malahide* but later changed the title to *Young Renny*. I could not deny the demands of readers who wanted to know more of that family. Still less could I deny the urge within myself to write of them. Sometimes I see reviews in which the critic commends a novelist for not attempting to repeat former successes, and then goes on to say what an inferior thing his new novel is. If a novelist is prolific, he is criticized for that, yet in all other creative forms — music, sculpture, painting — the artist may pour out his creations without blame. But the novelist, like the actor, must remember his audience. Without an audience, where is he? Like the actor, an audience is what he requires first, last and all the time. But, unlike

273

the actor, he can work when he is more than half ill and may even do his best work then. Looking back, it seems to me that the life of the novelist is the best of all and I would never choose any other.

I had written but a chapter or two of *Young Renny* when Spencer Curtis Brown wrote to me to say that Nancy Price was going to produce *Whiteoaks* and would like me to help with the production if possible. There was great excitement in our house — even down to the little ones. We could not leave them before Christmas, but we booked our passage for early January, even though Caroline was still using a stick.

It was a handsome, snowy Christmas and shortly before the holiday Edward Weeks came from Boston. He was a vastly entertaining guest. To the music of the gramophone he would dance as an Apache, draped in a colourful curtain and brandishing a carving knife, or he would, in a high-pitched la-di-da voice, deliver an imitation of certain lecturers. I never have been addicted to prolonged serious conversations. Like Gran Whiteoak I like people who can make me laugh.

Our housemaid at that time had been reared in a convent. She made a lovely and reverent crêche for my children, and though they are now grown up and married, I still have a crêche for them each Christmas. This same maid, no sooner had Caroline and I set forth on our journey than she lighted a fire in the drawing-room, put on her best dress and seated herself by the blaze with her embroidery, while Nanny and the children looked on in chilly disapproval.

We sailed from Boston. We had sherry and a welcome hot bath at the Weekses, lunch with the McIntyres, tea with the Sedgwicks, and so on to the *Britannic*. It was a rough and bitterly cold voyage. At Halifax it was twenty below zero. We stood on deck and watched a consignment of apples being loaded on to the ship. Suddenly one of the dock hands slipped and fell into the icy water. There was a shout, a splash, and he had disappeared, but soon he came to the surface again and was rescued.

It was misty and mild off the coast of Ireland and in London it was springlike. Shipboard friends, Sir Harry and Lady Armstrong, had urged us to go to one of the large hotels, where they were staying. We did, but before long tired of it and returned to our Miss Stuart's little private hotel in Portman Square. It was exhilarating to be in London once again. It was exhilarating to meet Nancy Price. She was enthusiastic about the play. We spent hours talking it over; she had suggestions to make which I was ready to follow. Caroline had brought her typewriter along and we worked hard together. I was so ignorant of the ways of the theatre that I had expected rehearsals to begin at once and the play produced in a few weeks. I had still to experience the delays, the disappointments of the theatre. I sometimes wonder why a novelist should trouble his head about it, but — having had one success, it is difficult to forget.

Not only did Caroline and I work hard at *Whiteoaks*, but we went to many plays and parties. We went to theatrical parties, but I was somehow disillusioned. I was too romantic about the stage. I expected too much. When I had finished the seemingly slight but tedious work on *Whiteoaks*, I returned with thankful spirit to my novel *Young Renny*. All through my stay in London I had been darkly yearning toward it. Once more engrossed in it, I turned my back on the stage and its harassments. *Beside a Norman Tower* (a story of my children) was to be published in the autumn and Daniel Macmillan had promised that it should be illustrated by A. H. Watson, who so charmingly captured the grace of early childhood.

At this time we were in one of our periods of uncertainty over where to live. Now it was a house in Jersey. Now it was a villa in Antibes. My experience is — never be led to go to any place to which you are advised. There is nothing so enjoyable to most people as to recommend situations (preferably at the ends of the earth) where the climate is perfect, the natives friendly and the scenery divine.

Two topics were engaging the minds of Londoners. One was the sudden death of the King of the Belgians while mountain climbing. The other was the disappearance of Frank Vosper from an ocean liner. He had been seen by two companions late at night in his cabin. It was known that he did not leave it through the door. Yet in the morning he was gone, though the porthole was too small for a man of his size to negotiate. Not long before, we had met him at a theatrical party, had liked him and admired him as an actor.

Before we sailed for Canada I signed the contract for the production of *Whiteoaks*, but I cannot remember whether or not the date was set. We returned a little subdued. We had taken passage on the *Adriatic* and this was to be her last voyage. There was a feeling of sadness among the officers and stewards, some of whom had served on her for many years. They declared, and I could see this was true, that none of the new liners, for all of their flamboyant elegance, could compare with her. But one thing was wrong and that was the plumbing. A heavy scent of disinfectant pervaded our cabins. They smelled most terribly like kennels. So much so that at times I was driven to growl like a dog.

But the fruit! Never have I seen such an abundance of superb fruit on a ship. I would wake at six in the morning to eye the massive mound of grapes, nectarines, pears and tangerines within reach. The result! I had no appetite for breakfast and, by the time we reached Boston, was quite bilious. In one of the most glorious spring skies I ever have seen, Ted Weeks came aboard and lunched with us. He was delighted, he said, by *Beside a Norman Tower*. He was interested but doubtful of my going back to the year 1906 in *Young Renny*. Later he changed his mind and gave it a welcome into the fold.

It was early March. Boston had been springlike, but in New York it was winter, with a wind that shook you and icy sleet that wet the face. And there was a strangely troubled meeting with Pierre. I was glad to leave that city and return to Toronto and my children.

They were delighted by their presents from London but most of all by our reunion — to be together again, to tell us of the dancing class of which they were the smallest. It was heaven to be home, I thought, but truly we had no home and there were a thousand things to do, before we again sailed for England. Dinners, clubs, speeches, a few nostalgic days at Trail Cottage. Then the discovery that my grandfather's books (the last and best of them) had been stolen. As I have said, I selected them before we left Springfield Farm, and, wrapping them carefully, laid them in five large packing cases. I was proud of their beautiful bindings. I pictured them on the shelves of my study in England and felt a glow of affection for the grandfather I had never seen. But, though I had wrapped them carefully, with the assistance of one of the removal men, I had had no lids for the cases. I would get them later, I thought, with my usual manner of putting things off — which I vary by impulsive and unpremeditated action. No one is less smug about his faults than I. I am dreadfully conscious of them and deplore them, but always too late.

We had no motor car. The garage had seemed an ideal place for storing the books and some furniture and china. Now on this spring morning I opened the door with confidence. The furniture was there. The barrels of china there. The books, no! I could not believe my eyes. I ran into the house to tell Caroline. She came. But no amount of searching discovered the boxes of books. It was clear that they never had been stored there, for during all those months the door had been locked.

Now was the strongest link with the romantic figure of my grandfather broken. I had his ring, I had two mahogany chairs, with crest inset, I had his photograph — that was all, with the exception of a few books.

Some months later a friend of mine came upon three volumes in a second-hand book shop and bought them for the sake of their binding. In them was my grandfather's name. In their margins, his notes, in his small, precise handwriting.

When I look at his photograph, I am conscious of his almost mysterious influence on my life. When I look on that profile, I see a man worldly, yet remote; passionate, yet without warmth; talented, yet without ambition. What a contrast to the simplicity of his wife — to the fire and tenderness and generous impulses of his son, my father!

So, in the loss of the books our visit to Canada came to an end. Yet in this visit was the renewing and strengthening of my friendship with Anne and Edward Dimock. I shall never forget their kindness at the time of Caroline's accident, nor cease to be grateful for the shrewd, yet cautious, interest Edward has shown in the management of my financial affairs, in which, with such good example, I have no ability to profit or to learn but remain as ignorant as were probably my ancient Celtic forbears, accepting without question what their gods sent them.

Chapter 18

The Cliffs
and the Heath

NEVER shall I forget that arrival in England. Unlike many of our other landings, there was no confusion and the weather was perfect. Sky and sea vied with each other in blueness. It was Sunday morning in Plymouth and church bells were ringing. Not many were disembarking there. We four stood on the deck of the tender waving good-bye to shipboard friends. Of the forty children who had been present at the children's party on board, mine were the most beautiful. Now, standing trim and straight on Nanny's either hand, they waved to the other children with no sentiment of warmth. The only person on board for whom they felt warmth of sentiment was a professor from Montreal who hated children. He had asked to have his deck chair placed far away from them. But to escape was impossible. Every child liked him on sight. They brought their toys and romped about his chair. Over the top of his detective novel he glared at them in hate, and they ran to him and clasped his knees.

Now Esmée waved a tiny hand at him. "Good-bye," she called out. "Have a nice time."

The harbour was bright as a sea-shell in the blazing sun.

"Is this England?" asked Esmée.

"Yes," I answered, drawing a long breath of the air. "It is England."

René was about to have his fourth birthday. He felt important.

"I was just going to say," he observed, "that it is England."

All the way across the harbour on the puffing tender we kept counting our luggage.

"There were eight trunks and seventeen small pieces," I declared.

Caroline interrupted almost hysterically. "No, no, there were *nine* trunks and *sixteen* small pieces. My new revelation is lost!"

Nanny cried, "Where is the children's trunk? Please let me count: one — two — three — four —"

The children too began to count.

In the customs we had difficulty in persuading the official that we had nothing to declare, after a whole year out of England. I urged my keys upon him, imploring him to search through all the mound of luggage, but he drew back in dismay and without further enquiry chalked the magic sign on all the pieces. Two porters threw themselves into the task of installing us in taxis.

Possibly I had over-tipped on board ship. But, whatever the reason, I had only a half-crown left when I had paid the taxi driver. In the hotel Nanny came to me.

"We must have a bottle of milk of magnesia," she said.

"How much is it?" I asked.

"Two and six."

I put the half-crown into her hand.

Now I was in a difficult position. There was my child, expectant of birthday presents. There was I, penniless, till the bank in Plym-

outh could be assured from London that I had an account there.
The teller had written to London; the thought of a telegram had
not occurred to him and when I had suggested it, he had drawn
back from such a headlong procedure. On the birthday morning
Caroline and I hastened to the bank and were informed that no
word had as yet come from London.

"But what am I to do?" I cried. "It is my child's birthday. He
is four years old to-day and I have not a penny in my pocket for a
present or to pay for the cake I have ordered from the bakery! It
has his name on it in pink icing."

"On my own responsibility," said the teller, "I will advance you
five pounds."

I could have hugged him. It was glorious to march through the
crowded street with a pocketful of money, past women shopping
with big baskets, past sailors returned from long voyages, past
cafés where people were drinking morning coffee, to the largest
toy shop.

It was a successful birthday. The garden behind the hotel was
delightful. On the lawn in front there were fine shade trees and
a thousand daisies for making daisy chains. But we could not remain there for long. A house must be found for the summer — a
house by the sea, with a garden for the children. This hotel was
no place for a little boy just discovering the delights of conversation and asking questions.

It was an old-fashioned hotel and many of the guests were
elderly gentlemen and permanent. One of them, a retired naval
officer, sat at the table next our own. His red felt slippers seemed
a warning for quiet. Every time the little clear pipe broke the
silence of the dining-room Caroline, Nanny and I would exclaim
in one breath, "Sh-h."

In embarrassment he would lower his head, but the very next

instant his voice would pipe out again. "Where are we going to live next? Are we going to live here forever?"

The old gentlemen would look round the barrier of their newspapers, their expressions saying, "God forbid!"

But where were we to find the perfect house? Caroline and I explored the seaside villages of Cornwall. At night we would sink down exhausted and always came the question, "Have you found a house for us?" Finally we did, in Seaton, not far from where we had once lived. The owner and his daughter were on a fishing trip to Norway. There was a vegetable garden, a flower garden, a cook, a gardener, and a glorious view. So, with our mountain of luggage, we disappeared from Plymouth and, after two weeks in a comfortable little hotel right on the sea, we moved into the house which was called Normanhurst. During that fortnight I had struggled with the weighty correspondence now a part of my life. Now once again in the privacy of a house I returned to the writing of *Young Renny*.

As to weather, it was a lovely summer, hot and sunny. I had rented a beach hut for the children and there they and Nanny spent most of the day, Caroline and I joining them for tea. Sometimes we walked along the cliffs to Beer, which we and the children loved for its gulls and fishing boats. Has it changed? It is twenty years since I have seen it. We went to Sanger's Circus and I was very much afraid of the lions. The children not at all. Two shillings extra I paid for each of our five seats — the reason (discovered too late), that they had red carpet laid on them. Still, we had a good view of Bonnie Black Bess ridden by Dick Turpin, and of all the galloping dancing ponies. It was a carefree life we led that summer.

The St. John Ervines lived conveniently near. Both were enthusiastic gardeners and their garden by the sea I never shall forget. There was more leisure for growing flowers in those days. Leonora Ervine had not yet taken on the many civic duties which now rest on her competent shoulders.

We went to the Braggs' at Hawkchurch for tea and saw the rectory where we had lived, standing beautiful and desolate. We had a mind to go back there. Yet I wanted to be somewhere nearer to London, for there now seemed some likelihood that my play *Whiteoaks* would be produced in the near future. But always there were fresh demands as to rights to be coped with, combined with the other vagaries of theatrical management.

My novel *Jalna* was being filmed in Hollywood by R.K.O. with a cast including C. Aubrey Smith, Nigel Bruce, Ian Hunter, Peggy Wood and Kay Johnson. These were excellent, but the part of the grandmother could scarcely have been more ill-cast. Not one of the attributes that made old Adeline Whiteoak notable belonged to the actress who played the part. Readers of the books wrote to tell me of their dissatisfaction with the film. A scene between Meg Whiteoak and Maurice Vaughan was introduced which really angered me. When the producers sent me an advance script, I wrote telling them, in quite unmeasured terms, of my disapproval. I never shall forget the polite answer I received. It was to the effect that the scene in question would be acted *so innocently* that I should find nothing in it to offend. Yet when I saw the film in London, my feelings remained the same as when I read the script.

While *Jalna* (the film) was simmering in Hollywood and *Whiteoaks* (the play) was simmering in London, *Young Renny* (the novel) was fairly boiling over in Boston. I cannot actually remember what it all was about, excepting that Ellery Sedgwick had wanted changes made to which I could not agree. Alfred McIntyre was on my side. The book, when published, had a good reception from critics and public alike, and has lately been admirably televised by the B.B.C.

Meanwhile the owner of Normanhurst was soon to return from Norway. We must find another house. Most earnestly we longed for something more permanent. But where? We toyed with the idea of acquiring a castle in Wales which might be bought for a song. We toyed with the idea of a villa in the south of France or on the island of Jersey. We ended by returning to our little hotel in Lyme, while Caroline and I set about the fascinating and exhausting business of house-hunting. From Sussex to the Cotswolds we searched. Then a chance remark of Leonora Ervine's came to mind. She had said that, if she were to leave Devon, she would choose Malvern above all other places in England. I cannot remember whether she gave any reason for this, but I remembered the remark, which she had probably by that time forgotten, and I said, "Let's see what we can see in Malvern."

The agent there had, he said, the very house for us. Not in any of the several Malverns but in the near-by village of Colwall. It had large grounds, with specimen trees from distant countries. The house itself would not be ready till the New Year, as some repairs were necessary, but, he promised, it was well worth waiting for. At this time I was in love with Frampton Manor near Stroud. It was an ancient house with an adorable little stairway leading to a small panelled room called Fair Rosamond's Bower. I liked everything about Frampton Manor though it did seem rather out of repair — a door fell on us as we were going through it — and there was at the back a canal which Caroline said would be dangerous for the children. I had pictured them sailing their boats in it. There was an apple tree at the front and apples of a pale golden colour lay on the lush green grass. I ate one and thought I never had tasted an apple so delicious.

We decided to lease the house in Colwall, after we had been captivated by the views in a splendid sunset — the Welsh mountains to the west, and to the east Great Malvern and the Malvern Hills. We thought we were lucky to have acquired such a place, even though it was almost three hours from London and we had been resolved to find a house near-by.

The problem now was to find a home for us where we could be comfortable till The Winnings (a corruption of The Winnowings) was ready for us. There were Nanny and the little ones expectant in Lyme Regis. This problem was solved by Mrs. Lyons Biggar, a Toronto friend visiting in London. She advised us to secure the house of her brother-in-law, Harry Biggar. He was Canadian archivist in Europe and was to be absent till the New Year. His young son, the actor John Vere, took Caroline down to Worpleston to see the house. She liked it very much indeed and late October saw us installed there for two very pleasant months. It was heaven to the children, for there was a nursery full of toys, a fox terrier full of high spirits, and a dear old butler, named Drury, who was overflowing with kindness. There was a cook who baked the best bread I ever have tasted. And all about the house was the lovely heath for our walks. How well I remember the four of us, laden with Christmas parcels for Canada, going in Indian file along the narrow paths to the post office, stopping to gaze wistfully at the gypsies' camp, the glowing fire with the pot above it, the dark children playing among the heather, the grazing ponies.

My mind was now at rest concerning *Young Renny*, for my Boston publishers wrote of their satisfaction in it. I was at work on a play called *Snow in Saskatchewan*. In my fancy I pictured this as a success but could not find a producer for it.

Yes, we were happy. The neighbouring families were friendly.

285

The children went to parties. But ahead of us lay the tumult of removal and the settling into a new home. We would remain there for years and years, we were sure of that.

We had become attached to the heath, to the two who so well had served us during those months, especially to Drury, the butler, who looked like a particularly benign bishop. He was very fond of the children and when we said good-bye, he presented Caroline and me with a handsome cloth for the tea table which he had himself made.

Chapter 19

The Winnings

WE LEFT for Herefordshire two days after Christmas. It was one of the most uncomfortable journeys I can remember, the weather unspeakably miserable, the officials glum, the train unheated and I acquiring a bad cold. When we arrived at the private hotel in Colwall, I was forced to go straight to bed. This hotel, or I should rather say guest house, had not long been open. I think we were the first guests. It had been a large private house whose owner had kept thirty-seven small dogs in it. The new owner told me that he had been hard put to it to get rid of the smell of kennel.

Cook's vans were at the door of The Winnings. Wet snow was dimly falling when I walked slowly along the village street, with its tall iron fences, its dripping conifers, its unfriendly-looking houses. How different it all was from that first visit in the flaming sunset. The front door stood wide open. Inside Caroline was watching a man who was trying to re-create a chandelier from a mound of crystals, to which it had been reduced for storage. This dining-room was an enormous room and when first we saw it, had been carpeted, curtained and papered in ox-blood red. The owner, Mr. Ballard, had willingly redecorated the house to our taste, with the exception of the dining-room, which he greatly admired. But

Caroline had been firm. So it too was done over. Our furniture looked sparse but elegant in the dining-room, where formerly there had stood an enormous table, many chairs, a piano and an organ. The walls had been covered by water-colour drawings done by the sisters of the owner. This Mr. Ballard was a man of strong character, a domineering man, I should say, but always very nice to us. His grandfather had been a noted engineer who had done much work abroad and from abroad had brought many of the specimen trees that graced the grounds of The Winnings. For some unknown reason he had had a tunnel dug there, but it led nowhere and was the home of bats.

What views I had from the window of my study! In the west lay the dark mountains of Wales. On the east the stark Malvern Hills. But in springtime they were not stark. They rose in mystery from a white storm of fruit trees in blossom. Many a good walk had Caroline and the children and I on the winding paths of those hills. George Bernard Shaw loved them and came each year to the festival at Malvern. Everything he did there was considered noteworthy, if it was merely to bend and stroke a cat.

We saw the first performance of *Saint Joan*, with Wendy Hiller, whom Shaw himself had chosen for the part. We sat directly behind Shaw at the first performance of *The Simpleton of the Unexpected Isles*. He appeared cheerfully interested during the first act, in the interval told me he was satisfied by it — after that he fell shamelessly asleep till he slipped out just before the final curtain.

Can genius be all excuse for rudeness? I did not think so when, in the hospitable house of the Reyner Woods, in Colwall, Shaw exclaimed when refusing tea, "I have not taken it since I had it here a year ago and I hope never to take it again!"

The Winnings was convenient to Malvern. It was convenient to

Stratford-on-Avon. We used to drive there for matinees, and have a picnic lunch on the way. After the play, tea and the lovely drive home. There was no end to the delightful places to which we could motor when the weather was fine, and our chauffeur-gardener Imms enjoyed these trips almost as well as we. Into Wales, along the valley of the Wye, to Evesham and Gloucester and Cheltenham. As well as being an excellent driver, Imms was a musician. He and his children all could play an instrument with facility. Proud were Caroline, the children and I when, on Remembrance Day, Imms sounded "The Last Post" in the Abbey Church.

The grounds of The Winnings were so large, there was so much to be cared for — flower borders, greenhouses, lily pond — pruning and grass mowing — one man could not do it alone. Imms was but the assistant to Fletcher. Fletcher was a fine, sturdy man whose thick thatch of hair was grizzled, yet he was called the "young" gardener, since he had come to The Winnings as a youth. He grew beautiful flowers and, in the greenhouse, grapes and tomatoes. When we were discussing what varieties of flowers to plant in the borders, he always would end by saying, "And there's allus *pansies.*" His eyes would shine with pleasure at the mere thought of them. He had a great admiration for my little Esmée. "Ah," he would exclaim with relish, "her's a grand little sowl."

What a tumult of blossoms there appeared in the spring! The magnolia trees, almond blossoms, daffodils and hyacinths, each urging their supremacy. An old quarry was in the middle of the grounds and it had been made into a retreat for the shyer flowers, and in its seclusion was a thatched summer house.

In riotous mood some former owner (one of the Ballards, of course) had had a large swimming pool made. This was surrounded by a high fence and there were two dressing-rooms, so decent privacy was preserved. The children would sail their toy boats in the pool, while Nanny sat knitting. The water had become a little green and slimy. I did not think it safe for bathing.

The Winnings was a wonderful place for children — the big rambling house, the grounds with their endless possibilities for hide and seek. But, better even than games with their little friends, the children delighted in a certain game they played with me. It was called the Knock Family. I was Mrs. Knock, Esmée and René were Matilda and Augustus Knock. This game was a denial of the teaching which should be instilled into all well-brought-up children. Mrs. Knock invariably went on a visit, after giving strict orders as to good behavior. The perverse part of the game was this — if on her return Matilda and Augustus had been good children, they were given the most ingenious punishments, but if they had been bad, they were treated to the most extravagant rewards. The result was a riot during her absence. Caroline refused to have any part in this disorder but shut herself away in her own rooms while the noisy game went on. At the end the children and I fell in an exhausted heap on the sofa.

Before long, to join in all our activities, came two puppies, a Scotch terrier and a Cairn. The Scotty was named Moulin, after a village in Scotland, the Cairn terrier — Duff. There is a story, "April Day," concerning these two included in a collection of my animal stories, entitled *The Sacred Bullock.*

Moulin and Duff were not the only dogs in the house. There was another, an old spaniel named Major, which we seldom saw but often smelled, for a most strange and permeating odour came from him. He became a member of our household in this way: We had engaged as cook a Mrs. Watts, who came from the village and whose husband was the local postman. He also delivered telegrams. He was a vague little man and always he had depended on his wife to rouse him in the morning. Now, though she bought the noisiest

alarm clock in Malvern, he overslept. This was serious for a postman. He must rise early for all he had to do. To deliver a telegram,
for which he received sixpence, he sometimes trudged a mile.
There was nothing to do but bring him to The Winnings, and, of
course, Major the spaniel too.

Now I would see, coming in or leaving by the back entrance, the
mystic figure of the little postman, his spaniel at his heels. Now,
hanging on a nail in the kitchen, was his official cap. It gave us a
sense of security to see it hanging there. It was wonderful to hand
a letter to him instead of going all the way to the post office to
mail it.

The cook would have been a contented woman, with her postman
safe beside her, in the dim chill of the domestic quarters had it not
been for Aggie.

Aggie came to us as an experienced house-parlour maid, after
a deal of anxious search, for good domestic help was beginning to
be scarce in that part of the country. When first I set eyes on her,
I thought, "One thing is certain. There will be no trouble from 'followers.' She's too ugly for that." Not so. Aggie had not been a week
in the house when, passing the kitchen, I saw her sitting on the
knee of a nice-looking rosy-cheeked young man. There she sat,
looking quite possessive, with her round pale eyes, turned-up nose,
codfish mouth and no chin!

Never have I known such a worker. She delighted in work. She
had a mania for work. She was a worker to end all work. Her
eyes watered with joy at the very mention of her favourite furniture polish.

The guest room was her treasure. She brushed the nap of
the carpet to perfect smoothness, then locked the door and hid
the key lest one of the family should ruffle its surface by a step.
In the bed of that room she kept a hot-water bottle, locked safely

in for an imaginary guest. She hated the dogs and they scuttled out
of the way at her sinister approach.

They might hide from her, but Mrs. Watts, the cook, could not
hide. All day long and till bedtime she was exposed to Aggie's
ceaseless flow of talk. Aggie was collecting sofa cushions for her future home. She had a dozen of them but no prospect of a sofa. From
a little seamstress she ordered an embroidered quilt which took a
month in the making, but when it was done, she refused to accept
it. Raising her voice, she browbeat the weeping seamstress into a
state of near collapse. Then, and then only, did the cook complain
to Caroline, who discovered how ill Mrs. Watts was looking. She
had been a healthy woman, but Aggie was killing her. So I was
forced to tell her to leave our service.

A scene followed in which Aggie unloosed a torrent of explanations and complaints in her terrible locomotive-clanking voice. I
tell this because it was the only time in my life when I felt a sudden violent urge to strike someone, a primitive urge to obliterate
that person. I remembered what she had done to the cook, how
relentlessly, stupidly cruel she was — oh, I do not think I remember anything — I just looked at the brass fire irons — I saw the
brass poker — and I said to Aggie, "Not another word out of you!
Go, before you get hurt!"

"Who are you to threaten me?" she screamed. "I'll see a lawyer
about this." But she fled.

I am writing this on the day after Christmas, the season of goodwill, yet I discover that my face is set in a small grin of relish as
I recall that scene — Aggie's staring codfish face, the shining
poker, Caroline's startled eyes, my own murderous urge.

Aggie left and we never again heard of her. Peace flourished. Her
place was taken by a niece of the cook's who was just as pretty as
Aggie was ugly, as untidy and lazy as Aggie was neat and hard-

working. So we were happy again — the cook, the postman, their spaniel, their niece, and my own family and dogs.

Especially were the children and Nanny happy, because a tiny kindergarten school had appeared, right next door to us. This had been built in the grounds of the Downs School for the small son of the headmaster. He was Geoffrey Hoyland and he had married the daughter of Dame Elizabeth Cadbury. These two clever people, who, indeed, owned the place, had made an unusual school of it, where the ninety boys were cared for and fed with real solicitude. It was a preparatory school. Their boy of four had no companions of his own age. They were delighted to have René as a neighbour, and now the kindergarten school appeared, as it were, overnight, where Jim Hoyland, my two children, and three little girls of the neighbourhood were given easy lessons by an indulgent but firm young teacher. Nanny would take my two and the dogs along a grassy lane that led from the grounds of The Winnings to the grounds of the school, for she would not allow the children to go even that short distance without her. While she led them into the schoolroom, she tied the leads to the outer handle of the door and so the little dogs awaited her return.

Later on, René was to enter the Downs School. Knowing this, I had an especial pleasure in going to the plays at the school and to the sports. How those little fellows could dive and swim in the big pool! W. H. Auden was then a master there. I had read some of his poems and meeting him briefly I told him I was glad that René was to have a poet as one of his teachers. He was rather a heavily built young man with hair so fair it was almost straw coloured. Of him, Geoffrey Hoyland remarked to me, with a troubled yet magnanimous smile:

"Well, he's young and I think he'll improve. Yes, he'll surely improve."

These little dogs were characters indeed. Moulin, the Scotty, pugnacious, a fighter born, but gentle and almost apologetic toward Duff, the Cairn, who, toward Moulin, was fiercely jealous and supercilious, but to us sensitive and loving. What grounds were those for dogs and children! Intriguing, with unexpected humps and hollows, sending out their wild sweet scents, and always in the distance the proud Malvern Hills, the dark mountains of Wales, where the sun set.

A pear tree grew wild in the grounds and we discovered that our terriers had an avid taste for pears. When we discovered this, we had been anxious about them for some days. They were unusually quiet and had no appetite whatever. What had happened to them, we wondered. . . . Then, loitering in the grounds, I came upon them fairly gorging themselves on the ripe little pears, their two faces raised heavenward as they munched, while the sweet juice trickled down their chins.

While the dogs, the children and Nanny, the cook, the postman, and their dog were occupied with their many activities, Caroline and I were not idle. She coped with the housekeeping and was critic and secretary to me, though much of the typing was done by professional typists. I have already mentioned my book about the children — *Beside a Norman Tower.* Now I completed another on the same volatile subject. This was *The Very House.* These were in no sense fiction and were a change and relaxation from my other work. Plays were disappointing. The trouble with my plays is that they offer no important part to tempt a female star, with the exception of *Whiteoaks,* and in it the star must take the part of a centenarian. St. John Ervine had said to me: "You must cut out that business of the false teeth. No actress will ever consent to do it. . . ." Yet Nancy Price and Ethel Barrymore faced up to it with admirable *sang-froid.*

I had hoped that Raymond Massey would be interested in *Snow in Saskatchewan*, but he was not. Now word came from Nancy Price that she could not secure a theatre for the production of *Whiteoaks*. I began to wonder if the play ever would be produced. There was too much of postponement in the theatre, I told myself, and I turned with relief and a fresh zest to the writing of my new novel, *Whiteoak Harvest*. The first English reviews of *Young Renny* now came to me. At that time I still read reviews with earnest attention.

The weather was glorious. We went to London, where all was astir for the King's Jubilee. We had feared that Caroline would not be able to travel, for she had given her heel a severe gash when a bottle fell from a shelf above the bath and was splintered. At the time I was in bed asleep. Caroline called Nanny, who understood something of first aid and bound up the foot. But my shock, when, next morning, I entered the blood-splashed bathroom, may be imagined.

Caroline should certainly have had a doctor, but she, usually a Spartan, was afraid — not of having stitches put in the gash but of having them *taken out*. She appeared in London, wearing on the cut foot one of Nanny's large flat-heeled shoes and carrying a stick. So we went, in glorious hot weather, to the Jubilee service in St. Paul's. In Malvern there was a blazing bonfire on the beacon and a procession, to which went Nanny with the children and dogs, all bursting with pride to see Imms playing so nobly in the band.

We were really settling down, we thought. There were so many interesting places within motoring distance — the Wye valley, the Cotswolds, the lonely roads and monasteries of Wales. I remember with delight a performance of *Noah*, in front of the open door of Tewkesbury Abbey, with lovely golden angels on the walls and God speaking in sonorous tones from the topmost tower. I remember too how frozen cold were my feet and legs. All the beauty of the performance could not quite make me forget these chilled members. Looking back on our life at The Winnings, I remember best the sweet-scented pleasures of the summer and the chill of the winter. When I took Esmée to her dancing class in Ledbury, I was almost frozen, but she was dancing and did not mind. Even when Caroline and I brushed up our dancing with the same teacher, we were chilly. To be sure, we had central heating at The Winnings, but the furnace stood in a niche outdoors, so that, as I sometimes remarked, it had to heat the mountains of Wales before any leftover warmth reached us. Indoors the house was now quite handsome, for we had brought over from Canada our furniture which had been in store there. Well I remember seeing it unloaded from the van. The removal men had taken out all but the last barrel. In it was well-packed the marble *Three Graces,* so loved by my mother. The men lifted out this barrel, then dropped it with a crash on the flagstones.

They were aghast at what they had done, but their feelings were as nothing to my shocked dismay. In that barrel was something that for many years had been treasured by my mother, that for many years had been the chief ornament of her drawing-room, that had survived our many removals and had twice crossed the ocean. In anxious silence the men righted the barrel, removed the lid and delved into the interior. Mixed with the packing material was a mass of shattered marble — graceful torsos, slender legs and arms — for my mother's sake my eyes were filled with tears as I turned away.

When I recall The Winnings, I see the lovely country which surrounds it. I smell the scent of magnolia and Spanish broom, see the storm of daffodils that swept the slope by the house in springtime, but I recall few people who were congenial to me. It was a contrast to South Devon, where we made many friends. But at

Colwall there were the Raynor-Woods and in their house I met our dear friends Zoë Puxley and Grizel Hartley.

We saw something of the Brett Youngs, who lived at Evesham. I remember his handsome dark blue eyes almost as well as I remember his excellent books. One day, when the St. John Ervines were visiting them, the two couples came to lunch with us. When they returned to the Brett Youngs' house, earlier than expected, they found the domestic staff relaxing in the deck chairs on the lawn. I do not think the Ervines would have minded this in their place, but it was very upsetting to the Brett Youngs.

Chapter 20

Whiteoaks —
the Play

THE FILM of *Jalna* was released. My New York agent and friend, Francis Arthur Jones, wrote telling me that it was drawing good crowds, but Kenneth McGowan wrote from Hollywood that it was treated with "respect but no raves." I did not wonder. In early November I finished the writing of *Whiteoak Harvest*. Eagerly I had strained toward its end, but when the last page was written, I did not know what to do with myself. Without those characters I was lost. It is as natural to me to write as it is to breathe, and all the excitement of production does not take the place of creation. The manuscript of *Whiteoak Harvest* was sent to my publishers. The manuscript of *Whiteoaks* — the play — was in the hands of Nancy Price, but she was unable, she said, to interest a manager in it. Again and again I wondered if ever it would be produced and reached the point where I did not much care. About my novels my feelings were very different. There my public was steady and warm-hearted. They understood me and I understood them, that is to say, I offered them lucidity and living characters and, in return, they gave me a belief in those characters which was equal to my own. In truth, considering the letters I continue to receive through the years, it seems to me that their acceptance of them exceeds mine. This applies only to the Whiteoak chronicles, because to them I have given the sustained work of a lifetime and my other books and many short stories are diversions, distractions. I make four exceptions — they are my novel *Growth of a Man* and my history of the Port of Quebec, both published later than the period of which I now write. The other exceptions are my first two novels, *Possession* and *Delight*. These four, so different, represent living, experience, and — in a way — failure, because they have been so overshadowed by the Whiteoaks.

In January, 1936, there were fogs and floods in England, the worst in many years. Gales of one hundred miles an hour swept the country. The dark days sped by with appalling swiftness. I suffered from severe chilblains. After two and a half years of waiting for a production of my play Nancy Price suggested I should write a new last act. I decided to put the play out of my mind, to forget about it.

As though with this decision, the weather cleared. Although it was mid-January the weather calmed. It became springlike and we had glorious walks with children and dogs on the Malvern Hills. One of these walks, however, was unfortunate and this was because of my own headlong behaviour. On this day the children luckily were not with us, so they did not see what happened. We were walking on the Downs Road when we met a young man with a Sealyham. It rushed at Moulin, who was on a lead, and attacked him. The two engaged in a fierce fight. To me it seemed that the Sealyham's jaws were closed on Moulin's eyeball and, in panic, I bent and took him by the jaws and tried to open them. He turned on me and viciously bit my left hand. It was well for me that I wore a stout glove, but, as it was, the lining had been gnawed into the wound. The young man, commiserating, now picked up his dog and accompanied us to our gate, while blood trickled from my hand onto the road. Moulin swaggered, as though he had won a great victory, and Duff fairly walked on tiptoe from excitement. The doctor came and cauterized the wound. The hand swelled till it was unrecognizable and I had another of those lessons which it has been my lot to learn, too late. Fortunately it was the left hand that was afflicted, so I was able to write, but for a fortnight I had considerable suffering.

The springlike weather left us and we had a real snowfall. It was a shock to Nanny when I bundled the children up and took them out into the snow to make a snowman. It was a shock to her when I allowed them — encouraged them — to take the drumstick of a chicken in their hand and pick it clean, but how they enjoyed it!

January of that year was an eventful and sad one for the country. In midmonth Rudyard Kipling died and, only a few days later, our King. I remember the moving dignity of the radio announcements of his last hours. Far away in our snowy hills we heard the voice. "The King's life is drawing peacefully to its close." Everything sounded more portentous in that setting.

When the accession of Edward the Eighth was proclaimed, we gathered, from oldest to youngest, in a half-circle about the radio to listen. There was Fletcher, the "young" gardener, massively solemn, his curly grizzled hair growing low on his forehead, his cap, the colour of the good earth in which he worked, held in his hand. There was Imms, alert, fair-skinned, listening most intently when the trumpets were blown. There was the cook, placid yet properly sorrowful. There was Bessie, with her look of the healthy young female trying to be serious. There was the little postman (cook's husband) in his uniform. There were the children, on Nanny's either side. There were Caroline and me. There were the dogs.

All listening to that proclamation, and it seemed that the hills of Malvern and Wales listened too.

Caroline and I went to town for the funeral procession. As she had gone to the Jubilee service with a badly cut foot, so I went to the funeral procession with a badly bitten hand. We had excellent seats and as the new King walked by with his brothers (one soon to be King) our hearts went out to him in sympathy and homage. His face was wan and almost deadly pale. He raised his eyes to those seated above and they looked large and blue, with blue circles beneath them. It is difficult to think of him as the same man he is today.

After the funeral came the usual activity of a visit to London, buying clothes for the children, seeing plays, and the film of *Jalna*. Then home and immersed in family affairs and the writing of short stories and more work on the play *Whiteoaks*. Spring was struggling to be born. In every sheltered corner there were flowers. A new radiance touched the hills in early morning and at sundown. I did not want to go to London. I wanted to stay at home and begin a new novel. I was the prisoner of the novel and no excursions into play-writing could liberate me.

Yet, when Caroline and I found ourselves once more established in Virginia Temple-Godman's delightful little house in Stafford Place, we looked forward to our stay there with a good deal of exhilaration. The cook and the housemaid were glad to see us. "Welcome home," they exclaimed, when they opened the door to us. That maid, Violet, was, I believe, the most beautiful girl I ever have seen. When she brought my breakfast tray, I was newly astonished by her beauty. She made the movie stars look commonplace. She made fashionable debutantes look uninteresting. She was tall and elegantly proportioned — her face, with no make-up, perfect in symmetry — her colouring — but it would need a painting to re produce the lovely pallor of her skin, her silky black hair, her violet eyes. . . . Where is she now, I wonder!

There was work to be done on the play. Nancy Price came to lunch and we spent hours discussing it. She was an unusual theatre manager, in that she valued the opinion, the taste of the author. She had had a great success with the Chinese play *Lady Precious Stream*. Now the Little Theatre, where it had run, was free for *Whiteoaks*. Now, where all had been stagnation, there was activity. It was like a fresh wind blowing. I braced myself and faced it.

I liked Nancy Price. We got on well together. We spent interesting hours in her office at the theatre choosing the cast. Always was she ready, at that time, to defer to me, to select the actor or actress whom I considered best suited in appearance, in characteristics to the part. One of the first to join us was Stephen Haggard, a sensitive and alert young actor who already had had success on the London stage, who had won high praise from James Agate and Charles Morgan. He was to play the part of Finch Whiteoak. He was slenderly built, with a fine forehead, intense blue eyes and a mouth in which humour, courage and a certain boyish aloofness were blended. I think he was conscious of his own worth, yet never content. Later he told me that he would like to give up acting and become a novelist. He did indeed write one novel. He lost his life in North Africa during the war.

As Nancy Price was herself to play the part of the centenarian, Adeline Whiteoak, and Stephen Haggard that of the boy Finch, there remained the other members of the family, so familiar to so many readers of the books that to cast them was made more difficult. Nancy Price frequently made a pungent remark about the applicants before they appeared in the office. There was something eager and touching about these actresses and actors. I had a yearning over them, a desire to engage them all. A writer, if he has clean paper and a quiet room, can do his stuff, but the actor must have a part, a stage, an audience before he can show what he is made of. Some of them came to our house in Stafford Place to express their eagerness, and invariably I liked them and wished I could create a part for each.

The next parts to be filled were those of the two uncles and the aunt — Nicholas and Ernest Whiteoak and Lady Buckley. I well remember our interview with Aubrey Dexter, who played Nicholas. Nancy Price and I were sitting in her office, after interviewing a number of actors. She bent to sniff a bowl of hyacinths on the windowsill. "I must have flowers about me," she said. Her secretary announced Aubrey Dexter.

"I hope you will like him," Nancy Price said to me. "He should do the part well and at least he's a gentleman."

He came in, a man of only thirty-five — but already becoming a little heavy, distinguished-looking, with a fine voice. He was, when made up to appear elderly, the perfect Nicholas.

Frank Birch was to play the part of Ernest Whiteoak and to help in producing the play. He showed keen good humour and endless patience under the trials he endured. Lady Buckley was to be played by an actress, Jane Saville, who seemed made for the part and who, out of one particular line ("and to ramble so *rudely!*"), always brought a round of laughter from the audience. Nancy Price's lively daughter, Elizabeth Maude, was to play Meg Whiteoak. The lovely young Jill Furse was, after many interviews, chosen for Pheasant.

Ellis Irving, a handsome blond Australian, was to be Piers Whiteoak. I have seen the play a number of times, acted by very different types, but Ellis Irving was the best Piers by far that I have seen. He was virile and overbearing without being ruffianly, as I not long ago saw an actor in this role.

303

The important part of Renny Whiteoak was to be taken by Robert Newton, at that time very different in appearance from the Robert Newton of to-day, who, I hear, goes in for "tough parts." The first time I met him he was accompanied by a beautiful red cocker spaniel which he told me he had named "Renny" because of his admiration for Renny Whiteoak, before ever the thought of himself playing that part had occurred to him.

The youngest member of the cast was Tony Wickham, a clever boy who gave a vivid and humourous portrayal of Wakefield Whiteoak and moreover looked the part.

So the rehearsals began, the tension increasing day by day — sometimes Nancy Price and Frank Birch seemed at the point of explosion — still we all continued on speaking terms. The walk afterward to Stafford Place was peaceful in the lovely evening light. It was the only hour which was peaceful, for scarcely had I arrived at the house when there would be telephone calls to discuss this and that. I thought with longing of our hills, yet I cannot deny that I enjoyed the life of the theatre.

The stage of the Little Theatre was not always free for rehearsals. One took place in the bar. Sometimes we had them in the Savoy Theatre. Several times in a Swiss Waiters' Club. And wherever we were, there was Nancy Price's Pekinese behaving as though the responsibility, the agony of production were his. At the most unexpected moments he would rush from under a chair and fling himself at someone's ankles, but he loved his mistress, and how she loved him! She would fold him to her breast and exclaim, "I love him better than my daughters!" Of course, this was not true, but, at the moment, I am sure she thought so.

At that time I witnessed a curious change in Miss Price. Under my very eyes she became Adeline Whiteoak — that is, in her way of speaking, in her triumphant, half-jocular arrogance. No longer did she rehearse the part, she *lived* it, off stage as well as on. She was quite conscious of this. Indeed, she gloried in it. The acquisition of a parrot, to play the part of Boney, added zest to her fancy. When the long run of *Whiteoaks* was over, she still retained the parrot as a pet and, for all I know, may have him to this day.

I went home for a brief interlude before the final rehearsals. It was a lovely spring. The magnolias were just coming into flower, the garden teeming with colour and sweet scents. Caroline met me with the news that she had bought an exquisite Chinese cabinet, that Duff had bitten the postman and also that he had asserted his masculinity by lifting his leg against a tree instead of squatting puppy fashion. This last had, for some reason, given great satisfaction to Nanny. Moulin's laxness in regard to leg-lifting had been a source of humiliation to her. It was, she had seemed to think, a reflection on the family. With a sombre look she would regard him squatting and had even been known to go to him and offer a steadying hand while he, with infantile abandon, relieved himself.

In mid-April *Whiteoaks* had its opening. Nancy Price and Stephen Haggard had had a devastating quarrel only the day before, but their scenes together on that first night were poignantly done. The play went well. There were many curtain calls and even one for the author. Afterward we had a large party in Stafford Place.

The next morning there was Violet hastening out early to buy the papers. There were we, having breakfast in bed, reading the notices. They were more than merely favourable. They were excellent. Yet, after a short run I had word from Nancy Price that *Whiteoaks* was to come off. This was a disappointment indeed, after the long months of work, of waiting, of postponement.

Then something happened which could not be explained. For the last two performances the theatre was full. There was a fresh demand for seats. Instead of closing, the run was given new life.

Ringing the Changes

It was necessary to find a larger theatre. St. John Ervine wrote in the *Observer*:

> This piece, which is to be transferred from the Little to the Playhouse to-morrow evening, is easily one of the best plays now running in London. If the author were Chekhov and the principal part were played by Mr. Gielgud, all the fashion-followers would be cramming themselves into the Playhouse to see it. That, indeed, is what they will now do if they are more than fashion-followers; for I have seldom seen a play so rich in atmosphere, rich in character, and rich in performance as "Whiteoaks" is.

For more than eight hundred performances *Whiteoaks* played and since then has been produced in many countries. It has been broadcast and televised, but no performance I have seen has given me a pleasure equal to those at the Little Theatre.

Arrangements were made for a New York production. Nancy Price was invited to go there to play the principal part, but she was too greatly involved in coming productions for the People's National Theatre. I regretted this because I felt that no other actress could give such authenticity, such magnetism, such humour to the part of Adeline Whiteoak as she. When later I saw Ethel Barrymore star in *Whiteoaks* in New York, I was the more firmly convinced. Never for a moment did Miss Barrymore make me believe in her. Yet the play had a fair run in New York and toured the United States and Canada.

Chapter 21

Farewell
to The Winnings

LIFE was pleasant in many ways in Herefordshire. For the children it was indeed delightful. They had had, that summer, a long visit by the sea on a lovely part of the Welsh coast. They had the happy days of the little school. They had children of their own age as companions. There was the meet of the Hunt. There was the Colwall Steeplechase — always something picturesque and stimulating for childish minds, though they did not think of these as such but took them as part of everyday life. As for the dogs — never could they wish for anything better. Burrows to investigate, wildwood to be lost in; scarcely a day passed when there was not a desperate search for one or the other of them. On Duff's part there were hens to be chased. One morning he killed five of Fletcher's pullets. Oh, there was no end to the worry, the shame, the delight those two little fellows brought us! And their reactions to each other . . . if Moulin were first in the car, all was well, but if Duff were first established and Moulin entered (though never so humbly), there was the devil of a row — possibly right in our laps.

As I say, The Winnings was a wonderful place for children and dogs, but for Caroline and me it was much too far from London and the winters were too cold. Our friend, Grizel Hartley, whose husband is a house master in Eton College, urged us to come to Windsor, where she knew of a lovely Elizabethan house for sale. Already we had visited agents and been enthralled and confused by the places offered us. Now we went to see this house in Windsor, which was owned by Mr. Loftus Earle. At first sight we fell in love with it. The house itself had been restored and added to by the former owner. There were lawns, a gazebo, an orchard, a lily pond, a sunk garden, greenhouses, and about twenty acres of pasture land let to a farmer in return for manure for fertilizing. These pastures, with Jersey cows grazing on them, gave a rural aspect to the surroundings, yet already there were schemes for "developing."

We had lunch with the Earles. In a few days my lawyer made them an offer which was accepted. We would take possession the following April. Now we *owned* a house where at last we should be permanent, and what a lovable and livable house it was!

The King abdicated and departed. We had a new King. H. G. Wells had his seventieth birthday and at a dinner given by the P. E. N. Club the best speech was made by Shaw, who was over eighty. A big dinner was given at the Savoy for *Whiteoaks*, which was playing to crowded houses. Christmas came and a box of scarlet maple leaves from Canada. I was woken early by the children marching round my bed with bugle and drum.

Now it was necessary to break the news of our impending removal. When we told of it to Fletcher, the gardener, he broke down and openly cried. "If ever a man had two kind mistresses," he said, "I've had 'em." We cried too.

There was general mourning over our leaving and we were surprised — not because those whom we employed mourned, but because we thought we had made no impression on that cold and restrained community. But I believe they thought that in losing us they were losing something odd, even bizarre, of which in time (say thirty years) they might become fond.

We were even parting with Nanny, for the time had come when we felt that the children would be better under the care and teaching of a good governess. In January I finished my book *The Very House* (begun two years before), sequel to *Beside a Norman Tower*, both records of the children's lives, made from everyday notes, the only notes I ever have used for any of my books. Now I wrote several short stories. We passed through the wettest February in seventy years, yet the flowers of the garden did not mind and put out buds in every corner.

At the beginning of April we left The Winnings. I knew that never again should I walk on such lovely paths, in such freedom from traffic, never again should I have windows with such views. Yet I strained toward Windsor, toward the house I owned, from which I should never again be parted.

Once more were our belongings in removal vans. Once more did we arrive in a new home exhausted. I went on ahead and Caroline arrived, with the dogs, the next evening. The following day was Sunday and warm as June. We sat on the terrace in the gentle sunlight, relaxed, planning for the happy days ahead.

Nanny was to bring the children by train to London, where I was to meet them and they were to say good-bye to her. I looked forward to that good-bye with apprehension. It took place at Paddington. Nanny did indeed shed tears, but the two little barbarians skipped lightly from one train to t'other, with never a look behind. This railway carriage was much nicer, declared René, than the miserable one Nanny had brought them on from Malvern. And from Esmée questions about the governess to come and whether there would be dancing classes.

The governess was a charming young woman, Neria Boislier, half Scotch, half French, speaking both languages beautifully. René called her "Mad" (short for Mademoiselle) and her stay with us was pleasant. French songs and games she taught the children. When she took them for even a short walk, they wore gloves, and when Paxton, the chauffeur, gave them cricket practice in the evening, she filled their ears with cotton wool, for fear they should take cold. "But, Madam," Paxton would complain to me, "they can't even hear my directions." The game usually ended with his giving them a ride — one on each of his two broad shoulders. He was a fine figure of a man, tall and lithe, with a face of stern authority. To the children he was a good-tempered companion in their games, to the dogs one who must be obeyed.

Caroline made Vale House beautiful. The gardens already were teeming in flowers and when the cherry tree beneath my bedroom window was in bloom, one had something to admire every waking hour. At night there was the song of nightingales. Far away seemed the rumblings of war.

In Windsor we made many friends. Already we knew the Hartleys. Grizel Hartley would ride in at our gate, looking superb on her handsome grey horse Silver Mist, followed by two golden retrievers. The first time this happened, our terriers flew to attack the setters, who, in panic, leaped into the goldfish pool. . . . Now in speaking of this pool I must tell of a strange thing I saw there. It was when I was strolling alone. It was in a quiet and lovely spot, between house and orchard, just beyond a pleached alley of old pear trees. I was thinking of what I was about to write but stopped — stunned by what I saw — indeed, *beheld* is a better word. There were forty-nine of the fifty fish, in all their pretty shapes and colours, ranged as an audience, still as death. And there was the fiftieth — largest and most handsome — and astride his neck, the frog which lived on a ferny island in the middle of the pool! The frog clasped his neck in its green arms and the worst was that the captive seemed to like it.

If the faces of goldfish can show consternation, the faces of those forty-nine who witnessed the amorous scene showed it. I felt that only a man could save the horrible situation.

"Paxton! Paxton!" I called, running like the wind through the pleached alley to the house, where I had seen him at the top of a ladder, doing something to a window.

I tried to explain, but I could scarcely speak for excitement. Tolerantly Paxton descended the ladder, and followed me. Sceptically he scanned the pool for signs of disturbance. There was none. The frog had disappeared, the goldfish busied themselves as usual about the lily pads. Paxton asked:

"Madam, are you quite sure you saw — what you describe?"

Quite *sure*? Why, my brain was still reeling from the dreadful certainty of what I had seen! Yet, to this day, I think nobody really credits it.

Among our friends in Windsor were the Herbert Hartleys; then the Ian McMasters, whose daughter, Julienne, came to share lessons with Esmée; then Clare Stuart-Wortley, granddaughter of Sir John Millais, whose house had once been the home of Ann Page, one of the merry wives of Windsor; Sir John Hanbury-Williams and his daughter, who lived in the Henry III tower of Windsor Castle; Mrs. Montgomery, who had been born there because her father, Sir Henry Ponsonby, had been secretary to Queen Victoria. Almost everybody seemed to have some connection with either Eton or the castle. Yet one of our most interesting friends had no connection with either. He was a Mr. Selkirk, a former owner of Vale House, and a character. He was an ardent Anglo-Catholic and would tell you with zest of the fine "show" put on that Sunday morning. He knew the exact number of splendid vestments owned by the rector, and I believe gave most generously toward the purchase of more. He was a bachelor and had in the house with him five dogs, all spaniels, with the exception of a handsome Irish setter named Roy who never left his side. He was wont to exclaim: "I have four faithful servants, five lovely dogs, I have friends. I have much to be thankful for." Yet he endured considerable physical suffering, for he had a digestive affliction and ate almost nothing. He would invite all four of us to a delicious lunch and look on benignly while we enjoyed it. When his bouts of suffering came on, he would take to his bed and Roy would settle down beside it. But, after a bit, Roy would grow impatient of inaction. He would rear himself up and plant his forepaws heavily on the poor suffering body.

"Roy, dear, you're hurting master," Mr. Selkirk would mourn. "Please, please get off him."

Roy would obey, but soon, in peremptory fashion, would again urge his master to rise.

"Roy, dear — don't do that to master," the weak voice would protest.

Still Roy would persist. Then, with a roar, Mr. Selkirk would shout, "Roy, you red devil, *get down!*"

Mr. Selkirk owned an old-fashioned launch with comfortable chairs and used to take us on picnics in it up the Thames. We would anchor at Cliveden and the children would feed the swans with scraps from the splendid picnic hamper brought by Mr. Selkirk. With Roy hugged to his side, he would point out the houses where, as a gay young fellow, he had come to parties. The children, with his man to help them, would be given turns in steering the launch.

He was of a breed which has all but disappeared.

Only one other person have I known who with such grace rose above physical suffering. This was Mrs. Graham Smith, sister of

Lady Asquith. She was small and delicately made, with an exquisite aquiline face, but was so crippled by arthritis that when she came to lunch with us, her chauffeur carried her into the house. But then, and when we went to visit her, she was gay and bright with a charming vitality. She was an artist of talent and, in spite of her difficulties, continued to paint.

Chapter 22

Life in Windsor
and a Trip to America

SCARCELY had we been a fortnight in Vale House when I began a new novel, *Growth of a Man*. This was very different from the Whiteoak series. It was the story of a young man's challenge to poverty, to scholarship, to ill-health. It absorbed me for more than a year, even though during that time I was contending with other things of a nature to shake a less dedicated urge. This book stands alone among all I have written. Alfred McIntyre, my Boston publisher, liked it best of my novels and Harold Macmillan wrote to me of his pleasure in it and his pride in publishing it. Yet it never had the success I had hoped for. In saying this I mean that those who read it and liked it were not only fewer than the readers of the Whiteoak chronicles, but it did not inspire in them the warmth, the affection, felt by many for the family at Jalna. I think it lacks the warmth and humour.

During the time when I was writing *Growth of a Man* I was continually excited and depressed by near-offers to take the play *Whiteoaks* to America. On my part I did not believe it ever would be produced there and I did not very much mind. What I wanted

314

was to be left to myself, to get on with my novel. I had had enough of uncertainties, the harassments of the theatre.

My study in Vale House was a restful and beautiful room. Though its windows did not give onto noble hills and distant mountains, through their small leaded panes I could see the cherry tree, the well-ordered gardens. Its walls were hung with tapestries and there was a musicians' gallery served by a short flight of stairs. But, though I had great pleasure in the room, it does not, in truth, very much matter to me where I write, provided I have paper, pencil and quiet.

Beyond a hallway, past my study, was the schoolroom, to which the children had been promoted from nursery days. It was an immense room with beamed ceiling and windows of old greenish bottle glass. Out of it opened a conservatory which was always full of flowering plants and, again beyond, a huge ballroom where we kept odds and ends and where Stephen Haggard intended, sometime later, to produce plays. He was quite carried away by the idea of this, but at present he had much more important doings on hand. He had left the cast of *Whiteoaks* for an engagement to play in *Candida* with Diana Wynyard and Nicholas Hannen — a lovely play, beautifully acted.

In the ballroom slept René's tortoise, which, for some reason known only to himself, he had named Augustus Denmark. It was a nice creature with only one fault — a desire to explore far afield. Much of our time was spent in anxious searching for Augustus Denmark. Yet he seemed to like us and would make a pleasant hissing noise when he opened his pink mouth to receive a dandelion we offered him. Mademoiselle settled the problem of our losing sight of him by tying round his middle a long pink sash from one of her dresses which trailed far after him.

In our first spring at Vale House, Moulin was the victim of a

315

terrible accident. We had sent the dogs into the garden for their bedtime run. A quarter hour later he came outside the windows of my study, where we were reading, and gave a sharp bark. Caroline went to the window. She could just make out a little dark form below. "No, no, Mou," she said, "you must not come in so soon. Run off and play."

After a little he gave another bark and again was told that he could not yet come in. But the third time he barked there was something of pain in that brief summons which made me feel its urgency. I opened the casement and leaned out and picked him up. He gave a sharp cry. I carried him to the light and discovered the end of a black thorn barely projecting from his right eye. Caroline looked and drew back and covered her face with her hands. It was too late to send for a vet. Setting my teeth, I was able to extract the deeply embedded thorn. He uttered a cry of anguish. The thorn was an inch and a half long. I still have it. The next day I took him to two vets, but nothing could be done and he became quite blind in that eye. The strange thing was that, when we had had the dogs photographed in Malvern, a year before, that same eye had been only a white spot in the photograph.

There always seemed something of interest to do in Windsor. Paxton would drive us to Chobham Common, to Burnham Beeches or to Ascot, where we would walk and children and dogs run wild and free. At the time of the Ascot races the children liked to be taken to a spot in Windsor Great Park where we could (and only we) see the royal equipage sweep past on the way to the races.

One day we were caught in a shower. Still René was for getting out of the car and standing on a grassy knoll.

"But," I objected, "you'll get wet and you can see the little princesses quite well from the car."

"I know," he answered firmly, "but they wouldn't see *me*."

He had, even then at seven, an unchildlike understanding and sympathy for pain in others. Once, during a game, I fell and cut my shin on a step of the gazebo. In pain I drew down my stocking to see the injury. René took one swift look, then said, "Cover it up. Hurts look so much worse on you than they do on me."

Esmée, speaking of some acquaintances who never appeared to go anywhere or have any visitors, remarked, "They lead a very confiscated life, don't they?"

He was entered for Eton, but she was all for dancing and looked like a frivolous Alice in Wonderland in her ballet dress.

I am afraid they were (he especially, though he loved her dearly) rather a handful for Mademoiselle. In any case she, after six months with us, discovered that her mother needed her at home. We all were regretful to see her go, and now for me came the ordeal of interviewing one governess after another. God knows why I chose the one I did, for certainly she was a misfit in our family.

Miss Stubbings was rather a pretty woman who had spent seven years as governess to a well-behaved only child now in her teens. She had forgotten (if ever she had known) all about high-spirited young children. I recall with amusement the evening of her arrival. It was dark and the children had eaten their tea. The schoolroom looked enormous, with its high vaulted ceiling and rather dim lights. I escorted Miss Stubbings to meet her future charges. Politely they came forward to greet her, two little figures in scarlet pullovers, with untidy yellow hair. After shaking hands she enquired what was their scholastic standing. "I really don't know," I answered, "but they can sing a song in French for you."

With eager abandon the children flung themselves into the song and dance, with wildly repeated refrain and stamping of small feet.

Miss Stubbings looked almost frightened. What most impressed

317

her was, I think, the smallness of the children. "They are very small," she said, and repeated, "very small indeed."

But she recovered herself and set about reforming them. From that time I was constantly told of their naughtiness. But I'm afraid that poor Miss Stubbings often did not know whether she was on her head or her heels. It was impossible to achieve order in that schoolroom. Yet the children were always polite — an endearing quality to my mind. One heavenly day I discovered Esmée in the schoolroom trying to memorize a long poem as a punishment.

A few minutes later I met Paxton in the hall. I was so exhilarated that I had to exclaim, "Paxton, I have discharged the governess!"

With equal pleasure he returned, "Thank God, madam!"

She departed and, in her place, appeared Mademoiselle Berthy Müller. She was a handsome girl, very fair, but she had given her heart to Italy and used a brunette face powder to make herself look dark like an Italian. She was clever and spoke four languages with fluency. She was high-spirited too and full of fun, once she got used to us. When first she came, she was in a dreadfully nervous state, having been employed in a family where the mother was a martinet (and an American, by the way, which is odd because Americans are seldom given to excessive discipline). When I would enter the schoolroom, Mademoiselle would spring to her feet, rigid, her hands clenched at her sides, as though prepared for an ordeal. But I soon got her over that and a normal feeling of gaiety returned to the house.

Early in the following year my play *Whiteoaks* was produced in Canada and the United States with great success. Stephen Haggard joined the American company, not only to direct it but to play the part of Finch Whiteoak, which he had created in London. Now, in London, the play, which had seemed likely to come off, again showed vitality and was continuing its long run. Letters from

Canada told of the splendid reception there. Then came the news of one still more enthusiastic in America. Everyone was urging me by letter and cable to go across. Victor Payne-Jennings cabled: "Barrymore tremendous success as Adeline. Urge you come America. You will never forgive yourself failing to see Gran Whiteoak so magnificently realized."

But I was reluctant to go. Rumours of war gave our life a terrible uncertainty. Sir Samuel Hoare had said: "We will put an end to this haunting fear of war." Yet Austria had soon succumbed to Hitler and there were suicides at the rate of a hundred a day in Vienna. What if we were in America and the children in England when war might come? Aside from that I yearned for rest and relaxation in the south of France. I had been working hard.

Stephen Haggard cabled that I must come to see the success of *Whiteoaks.* Caroline was eager to go. So finally I was persuaded. Never, I think, has the author of a successful play been less inclined to see a production of it. However, we booked passages and made our preparations.

In those days before sailing, one thing after another cropped up to exhaust us. In running downstairs early one morning to let out the dogs, I caught my toe in the cuff of my pyjamas, fell and broke a bone in my hand. The housemaid fell and broke her wrist. Worst of all, Caroline's little Cairn terrier, Duff, became terribly ill from gastritis. Scarcely did we think he could survive. In the night before sailing I was up with him for two hours.

Now this little Cairn had more intelligence than any dog has a right to have. He might disobey; he might defy; he might be savage with Moulin; but he could give you a look that went straight to your heart. He had luminous eyes with long black lashes. Once he actually spoke to me. It was several years later than the occasion of which I now write. We were by that time living in Canada, and looking up into my face, he said (not distinctly yet still understandably), "I want to go out!"

But on that night in Vale House he seemed to be near to death. I lifted him out of his basket and sat him on a low stool and tied a towel, like a bib, in front of him. He had not been able to retain his medicine and it had been a struggle to give it to him.

"Now, Duff," I said, almost too weary to speak, "take this, like a good little dog — to please me."

He raised his lovely eyes to mine and took the medicine.

The following morning he had the strength to creep from his basket, for he knew we were going away. Caroline, with a thousand things to do, snatched a hurried good-bye, thinking she never again would see him alive. When we reached New York, we had an air mail letter from Minter, the parlourmaid, saying he was much better.

Paxton drove us to Southampton through lovely April weather and, for the first time, we sailed in an American ship. On board there were a number of Jews, escaping from Hitler. There were many German-Americans on board. The food was delicious. At the table nearest us there sat three stout elderly people — two women and a man. I shall never forget how largely, with what zest, they ate. They devoured caviar as though it were porridge. "Don't stare so," Caroline kept saying to me. "They'll notice." But I could not stop. Out of my thinness and my peckish appetite I watched them wade through massive dishes of food. . . . Then the sea grew rough. The ship rolled. The three at the next table were laid low with seasickness. "That'll teach them," I gloated.

After three days' absence they returned, looking sallow and subdued. With a trembling hand the man picked up the menu. He ordered caviar. With renewed zest, as though to make up for lost time, the three attacked it, and all the courses that followed.

In New York we were met by my agent, F. A. Jones, and, as always, the difficulties of landing melted under his genial touch. Our rooms in the hotel seemed full of flowers. There were many invitations. Stephen Haggard, happy in the success of the play, came to lunch, bringing with him his young wife. Pretending he was my secretary, he answered telephone calls of reporters with alternate facetiousness and pomposity. Edward Weeks came up from Boston to go to *Whiteoaks* with us, then on to Club Twenty-one. But the play I most enjoyed at that time was Thornton Wilder's *Our Town*.

Looking back on that visit, it seems a medley of palatial apartments, thronging faces, late hours and rich food. Early in May we went to Toronto. We travelled in the train with Hugh Eayrs, who had been in a hospital in New York. He was then a sick man. Caroline and I had not been able to secure good accommodation on the train and he, in his accustomed generosity, insisted that we should have his room. On the journey he was gay and witty as always. He told me he had been able to arrange with the C.B.C. for twelve hour-long broadcasts from the Jalna series on successive Sunday nights. For these Barbara Everest flew up from New York each week-end to play the part of the grandmother.

In Toronto *Whiteoaks* with Ethel Barrymore had had a warm reception, even though on its opening night there was a blizzard. Traffic was blocked by cars and the first-night audience was a blaze of diamonds and ermine such as is seldom seen in the theatre nowadays, when people may look as dowdy as they choose.

Miss Barrymore told me that she had been thrilled on the tour through Western Canada, where halls were packed to the ceiling by audiences who never before had seen a play but only moving pictures.

Now there were, for me, more crowded rooms, a few happy hours with relatives and friends, a few blessed days at Trail Cottage. In Toronto I was awarded the Lorne Pierce Medal, an honour I greatly value.

On May 17 we sailed for England on the *Empress of Britain*. Crowding newspaper reporters, photographers and agents in our stateroom made me think — "If this is the outcome of a modest success, Heaven preserve me from a great one."

I was extraordinarily tired. My throat, where is my weakness, had felt the strain. Pierre had come to the ship and remained on board till the last. Our good-bye had been painful. One night on board ship I was woken by a sharp pain in the throat. It was so sharp that I lay startled, wondering what had happened. I had no further pain. I fell asleep.

The following night was the night of the gala dinner. I was wearing a white evening cape. When I tried to fasten it at the neck, I found that I could not. It was too tight. Then I discovered that there was in my throat a lump, about the size of a bantam's egg. A swollen gland, I thought, and yet it did not look like a swollen gland. Also it was painful, though not enough to spoil my pleasure, especially the pleasure of returning home.

Paxton met us at Southampton. It was the month of May. It was warm and sunny. It seemed to us that every tree and shrub, every smallest plant that could bear a blossom was rejoicing in that power. Never, we thought, had England looked so beautiful, so peaceful.

Before we left home I had said to the children, "I do hope that you will make things easy for Mademoiselle while I am away. Be as good as you possibly can and when I come home I will give a prize to the one whose behaviour was best."

Now I asked hopefully of Paxton, "Were the children good?"

His clear-cut features became stern. "Madam," he said, "they were terrible. From morning to night they were terrible. I had to chase them or they would never have gone to bed."

"And the dogs — were they good?"

"They were terrible too," Paxton said grimly.

It was impossible to feel angry at the four lively little beings who gave us such a welcome. I said to the children, "I hear that you have not been very good. However, as I have promised a reward to the child who behaved best — I mean, to the one who was least bad — I shall keep my promise."

We four went to Hambley's toy shop in London and Esmée chose her reward, for according to reports her behaviour had been the less shocking of the two. René's birthday, however, was near at hand, so we bought his birthday presents on the spot and there was no envy in the heart of either child. It was bliss to be home.

The glorious weather still held. There was the fourth of June at Eton. Three hundred pounds were spent for fireworks. There was perfect weather for Ascot. There was the two-hundredth anniversary of the birth of George III. There were trips up the Thames in Mr. Selkirk's launch. But nothing could make me forget the pain in my throat which persisted. I had terrible dreams.

I consulted a doctor who told me that the trouble was caused by a cyst that was imbedded in the thyroid gland and was attached to the windpipe. The only cure, he said, was an operation, but the thought of this was horrible to Caroline. She was convinced that rest and a summer by the sea would make me well. So — for her sake, I agreed, though I felt in my heart that this hope was futile. The doctor warned me, and unfortunately did this in Caroline's presence, that though the cyst was at present "benign" (what a word to use!), it might at any hour become malignant. If its character changed or it suddenly grew more painful, I was to hasten home.

We had secured for six weeks a cottage on the Cornish coast. Caroline was packing my manuscripts for the journey when she was struck in the eye by the corner of a parchment envelope. The injury caused by this gave excruciating pain and later on badly affected the sight. Our plight was sorry indeed. Shortly before leaving for Cornwall I had lunch at Sir Edward Peacock's and told him and Lady Peacock our misfortunes. She begged me to have the operation at once. "Otherwise it will prey on your mind," she said.

At the time I did not realize how true this was, but when we were settled in our cottage by the sea, I did indeed realize it, in the cloud that hung over me, in Caroline's look of foreboding when she would say good-night to me — and I guessed of the tossing sleepless hours that lay ahead of her.

This cottage, named White Horses, stood high on a cliff. There were few others near-by and there was a glorious stretch of sandy beach for the children. Mademoiselle had gone on a holiday to Italy and, in her place, Nanny B. had come to look after them. They led a wonderful life, in and out of the sea, sailing their boats, building castles in the sand. They would walk with us over the springy turf that was starred by tiny pink flowers, to watch the surf-riding at Polzeath. That is to say, Caroline and I would walk while they and the dogs circled about us. Oh, those little dogs! Surely they never would forget the mad exhilaration of those six weeks by the sea, as we certainly could not forget what we endured because of their pugnacity and the dangers which beset them. There were, as the season drew on, many other dogs and one of these, a ferocious bull terrier, selected our two as his especial victims. It was useless for his master to cry out that he would not harm them. We knew that he wanted to kill them — just as they wanted to kill him. I can picture them still, flying across the level sands in pursuit of some meek old spaniel, while his master and mistress waved their arms in impotent rage and we walked quickly in the opposite direction, pretending that they did not belong to us.

Moulin, the Scotty, was really the fighter and when he was laid low for a few days, we had peace. It happened in this way: New arrivals in the house nearest to us brought with them a half-grown Scotty. On his first morning there he greeted our two with a friendly wag. Now Moulin advanced to him (as was his way) with a jocular air. He sniffed him, then, as though angered by the smell of the newcomer, sprang on him with a growl. We separated them, but Moulin, astride the other, had been bitten on the belly. It was not a bad bite, but he fancied he was killed. For days he lay on the couch in the living-room — an invalid.

Always we were afraid that the dogs would fall over the cliff, or into a crevice where the dark water whirled, or be lost in the network of burrows beneath the grassy surface of the cliff, but miraculously they survived.

Mrs. McDonald, our cook, was one of the nicest of women. She had a tiny daughter, Margaret, who was very fond of Paxton. Each morning he would walk to the village for the mail and she would be allowed to trot a short distance to meet him. What was her shock one morning to discover, just as she adventured forth, that he was almost at the door. Incensed by this lack of co-operation, she stamped her tiny foot at him and called out peremptorily:

"Paxie — go back! Go back!"

And the tall man shamefacedly hastened back and, turning, was properly met. It was ridiculous but somehow pleasant to see the obedience of one so stern-looking, to a tiny child.

I remember a violent electrical storm which woke us in the middle of the night. Esmée came and crept into bed with me.

Paxton went to the kitchen and made tea for everybody and carried it from room to room.

These things come back most vividly now, when I have lately heard of Paxton's death and I recall his kindness to us.

That summer I corrected the proofs of *Growth of a Man*. Caroline at the time remarked that Chapter Sixteen of this book was the best thing I ever had written. I also found time to write a few short stories. Sometimes I escaped to a rocky place beneath the cliff and there, in solitude, indulged in the liberated and brooding, almost pagan, worship of nature.

When we returned to Windsor, I set about preparations for René's going to school. He was barely eight and had been so sheltered that it was hard to cast him into the rough and tumble of even such an excellent school as the Downs. But it was necessary, as all his friends went off at that age and the thought of it exhilarated him. He and I went to London and bought his school outfit at Daniel Neal's, grey flannel suits for weekdays, navy blue serge and fine white flannel shirts for Sundays. The number of things he must have seemed endless.

In mid-September Paxton motored us to Malvern, and René's little figure was swallowed up in the school. It seemed unreal. Yet everything at that time seemed unreal. We lived from day to day, not knowing at what hour war would burst upon us. One day Hitler spoke for six hours. Mademoiselle hated him, but she understood German and she could not keep away from the radio. On and on the voice raged, like the voice of doom, till he was hoarse as a frog. At the end of September there were scenes of great emotion in the House of Commons when Hitler's invitation to a four-power talk was announced.

Almost were we bewildered by relief when a peaceful settlement was reached and Mr. Chamberlain returned to England.

All the countries rejoiced — all but France, and she was sceptical. Scarcely had we reached October when another ferocious speech by Hitler came over the wireless. I tried to shut the terrible events out of my mind by living in the book I had begun immediately after our return from Cornwall. This was *Whiteoak Heritage*. *Growth of a Man* was now in print.

Now we were expecting war at any time. Paxton was out all day delivering gas masks. All our household had been measured for them, but when they came, none was small enough for Esmée. Distracted, I enquired from officialdom what I should do with her if a gas attack came. I was told to dip a sheet in water and wrap her in it. The thought, the sight of the masks frightened her. To counteract this I made a game of them. We played games of croquet wearing them. We took amusing snapshots wearing them. These I still have. A Windsor newspaper remarked that certain people did not appear to realize the seriousness of the situation. But our cook was putting groceries away in glass jars to protect them from gas.

Meantime Caroline and I were preparing for the operation I must undergo. We had consulted Mr. Horace Evans of Harley Street, who later became physician to Queen Mary and was knighted. Good looks, charm and kindness were his. He arranged for me to enter the London Hospital in Whitechapel, where the best surgeon for that sort of operation was available.

I alighted from the train at Paddington, my arm full of gorgeous chrysanthemums. Turning swiftly on the platform, I inadvertently pushed the flowers right into the face of a woman waiting there. With cockney sarcasm she exclaimed:

"Thenk you! Thenk you very much indeed!"

It seemed to us that the taxi never would reach the hospital. Darker, grimmer became the streets. Lower sank our spirits. Should

I ever come out of Whitechapel alive? We held each other by the hand. The flowers nodded gaily.

This hospital had long ago been founded for the very poor but was now one of the largest in London. The private ward which I entered was new and quite small. The dark exterior gave no promise of the cheerfulness inside. I never have seen a hospital so little like a hospital. From that moment I was freed from apprehension.

The tiny sister in charge took me under her wing. My nurse was a beautiful Irish girl with whom I was soon on terms quite unlike those of nurse and patient. I was to have a week's rest before the operation. Caroline spent the time of my stay in hospital with our friend Norah Reid, in her house in Seymour Street. Norah had had a varied life: on the London stage; in India and Burma, as the wife of a cavalry officer; in London again, in the antique business. During the war she acted as hostess at Garnons, the home for convalescent Canadian officers in Herefordshire. Now, for the past ten years she has acted as my secretary. With her keen sense of humour, with our similar tastes, it has been an association the most happy.

Caroline was apprehensive lest war should break out while I was in hospital. "Never fear," said the young doctor blithely, "we'll get her out."

The surgeon was Mr. Charles Donald, a Scot, a dark, handsome man. He made a very good job of the operation. The hard thing for me to bear was that, following it, my Irish nurse had to give place to special nurses. The night nurse was of the cold-blooded variety. Through my suffering I was conscious of my hate of her, and of her indifference to my pain. I was no more to her than the poor animal is to the vivisectionist. Yet every so often she would thrust a needle into my arm to quiet me. There was at the side of the bed a deep abyss, into which a great bird was peering. I wished the nurse would fall into this. But I did not want the young doctor to fall into it and I warned him against it when he came to visit me.

Once when I went to see St. John Ervine in a London nursing home where he was recovering from an eye operation, he told me of this strange fancy: He had been lying for weeks, his eyes bandaged, in a darkened room, but he could see a wall and, in front of it, a flat expanse of dun-coloured earth. The only object that was not flat was a grave close by the wall.

I was in the London Hospital four weeks and every day Caroline came by bus from Portman Square to spend the day with me. My recovery was good. Friends came to see me — Betty Macmillan, blond and beautiful — Jane Priestley, darkly beautiful. Mademoiselle brought Esmée, on her birthday. They had been to Harrod's to buy a canary in a gilt cage, my present to her. They had been to the Tower. Having seen the block where queens were beheaded, Esmée was not impressed by my bandaged neck.

My worst experience (after the operation) was on Guy Fawkes night when the celebrants, in the narrow streets below, tormented my nerves.

There was great excitement when Gracie Fields came to visit the hospital. Some of the nurses collected on the windy roof to view her arrival. Gaily she waved to them and called up:

"Hi, girls — I can see your pants!"

I feared that I would get a large bill from the surgeon, Mr. Charles Donald, so I said to him one day, when, toward the end, he came to visit me:

"Do you know, I once sent a cheque to a tradesman who never cashed it, and when I asked him why, he replied that he preferred to keep it, for the sake of my autograph."

329

The surgeon brooded on this for a bit, then he said, his Scotch accent deepening:

"Weel, it must have been a vera small cheque."

One thing that endeared Mr. Donald to me was that he had read my books and admired them. When I returned home, I sent him a copy of *Growth of a Man*. I wrote his name on the flyleaf and added my thanks "for only partial decapitation."

In his graceful note of acknowledgement he assured me that, whatever else he had removed, he had left "the grey matter" in my possession.

It was heaven to be home again. It seemed no time till René had come for the Christmas holidays. He was now an English schoolboy with a pink and white complexion and full of high spirits.

Here I must remark on the good care that had been taken not only of him but of his clothes. Not a button was missing. There was not one hole in his socks!

What a happy reunion it was! Paxton would drive us to Burnham Beeches, or to Ascot and we would walk on the heath. The weather was springlike. Sometimes Mademoiselle would take the children to Richmond to skate. Children and dogs were happy. They knew nothing of the threat of war that struck at us from every side — from newspapers, from radio, from pulpit. We were told by the government to store food and water. Late in January Caroline and Paxton motored to Devon to inspect cottages. We had been advised to get a retreat in the country, as Windsor was so near London. My progress toward health had, for some reason, ceased. I suffered at night from devastating headaches. I could not sleep and could write no more than a few lines in a day. Caroline was convinced that the change to beloved Devon would help me. But all the cottages had been snatched up by the time she arrived. Not only that, but she was caught in a heavy snowfall, first and last of the season.

My health deteriorated. I could no longer take walks, excepting in our own garden. It now seemed certain that war would come and it was equally certain that we should be of no use to the country. Caroline, who has always made our decisions, now made the painful one that we should let Vale House and go to North America. There I might regain my health. There we might find sunshine and peace. It would probably mean an absence of no more than a year. Then we should return to the house which we loved more than any other we had known or ever could know — the house to which we had given a part of ourselves.

A dozen times we made up our minds to go, and an equal number of times unmade them. But from the hour when we broke the news to Paxton and Mrs. McDonald we were swept on an invisible tide toward a new chapter in our lives.

A desirable tenant was found for our house in Lord Dunboyne, an Irish peer. As he wished to furnish Vale House, it was necessary for us to store our furniture. So once again Thomas Cook's vans stood at our door. Once again a house that Caroline had made beautiful was left bereaved.

Chapter 23

Change

It HAD been my idea to go to Boston. So I wrote to Edward Weeks asking him if he could find a furnished house for us. He cabled back that he could and he would. We talked about it across the Atlantic Ocean and it was as though he were in the room with me.

Now for the upheaval!

Fortunately the spring, though chilly, had brought me better health. I was able to take part in our preparations, which every day grew more complicated. Our car, the Armstrong Siddely that had given us so much pleasure, must be sold. How strange it would look on the roads of to-day, with the gaudy streamlined cars! Very solemn, I fear, but how comfortable it was — how quiet — how powerful. In it you felt as safe as Noah in his ark.

When Vale House was empty, it had no resounding emptiness of a vacant house, but, with its beamed ceilings, its lovely windows, it stood gracious, receptive, waiting (so we thought) for our return. It was the end of March and every corner of the garden made our good-bye the more heavy-hearted. The very goldfish in the pond, the very blossoms on the fruit trees reproached us.

Then there were the good-byes to our friends, to Mademoiselle (for she could not come with us), to Paxton. He had driven us to Malvern, where we were to collect René, and there we were at the Abbey Hotel, with two children, two dogs and a sick canary. Also Caroline was ill in bed. She was heart-broken at leaving Vale House. Yet it was she who had made the decision to leave. And so it is, she has the more decisive nature, mine the more resilient. In truth I am scarcely ever decisive but have wobbled through life, letting others make up my mind for me. I was very much troubled about the little bird, Jackie. Certainly he was not in a condition to travel and Esmée and I agreed that it would be well to leave him with one of our friends, with whom he might recover. But we found that no one wanted the present of a sick canary, even if contained in a handsome cage.

The day of departure was almost at hand. I went with Paxton and the dogs for their last walk on the Malvern Hills. I was too tired to walk so I sat in the car and watched them as they frolicked along the steep and narrow paths, Paxton striding after them. The hills never had looked more beautiful, as they rose in their austerity above the springtime verdure. When Paxton and the dogs returned, I noticed how sad, how worn was his face. He looked ten years older in the past few weeks.

We were on the train, passing through Colwall, and there on the platform we saw the Geoffrey Hoylands. They had come for a last glimpse of us. "And will the dogs learn to bark with an American accent?" asked Dorothea Hoyland Like children, they ran alongside the train till they were left behind, but it is a charming recollection of them.

What train is so comfortable as an English train? None that I know. There we were ensconced in our compartment — the dogs on guard, the seat beneath them protected by a travelling rug; the children lively in anticipation; Caroline, with head thrown back, eyes closed, the picture of sorrowing departure; me, with the sick canary on my lap. From Caroline's closed eyelids tears appeared and trickled down her cheeks, in sorrow of leaving the land she loved best. René saw her tears and sobs shook him. Esmée saw them and she began to cry. I too wept for the pity and strangeness of life. Caroline's eyes flew open and she gathered both children into her arms and comforted them. The dogs yawned in nervous tension. The canary scratched in the gravel on the bottom of his cage. The sunny springtime fields flew by. We were on our way.

The waiter carried our lunch to the compartment and, with the help of the dogs, we made short work of dispatching it. Moulin and Duff had one little fight, but we were able to separate them without the canary's being alarmed. I was heartened to see that already he was looking better.

All the way to Liverpool no other passenger ventured into our compartment. Even when I had taken the children to London for a play or to shop, we had a method for keeping out other travellers. We would board the train promptly, choose an empty compartment and I would station a child at both windows. Each time another passenger made as though to enter, I would say, "Naughty faces, children!" and the two villainous little faces at the windows effectively frightened off the intruder.

In Liverpool we were joined by a Scotch maid whom we called Pilly. Her round rosy face gave us a feeling of confidence which, as we later discovered, was sadly misplaced, but she was good-humoured and quite at ease with both children and dogs. She was a woman not dumbfounded by any situation, and she could turn on an authentic flow of tears, as from a tap.

Whenever we were in any sort of stress Duff was sure to give trouble. Now in the Adelphi Hotel he disappeared. He had been left in care of the children while we attended to other affairs, but they forgot to shut the door of their room. He set out to explore. After a distraught search he was found, hiding under a bed, in a distant room. Then was there rejoicing, he seeming as pleased as anyone.

I had been told that the quarters provided for dogs on board ship were fit for a king, but indeed they were terrible — two cages, "aft," where snow or rain beat down. But the butcher fed them enormous meals of cabbage; Caroline and I took them for exercise on the lower deck; and, twice a day, Pilly brought them to our stateroom for a visit. How clearly I can see them, as Pilly dragged them back to their dismal quarters, their eight feet despairingly planted, for they would not take a step.

Jackie, the canary, lived well with the butcher.

The children made friends with other children but every afternoon went with me to the horse races. On one occasion Esmée won eight shillings — a bitter pill for René!

At 5:20 A.M. on April 10 we were up and dressed but did not disembark for long hours. Fussy officials, collectors of taxes cared not a fig how long they delayed us. There were press interviewers, press photographers. In the newspaper pictures later we looked like immigrants of the less desirable sort. Straining on their leads, both dogs made puddles before I got them off the ship.

In the bitter cold, for an hour and a half, Ted Weeks awaited us on the dock. Then, with his masterful hand on the helm, we were piloted through the customs and installed in a pleasant house in Chestnut Street, across the road from his own. Caroline went to bed with a raging headache and I washed the children's hair.

We settled comfortably into the house in Chestnut Street. From somewhere a cook appeared, a fine upstanding woman, and

335

I engaged a Harvard student to come as tutor to the children, for I felt that their education should not be neglected. He was a nice young man, but he knew nothing about teaching young children and the lectures he delivered to them appeared to make no impression. What did impress them was the excitement of the new life in Boston. There was always something to do — the walk across the Common to visit the shops — the little white boats in the park. It had been spring when we left England. When we arrived in Boston, it was wintry cold, but when spring did come, it burst upon us with a dramatic rapidity which I have never seen equalled. One night when we went to bed there was no leaf unfurled. The air penetrated with a cruel chill. The sky was a sombre November sky. All night it rained and, like a miracle, it was a warm rain. When I walked through the Common, it was a new world. It was not only spring. It was summer. The wet leaves of the trees had opened wide to sun themselves. The air was full of new earthy scents.

That morning there was a parade of Boston policemen and I thought I never had seen a body of finer men. Doubtless they were of Irish extraction. How law-abiding Boston is to-day I do not know, but certainly those men looked capable of keeping any city in order.

One day René remarked to me, "I woke early this morning and I entered into the mind of every person in Boston."

"And what did you discover?" I asked.

"Well," he said, "I think God would have been disappointed. Perhaps sorry he made us."

At that moment the dogs encountered two other dogs and the conversation never was finished.

In particular my Scotty disliked Ted Weeks's old spaniel Micky, and Micky had an equal detestation of him. It was a lovely sight to me to see the editor of the *Atlantic Monthly* on a fine Sunday morning sitting on his front porch, in his shirt sleeves, reading a newspaper. The scene was so peaceful — like something in a village. But all was not peace. Through my front door would escape my Moulin; from Ted's porch would leap Micky. They would meet in combat on the road. I remember one particularly ferocious fight when Ted and I rushed out to separate them. Each of us felt concern for his own dog. I found blood on Moulin.

"Your dog has bitten mine!" I cried in anger.

"He has not," Ted retorted, with equal heat.

"But he has!"

"It is impossible."

"There's blood on my dog!" I was now furious.

"Then he bit *himself*," declared Ted, "for my dog has no teeth."

One morning, walking in the Public Garden, René and I came upon a curious sight. A small crowd was collected about a lawn sprinkler where, in the midst of the fine downpour of water, a young robin stood. He was full fledged but with little sense. He had run under the sprinkler for a bath. Now, his plumage heavy with water, his wings dropping, he was drowning before our eyes. It was a pathetic sight, yet no one of those standing there moved.

"Run in and rescue him — quick!" I said to René.

He dashed under the sprinkler, picked up the robin and set it down in a sunny space. It shook itself and, after a few moments, hopped away. The onlookers smiled a shamefaced approval at the dripping small boy.

It was such a tiny incident but showed how thoughtless mob inertia can make people tolerate what should move them to action. I don't believe those people actually wanted to see the young robin drown, but no one would venture under the sprinkler to save it.

Life was so pleasant in Boston, the weeks flew by. But the weather was growing hot and we must find somewhere to spend the summer. Two houses were available in New Hampshire which Caroline made the journey to inspect. One of them greatly pleased her and there we moved in early June. There were she and I; the two children; their young tutor; Pilly and the cook; the dogs and the canary. . . .

Seven Millstones was a white New Hampshire farmhouse, surrounded by almost a hundred acres of field and woodland, on the edge of a lovely lake. Sometimes we would glimpse a deer leaping into the shelter of the dense undergrowth and trees. The dogs ran wild. The children ran wild. To be sure, they had a few lessons each morning, but the day was filled with bathing, boating and picnics.

The sun blazed down by day; the moon, the brilliant stars, the dancing fireflies enchanted us by night. Scarcely could I sleep for the beauty of the nights, that and the torture of mosquito bites. I am still convinced that I had more and larger bites than the other three, but certain it is that our blood, fresh from England, whetted the appetites of those wicked insects. We became quite callous toward the complaints of others and when one of us would display an especially large red lump, the three others would chant in chorus — "Nobody cares! Nobody cares!"

I had less of the blazing outdoor life than I should have wished, for I lived in an attic room, writing-board on knee, till lunch time. I was hard at work on *Whiteoak Heritage*. Beneath the sloping roof my window gave onto the flowery field where buttercups and devil's paintbrush and poison ivy flourished, and beyond the field lay the lake and beyond the lake the mountains.

But though I was working and must spend my mornings indoors, I so gained in health and strength that when summer ended, I was well indeed. So were Caroline, Esmée and René. He had lost, in those blazing months, the pink and white of his complexion and now presented to the world a little face sunburned and freckled.

So congenial had we found life in Boston that we might have returned there but for the coming of the war. Then our almost passionate wish was to be among our own people. Canada also had declared war. I wrote to my Uncle Walter and he, thankful to have us near him once more, acquired for us a small stone house, set among primeval pine trees, near the village of Thornhill, about fifteen miles from Toronto. He and Sidney Kertland, the architect who undertook the additions to the house for me, motored down to New Hampshire to take as many of us as could be crowded into the car to our new home.

It was a strange, bewildering time. For months life had been comparatively free of care. We had lived in a kind of pleasant disorder. Now we were ruthlessly pushed into the business of packing, consulting timetables, travelling, and again settling into new surroundings. Caroline, Pilly and the dogs were to travel in the car with my uncle and Sidney Kertland, after closing Seven Millstones. The children, the canary and I were to go by train.

And so we said good-bye to the house where we had spent such happy months, and not long afterward were told that it had been burned to the ground in an incendiary fire. It seemed unbelievable and yet we had suspected from gossip that it was a strange, vindictive neighbourhood.

Hugh Eayrs met us in Montreal — that is to say, the children, the canary and me. 1 was very anxious about the last, as the

339

weather was extremely hot and the train, because of air condition-
ing so cold. However, I need not have worried. After the long
train journey to Toronto on the following day Jackie was the least
tired of any of us, hopping brightly from perch to perch and scat-
tering seeds.

In truth, when Hugh took matters in hand, there was no
need to worry. Under his benignly humourous influence, one's
difficulties were smoothed away. It was only in his own life that
this was not so. Scarcely six months passed, after our coming to
Canada, when he died.

The furniture we had left stored in England now was brought
to us in huge "lift vans." While we lived in the original small
house, workmen, under the direction of Sidney Kertland, added
to it a garage and a number of rooms. The best of these was a
really splendid library, with a stone stairway leading to my own
bedroom and a gallery. The windows looked on the grandeur of
the pines, on the stream that flashed in the winter sunshine.

It was a winter punctuated by the noise of building, of partitions being torn down, of walls being built, but when spring at
last came to us and there were hepaticas in our bit of woodland
and marsh marigolds by the stream, all was at last in order. The
house had an air of serenity.

Yet the war news was frightening. Vale House was taken over
by the government and six families from London installed in it.
We had long melancholy letters from Paxton. He was bitter over
what was being done to that lovely place. He would tell us how
his heart ached when he found in the garden forgotten little toys
that had belonged to the children.

But now we were settled in this house in Canada where, we
thought, we should be content to spend the rest of our lives.
How peaceful it was — guarded by its pines! There were as yet

no building projects to destroy the beauty of the surrounding country that reminded one of Gloucestershire.

And there for years I lived and wrote quite a number of books. And now this one. Thinking it over, I am convinced that I know little about the writing of an autobiography — that I am without skill in presenting my own life. But I have tried to see myself objectively, as a character in a book, my weakness and my — I hesitate to write the word *strength*, but will instead use the word *resilience* — my vacillations and my temerity. I realize that I have possibly given too much space to the telling of little things, but these had a way of pushing themselves in. They were important to me.

I feel no urge to write of my life during the years of the war or after. Each of us lives through several lives in his time. This latest period of mine is mostly a record of books written, of seeing my children grow up, of seeing a different sort of world rise into my astonished view.

Strange were those years of the war, in that sheltered spot — outwardly sheltered, yet inwardly so shaken by the blasts of news, waiting for which we sat tense before the radio. The bombing of London — the fall of France —"There'll always be an England —"

New and steadfast friends are added to the old friends. Again we are settled in a house where we feel we shall be content for the remainder of our days.

But — I wonder!

And so, on that note I shall end.

I wonder. . . .